Loss and Decline
in the Novels of Anne Tyler

LOSS AND DECLINE IN THE NOVELS OF ANNE TYLER

The "Slipping-Down" Life

Susan S. Adams

The Edwin Mellen Press
Lewiston•Queenston•Lampeter

Library of Congress Cataloging-in-Publication Data

Adams, Susan S.
  Loss and decline in the novels of Anne Tyler : the "slipping-down" life / Susan S. Adams.
    p. cm.
  Includes bibliographical references and index.
  ISBN-13: 978-0-7734-5788-1
  ISBN-10: 0-7734-5788-7
  1. Tyler, Anne--Criticism and interpretation. 2. Women and literature--United
States--History--20th century. I. Title.

  PS3570.Y45Z53 2006
  813'.54--dc22

                                                                    2006043806

hors série.

A CIP catalog record for this book is available from the British Library.

Front cover photo: A formerly genteel house "slipping-down" from its gracious past

The Edwin Mellen Press
Box 450
Lewiston, New York
USA 14092-0450

The Edwin Mellen Press
Box 67
Queenston, Ontario
CANADA L0S 1L0

The Edwin Mellen Press, Ltd.
Lampeter, Ceredigion, Wales
UNITED KINGDOM SA48 8LT

Printed in the United States of America

For Jill and Greg; Amanda, Scott, Andrew, and Matthew;
Louisa, Davith, and Liam

"They were traversing the curve of the earth, small
and steadfast, surrounded by companions."
(*Dinner at the Homesick Restaurant* 278)

Table of Contents

Foreword

In her careful study of Anne Tyler's sixteen novels, Susan Adams has an ambitious goal. She intends to establish the literary merit of a writer whose works have often been considered merely popular, sometimes even quirky, and who is certainly not destined to have an enduring reputation. Adams succeeds admirably, marshaling her impressive knowledge of Tyler's *oeuvre* and the relevant secondary critical material to prove that Tyler, while resisting traditional American economic and social values, nevertheless speaks to the core of what it means to be successful – and happy – in America today. Tyler's characters are perpetually "slipping down" economically, socially, and even physically, but they grow in confidence, happiness, and sometimes joy. Tyler's insights into what makes a meaningful life, Adams persuades readers, should secure her place in the literary canon.

To frame her argument, Adams situates Tyler in the admirable company of Anthony Trollope and Charles Dickens, showing that she shares these authors' interest in ordinary characters and their less-than-glamorous (but always fascinating) lives. She also systematically outlines the critical history of Tyler's novels, organizing critical response into two camps: those who think Tyler sentimental and unrealistic and those who see her challenging, to her peril, core American values. Adams falls into the second camp, although she (unlike many critics) thinks that the status quo, particularly in America, *needs* challenging. Tyler, Adams believes, resists the seductive call of the American Dream and, more often than not in her novels, has her characters fall from family acceptance, success, and grace in order to remake their lives.

Adams concentrates on the role of family in these fortunate falls and quite correctly stresses the ways in which Tyler has her characters redefine their notions of family. Building on the work of critics such as Mary Ellis Gibson and Anne G. Jones, Adams points out that many of Tyler's characters move from the claustrophobic nuclear families of their birth to supportive and creative families of their own making. Tyler's protagonists also feel, paradoxically, the fortuitous effects of economic decline and find satisfaction outside the material. The happiest people in Tyler's novels, Adams reveals, are those who step off the ladder to success, accepting that self-knowledge should be the goal, not material prosperity. For Adams, "slipping down" in Tyler's world is the only way to truly succeed.

Acceptance of societal change is another important part of this particular formula for success. Tyler's characters must leave behind–sometimes literally–the restrictive mores of their families. Adams insists that Tyler's heroes and heroines must learn to adapt, even to change, and not simply accept psychologically and spiritually constrictive lives. This adaptability can become a useful model for positive change in American society as a whole, Adams asserts. Along with critic Margaret Morganroth Gullette, Adams believes that Tyler's characters learn both to accept the changes that come with age and also to leave behind fairy-tale notions of happy endings. Heroism and happiness do exist in Tyler's novels, but her heroes are ordinary men and women, and their happiness is often hard-won and sometimes fleeting.

As Susan Adams makes the case convincingly in her new study, death, loss, pain, and, most importantly, acceptance of diminished possibilities all lead to growth and maturity in Tyler's novels. Tyler resists the American rhetoric of infinite expansion and shows that when her characters light out for the territories they (almost always) find themselves eventually drawn back home. Economic success does not lead to satisfaction, and family values can be a prison in Tyler's world.

However, the characters who step outside the rat race realize that new, more sustaining families can be made by will rather than biology; those who acknowledge that the limitations of age offer new possibilities for growth can find freedom. In her thoughtful delineation of these themes in Anne Tyler's novels, Susan Adams makes an important contribution to Tyler studies. Following in the tradition of Tyler scholars like Joseph C. Voelker and Alice Hall Petry, Adams adds both a discussion of Tyler's novels from the last decade and provides a new emphasis on the lives of Tyler's "slipping down" characters. Most importantly, her book asks readers to question, as Tyler does, the sometimes-empty promises of the American Dream and to reconsider what it really means to be a success.

Caren J. Town
Professor of English
Georgia Southern University

Acknowledgments

I would like to thank the Northern Kentucky University Faculty Senate for granting me a year-long sabbatical leave to write a major portion of this book. Thanks are also due to former Dean of Arts and Sciences Dr. Gail Wells and former Provost Rogers Redding of Northern Kentucky University for their support of faculty research and scholarship -- and, especially, to Dr. Danny Miller, Chair of Literature and Language, for his personal interest in, and encouragement of, my scholarly endeavors throughout the years.

I would also like to thank Alfred A. Knopf Inc., a Division of Random House Inc., for granting me permission to use excerpts from each of Anne Tyler's novels.

As always, my husband Michael C. C. Adams deserves special thanks. He remains my most loyal and helpful colleague, reader, and critic (despite his own heavy workload and the many other roles he plays in my life). His suggestions are always intelligent and wise, even if I fail to carry them out as fully and effectively as they require.

Chapter One
Introduction

Anne Tyler is one of the most popular American novelists alive today. Her readership has continued to grow (Croft, *Bio* 85), as have her prizes: the 1989 Pulitzer Prize for literature for *Breathing Lessons*; the 1981 Janet Heidenger Kafka Prize for Fiction by an American woman for *Morgan's Passing*; the 1983 P.E.N./Faulkner Award for *Dinner at the Homesick Restaurant*; and the 1985 National Book Critic Circle's award for *The Accidental Tourist* as the most distinguished work of fiction of that year (Bail 11). In addition, several of her works have been made into movies (*The Accidental Tourist* and *Earthly Possessions*) and made-for-television dramas (*Saint Maybe, Breathing Lessons*, and *Back When We Were Grownups*). Nevertheless, her place in literature continues to be the subject of debate.

While contemporary novelist Anne Tyler's literary reputation is still uncertain, she has already been compared to many of the great writers of the American tradition. Frank W. Shelton notes that Tyler acknowledges the influence of Eudora Welty on her subject matter, but Shelton believes Welty's influence extends even further, to the very "ordering poles of her fiction: a sense of distance on the one hand and a gift of sympathy on the other" ("Necessary" 175). Alice Hall Petry has discussed Thoreau's theme of simplicity in Tyler's work (*Understanding* 7), a theme which Barbara Harrell Carson suggests Anne Tyler deliberately incorporates in order to challenge and counter in her novels (24). Petry also discusses the "Hawthornesque burden of the past, coupled with a terror of the future" in a work such as Tyler's *Searching for Caleb* (*Understanding* 129)[1], while Sanford E. Marovitz looks at Emerson's transcendental influence (through her parents' teachings) on Tyler's language and thought throughout her career (207-21).

More often, however, Anne Tyler has been compared to writers outside the American literary canon. Edward Hoagland locates Tyler's novels inside a tradition he calls "the literature of resignation," characterized, he believes, by "wisely settling for less than life had seemed to offer . . . [and] exemplified by Henry James among American writers." Hoagland adds, however, "It is a theme more European than New World by tradition, but . . . it has gradually taken strong root here and become dominant among Ms. Tyler's generation" (144). Margaret Morganroth Gullette identifies Tyler as a "meliorist" in the manner of George Eliot (rather than someone "resigned" to less, as Hoagland believes), theorizing that Tyler, like her earlier British counterpart, shows that the "individual's life is capable of improving over time" (*Safe* 150-51). The quiet comedy and familiar domesticity of Tyler's works have led, as well, to her frequent designation as "the Baltimore Jane Austen" (McCullough 10). Critics have noted that her interests, like Austen's, are "in marriage . . . in courtship, child raising and filial responsibility . . . . If meddlers aren't enough to make things happen, she will throw in a pregnancy or abrupt bad luck or a death in the family, so that the clan must gather and confront one another" (Hoagland 140).

But the most frequent literary comparison of all is that between Anne Tyler and the great nineteenth century British author Charles Dickens, as Barbara A. Bennett (57) and Alice Hall Petry (*Understanding* 6) have noted. Joseph Mathewson says of Tyler's work:

> There is almost that kind of size and eccentricity to Miss Tyler's characters [as can be found in Dickens's works]. Her writing has a lot of Dickens's humanity, too, as well as a certain lack of fear, which came more easily to his own century than it does, alas, to ours. (124)

Wallace Stegner also writes of Tyler's "Dickensian gallery of oddballs, innocents, obsessives, erratics, incompetents, and plain Joes and Janes, [who] . . . see the world a little skewed, but their author sees them with a sad precision and presents them with such amusement and lack of malice that they come off the page as exhilaratingly human" (148).

Such comparisons as these pay high tribute to Anne Tyler's abilities as a writer and would seem to suggest that her literary stature is assured beyond today's popularity with the reading public. Yet that is not the case. For one thing, there is the fundamental question of whether contemporary authors will continue to matter in the same way as in the past. Charles Dickens, George Eliot, Jane Austen, as well as Henry James, Henry David Thoreau, Ralph Waldo Emerson, and Nathaniel Hawthorne, were all writing at a time when books, fictional and non-fictional, indisputably mattered – something that can no longer be said with complete conviction in our own time. As Daniel Pool explains, "In an era before television, radio, movies, records, compact discs, or even a car to get away from the house, and when newspapers were still expensive . . . . novels had an impact" (32). Charles Dickens was the media star of his age, leaving an impressive estate of 93,000 pounds, Daniel Pool reports (184). Critics concur that Dickens and other authors of his period were viewed as vital to the progress of their age and contributed to the rise of the middle class in Great Britain:

> [they] provided information, showing readers how to act in social situations. Novels introduced disparate classes to each other, showing the increasingly juxtaposed "two nations" [of the rich and the poor] how others actually lived and thus helping to promote mutual understanding and to catalyze social change. Novels explored difficult social issues and attempted to move toward solutions. (Hayward 29-30)

It was a time of great social unrest, reform, and vitality during which the nineteenth century author and reader, both, "were involved in a volatile process of self-discovery and self-creation. . . . Both public and author were evolving," Roger Fowler explains in his study of Charles Dickens (64). Through it all, the nineteenth century writer was seen as essential to the process of establishing societal identity and growth.

But can the same be said today, in an era when authors seemingly have been replaced by computers, movies, TV news, and TV sitcoms in readers' lives? What does Anne Tyler's popularity with the reading public mean? Does her success as a contemporary novelist really matter to society (one Anne Tyler, unlike Charles Dickens, determinedly shuns, avoiding the limelight even at a time when authors rarely get much media attention anyway)? Anne Tyler herself holds out little hope that she can influence her times through her writing. In an interview with Paul Bail in 1997 she said, "Much as I would love to think that a novel could make a positive political change, I've never seen it done, and I believe it is always a mistake to aim for anything more than pure storytelling when writing fiction" (qtd. in Bail 10). While Anne Tyler clearly does not see herself as a contemporary Charles Dickens writing to change her readers and her age, neither does she feel the despair of Don DeLillo's author/protagonist Bill Gray in *Mao II* when he says:

> Years ago I used to think it was possible for a novelist to alter the inner life of the culture. Now bomb-makers and gunmen have taken that territory. They make raids on human consciousness. . . . News of disaster is the only narrative people need. The darker the news, the grander the narrative. (41-42)

Clearly, Anne Tyler still thinks fictional narratives about more gentle and ordinary human experiences (beyond explosions, wars, disasters, and destruction) still matter, as she has kept on writing her quiet, domestic fiction steadily, from one decade into the next, from the 1960s into the new millennium.

Further, the reading public seems to agree that her fiction is worth both the time and money they spend on it, as her popularity has steadily increased throughout her career. Robert W. Croft reports,

> Like *The Accidental Tourist* before it, *Breathing Lessons* became a bestseller. *Time* named it one of the best fiction books of 1988 and the next year cited it as one of the ten best fiction books of the decade. Hardcover sales of the novel nearly doubled those of *The Accidental Tourist* (222,000), while paperback sales of the Berkley edition had topped 1,000,000 within two years of its October 1989 release. Sales figures for her earlier books continued to climb as well. By September 1991, each of her previous novels had sold more than ten times its original hardcover sales in their Berkley paperback editions . . . . (*Bio* 85)

More recently, as well, Tyler's appeal has been affirmed with *Back When We Were Grownups* making the bestsellers' list after its publication in 2001. Tyler's readers continue to agree that the ordinary, day-to-day lives of her characters really *do* matter, if only to themselves, the author, and her characters, if not to American society as a whole.

As Flannery O'Connor once said, "people without hope not only don't write novels, but what is more to the point, they don't read them. They don't take long looks at anything, because they lack the courage. The way to despair is to refuse to have any kind of experience, and the novel, of course, is a way to have experience" (77-78). The experience reading provides, while no longer seen as leading to cataclysmic social change and the progress of civilization, as in the nineteenth century, nevertheless is still valued by the reading public at large as an experience worth having. Those who study its effects agree – and believe, as well, that it does impact readers' lives, at least in subtle, if not apocalyptic, ways. According to Shirley Brice Heath's interviews with contemporary readers,

> reading serious literature impinges on the embedded circumstances
> in people's lives in such a way that they have to deal with them. And,
> in so dealing, they come to see themselves as deeper and more
> capable of handling their inablity to have a totally predictable life.
> (qtd. in Franzen 49)

In her study of modern-day readers, Heath found that fictional works helped individuals deal with the unpredictability of their lives and were seen by them as central to their personal development. They believed that novels became, for them, "the only places where there was some civic, public hope of coming to grips with the ethical, philosophical, and sociopolitical dimensions of life that were elsewhere treated so simplistically" (qtd. in Franzen 49). Even today, in our fast-paced, high-tech age, literature is still viewed by many as providing readers and writers alike with a means of addressing complex issues of importance to them and their society – issues, in Tyler's case, of interpersonal relationships, everyday survival, and human courage.

It is in the interaction between readers' lives and those of the characters they relate to that literature's impact can be found. Critic Jonathan Culler theorizes that literature "challenges the limits we set to the self as a device of order and allows us, painfully or joyfully, to ascede to an expansion of self" (130). That serious fiction still provides readers with a sense of an "expanded" self and an enhanced perspective on life at the outset of the twenty-first century, no less than in the nineteenth, should come as no surprise; as Jonathan Culler says, those who have valued reading fiction always "have assumed that there was a relation of this kind: that the meanings experienced when reading a novel would have a bearing on the reader's own life and would enable him [sic] to look upon it in new ways" (191). Anne Tyler's popularity suggests that her readers have found that the fictional experiences she provides them have been ones definitely worth having, ones that seemingly have addressed significant issues in their own lives and helped them deal with their personal lives "in new ways."

While Anne Tyler has said that she does not believe she can change the course of civilization, it is still important to her, she admits, to connect with her readers through her novels. She no longer reads reviews of her works, she told Alice Hall Petry in 1989, because "I don't want to know how often I've missed connecting" (qtd. in Petry, *Critical* 49). Earlier, she had been surprised by responses to the ending of *The Clock Winder*, telling Clifford A. Ridley, "I think of it as a sad ending, and I've been surprised that not everybody does" (24), and she would, no doubt, have been devastated to read (were she still looking at her reviews) David Klinghoffer's assessment of *Breathing Lessons* as a novel in which "the author's distaste [for the Morans] is palpable. So is her condescension" (139). Examining Anne Tyler's own reviews of other authors' works, Elizabeth Evans finds that "to Anne Tyler, fiction is not something merely to divert or entertain readers; fiction should engage readers, make them react to and connect with what they read. . . . for Anne Tyler it does not work unless the reader finds some aspect to like in the characters" (235).

And so Anne Tyler herself, it seems, not unsurprisingly, believes in the serious nature of the literary enterprise she has undertaken and its resulting effects on readers' lives, even if she does not believe she can change her culture in any major way. In one of her reviews, Tyler has said that she feels there is a contract "between writer and reader that the writer will do his best to draw the reader in and the reader will do his [sic] best to follow" (qtd. in Elizabeth Evans 240). In such a relationship, it is essential to Anne Tyler that the reader be able to stay engaged with characters and follow clearly both plot development and the author's perspective on life. As she told Bruce Cook, "I disagree with [novelist William Faulkner]. I want everyone to understand what I'm getting at" (158). Her aim in writing fiction, then, is neither to dazzle nor obscure but to connect and communicate clearly with her readers. She does not share contemporary novelist Jonathan Franzen's concern that his works be seen as high art – his motive in turning down acceptance of *The Corrections* (2001) as an Oprah Book Club choice (Giles 68). Tyler's primary worry is not the safety of her literary reputation but that she be able to reach out to readers and be understood by them. She admits,

> it does matter to me that I be considered a serious writer. Not necessarily important, but serious. A serious book is one that removes me to another life as I am reading it. It has to have layers and layers and layers, like life does. It has to be an extremely believable lie. (qtd. in Michaels 44)

Tyler's goal is to be "believable," involving readers in her fictional worlds and making sure, as she writes each work, that "a reader could make sense of it" (qtd. in Lamb 58). Most of all, then, Tyler wants to be understood.

In this goal Anne Tyler seems, at first glance, to have been overwhelmingly successful. Not only does she have a mass market following, but many well-known writers and scholars, in addition, have praised the warmth and clarity of her fiction. Author Gail Godwin, for instance, in her review of Tyler's *Celestial Navigation*, writes that Anne Tyler "has a way of transcending [her characters'] peculiarities with such loving wholeness that when we examine them we keep finding more and more pieces of ourselves" (71-72). Acclaimed novelist John Updike, commenting on *Searching for Caleb*, agrees:

> So, too, Ms. Tyler's details pull from our minds recognition of our lives. These Pecks, polite and snide and tame and maddening and resonant, are *our* aunts and uncles; Justine and Duncan's honeymoon, when they are "isolated, motionless, barely breathing, cut loose from everyone else," is everybody's escape from a suffocating plurality of kin into a primitive twoness; the America they truck their fraying marriage through is our land, observed with a tolerance and precision unexcelled among contemporary writers. ("Family" 78)

Updike concludes, "Anne Tyler has the rare gift of coherence . . . " ("Family" 78).
Critic Wallace Stegner, too, finds in *Breathing Lessons* that "all you need – all *she*
needs – are ordinary people going about their everyday affairs in ordinary cities such
as Baltimore. . . . First [her characters] surprise us, then we recognize them, then we
acknowledge how much they tell us about ourselves" (148). Not only do these
writers feel that Anne Tyler is able to connect with readers' lives and enable them to
see themselves and their world more clearly and thoughtfully, but, as writer David
McCullough suggests in his review of *Saint Maybe*, ultimately she has been
recognized as "one of the most important – and one of the most downright enjoyable
– American writers at work today" (10).

Her artistry, however, is deceptively simple, Frank W. Shelton finds,
delighting in the thematic richness and narrative range of Tyler's works, explaining,
"Every appreciative reader of Tyler's novels notes her warm sympathy and affection
for her characters; at the same time, however, she observes those characters from afar
and allows them their privacy" ("Necessary" 175). In her review of Tyler's *A
Patchwork Planet* (a novel she believes needed a little more final editing), Hilary
Mantel ultimately agrees with Shelton, praising Tyler's sophisticated craftsmanship
and narrative power, arguing:

> Fifty pages of Tyler, even if they are superfluous in one way, are
> likely to be sharper, wiser, and more perfectly composed than the
> pages of almost any other English-language novelist. Anne Tyler's
> work is so easily enjoyable, so consistently entertaining, that it has
> sometimes been viewed as trivial and escapist. But she is in no way
> a superficial writer, and to interpret her as such is to misunderstand
> the values of [her] comedy. (26)

Herein, however, lies the difficulty critics have found in dealing with Anne Tyler's
fiction. Despite her clarity and artistry and enjoyability, despite the numerous

comparisons which have been made between Tyler and the great authors of the past and present, there remains much suspicion about the seriousness and value of her works. Is the experience she gives her readers a rich, substantive, challenging, and expansive one, as Mantel and others believe, or is it, instead, as her detractors charge, simply easy "escapism" – or worse, a regressive experience, negating the possibility of development and change?

Alice Hall Petry summarizes the problem of understanding and then evaluating Anne Tyler's fiction when she reports on "the often wide gap between popular and scholarly responses to her work, for although the common reader often admits to 'loving' Tyler's novels (a reaction rarely inspired by, say, the books of John Hawkes), the professional critic and the scholar have not always been so enthusiastic about her" (*Critical* 7). Anne Tyler's very popularity with readers, it seems, is itself a problem. What exactly makes her such an "enjoyable" writer? Does the Pulitzer Prize award for *Breathing Lessons*, Tyler's "weakest book in years," Petry asks, "lend credence to Susan Gilbert's thesis that Tyler was being rewarded publicly for avoiding touchy political issues, for suggesting conservatively that no individual or group could, or should, try to change our society" (*Critical* 13)? Is Tyler's perspective, as Susan Gilbert believes, not an empowering and enlarging one for the reader at all but actually a "static, politically conservative line on life, a nostalgic vision of an America of private houses and lawns" (139)? While rejoicing in Tyler's artistry, John Updike at the same time admits to finding her:

> soft, if not bullish, on America; its fluorescent-lit banks and gas stations, its high schools and low life, its motels and billboards and boring backwaters and stifling homes and staggering churches and scant, innocent depravities and deprivations are all to her the stuff of a tender magic, a moon lit scenery where poetry and adventure form as easily as dew. Small towns and pinched minds hold room enough for her; she is at peace in the semi-countrified, semi-plasticized,

northern-Southern America where she and her characters live. ("Loosened" 88)

Is Anne Tyler, then, too accepting of what she should find unacceptable (the "stifling," "depraved," "deprived," "pinched," "semi-countrified," and "semi-plasticized" in the society she writes about), as John Updike implies here? Does she have "a tendency to present a false or sentimentalized view of reality and an inability to sound the depths of human experience," as other critics have suggested (Templin 180)? Is she, as Charlotte Templin reports Tyler's critics of charging, "Unable to treat the full range of human experience and . . . deliberately trying to please and to charm by painting a rosy picture of reality and ignoring the darker side of human experience and the deep flaws in American society" (190)?

Charlotte Templin argues that, while Tyler may not be politically conservative, as many believe, or even "apolitical," that "it would be more accurate to say that she shares the politics of the American majority" (194). She clarifies her point by saying that Tyler's readers:

> are part of a broad section in the middle of the spectrum of American political opinion that excludes the ideologies of the left and the right. If not "bullish" on America, they at least accept the basic premises of American culture and relate to the theme of family life . . . and day-to-day middle class existence. (Templin 193-94)

Does Anne Tyler, then, simply give a complacent, unquestioning, middle-class audience what it wants, without extending it in any way, as John Updike suggests again when he accuses Tyler of "celebrat[ing] domestic claustrophobia and private stagnation" in American life, ultimately, at the end of her narratives, "leav[ing] the reader just where she found him [sic]" at the outset of her novels ("Loosened" 89; 88)?

In other words, many scholars and critics seem to find Anne Tyler, at her best, when they grant her artistry and literary achievement, more the Anthony Trollope than the Charles Dickens of our times. In fact, it might be useful to explore this seeming connection (one, however, that has not to my knowledge yet been made) between the acclaimed Victorian novelist Trollope and the contemporary writer Tyler to help determine just how they might, and might not, be alike. Daniel Pool describes Victorian authors Anthony Trollope and George Eliot both as "solid chroniclers of normal life, upholding the future of decent English life against the new sensationalists [such as mystery writer Wilkie Collins]" (161), just as Anne Tyler has been described as being the chronicler and endorser of what has been deemed the "familiar world" of "contemporary middle-middle to lower-middle class life in America" (Towers, "Roughing" 145). Further, by the late nineteenth century, Anthony Trollope had become "the acknowledged leader among 'realistic' novelists" of his period, anchoring his reputation by developing a "close identification with his public" (Skelton 151) and creating narratives filled with characters he "regarded . . . as real people whom he had lived with and argued with and worried with as he described them" (Fredman 33) – traits which have all been ascribed to Tyler and her fictional creations, as well (Towers, "Roughing" 145; Hoagland 144; Shelton, "Necessary" 175). In fact, Anne Tyler has told Wendy Lamb that she "feel[s] very fond of my characters. . . . I end up knowing them, much more than I put in [a] book" (55), and that she "carries" them around with her "as if they were real" (56) while she writes a novel, just as Anthony Trollope spoke of doing a century earlier.

In addition, in drawing his portraits of men and women, Anthony Trollope became famous "as author and narrator [for] exhibit[ing] the key quality of Palliser, his central character," the quality of "tolerance" (Hughes and Lund 26). This tolerance, or "generosity towards his characters," this "pluralistic appreciation of the value – as well as the limitations – that each [character] in one context or another proves to have" (Miller 26), made Anthony Trollope as famous in his own times as Anne Tyler has become in ours for her "tolerance and precision" (Updike, "Family" 78) in depicting a wide range of characters of both sexes and many walks of life (from bank robbers to preschool teachers, sculptors to nursing home attendants, furniture makers to fortune tellers).[2] She has been celebrated for the way "she has forged a kind of trust with her readers" (McPhillips 150) and for creating through her works "a veritable Quaker meeting-house in which every voice may be heard as possessing equal opportunity for authority" (Gerstenberger 139) – bank robbers included.

And yet Anthony Trollope was never seen, in his own times or since, as an "apolitical" writer in the way Anne Tyler, at times, has been judged as being, but as very much engaged in a political struggle, the outcome of which was the "steady advance of the middle class in their power struggle with the aristocracy" in nineteenth-century Great Britain (Skelton 151). Throughout his career, until *The Way We Live Now* (1874-75), Anthony Trollope affirmed through his characters "the middle-class virtues of work, moderation, and sense" and projected a "standard Victorian optimism" through his writing (Skelton 152; 155). His object was to enable his readers to cope with a changing society, develop proper manners and values that would lead to their rise within the social hierarchy, and yet resist, through his assistance, many trendy and, in his eyes, ill-thought-out "reform sentiments of his times [especially concerning the Church of England]" (Gilmour 117). Anthony Trollope wished to elevate his readers and improve his era by spreading his own "faith in the system of English life in the nineteenth century" (Hughes and Lund 26) – and, thus, despite his involvement in one of the most radical movements of his times, the empowerment of the middle class, he has been labeled widely today as a "conservative." So, too, some of Anne Tyler's sharpest critics believe that she also is a conservative writer, as well – that she is not apolitical, at all, simply standing aside from engagement in the vital issues of her times, but, rather, bolstering American middle-class values and resisting change in American society today.

Certainly there are those who believe that Anne Tyler's novels, no less than Anthony Trollope's in the previous century, convey a "seductive conservatism . . . [and act as] insidious preserver[s] of the status-quo," as Cathy Comstock has said of Anthony Trollope's *Barchester Towers* (8). For example, Susan Gilbert believes that Anne Tyler's message is really one of maintaining American life just as it is, arguing that Tyler's works suggest:

> that only meddlesome, silly people try to change things. The wise see to the unchanging heart of things and accept. Beyond change are the streets, the schools, the drop-outs, the disappearing husbands, the children without fathers, the teenage mothers unable to provide for themselves or for the children they bear [all depicted by Tyler and seemingly affirmed, just as they are, in her novels]. (142)

Here Susan Gilbert asserts that Anne Tyler washes her hands of America's social problems and glosses over the ugly realities of contemporary life in the United States for her readers. Critic Gayle Greene agrees that Tyler, and a number of other best-selling, contemporary American white women writers she criticizes, is so escapist that she finds that Tyler's fiction "hardly acknowledges the world, let alone challenges it" and "tends to nostalgia" rather than allowing for possibility and change in American life (200).

Because reading literature does affect our vision, our lives, our society, if only, nowadays, in more modest and subtle ways than film and television seem to do, it really does matter, in the final analysis, whether Anne Tyler's fiction works to affirm middle-class readers' lives and conservative American cultural values (as Susan Gilbert and Gayle Greene suggest above) or, as we will now see others assert, offers a challenge to her audience and her times to grow, develop, change, and improve. It is surely ironic that an author who has sought as determinedly as Anne

Tyler to be understood by her readers has ended up "variously [being] deemed a feminist, a nonfeminist, a postmodernist, a Victorian, a realist, a naturalist, and a romantic" (Petry, *Critical* 14). Paul Bail, too, comments on this confusion in assessing Anne Tyler's fiction, explaining, "There is a certain ambivalence in the critical and academic community toward Anne Tyler's writing, some considering her to be a unique and independent voice in American fiction, others feeling she is too popular and saccharine and not political enough" (21). Ironically, Bail notes, some of Tyler's sharpest critics (feminists such as Susan Gilbert and Gayle Greene) use "criticisms . . . [which] have traditionally been used to devalue women's writing, namely, that it is domestic and regional and utilizes a small canvas and that it is quiet and uplifting" (21).

Yet Alice Hall Petry, aware as she is of the critical controversy surrounding Anne Tyler's works, asserts that Tyler's narratives essentially do challenge readers through their depictions of women's economic need and psychological desire for "meaningful work" and also "by avoiding too-easy, 'feel-good' happy endings," stating that Tyler, finally, is a writer who "emerges much more of a feminist and realist than many commentators have been wont to admit" (*Understanding* 96). Mary Robertson agrees that Tyler only seems conservative on the surface while, in reality, her works are designed to call traditional values into question:

> A social critic might find that Tyler's very limitation of subject matter confirms an ideology of the private family to the detriment of political awareness, and a feminist reader might think that only female actions having more public importance than Tyler's seem to have can help the causes of women . . . however . . . Tyler's unusual use of narrative patterns accomplishes much that should interest the feminist and the social critic alike. (184)

Robertson goes on to argue that Anne Tyler's narrative patterns overturn readers' conventional expectations of family novels and their perceptions that the nuclear family unit operates "as the most significant agent of character development and social representation" at work in our society (190). Julie Persing Papadimas, too, finds that Tyler's domestic novels redefine the nature of the American family to reveal the "changing definition of the family and the sense of transiency that permeates life in the United States" today (45).

Other critics argue that Tyler's works enlarge and redefine the very nature of selfhood widely accepted in contemporary American society. Barbara Harrell Carson believes that Anne Tyler's plots are ones that challenge readers' expectations, overturning "the myth of the heroic isolate [which] has so permeated our self-conception that we are hard-pressed to find in the American mainstream literature works celebrating a different approach to selfhood" (24). Carson describes Tyler's affirmation of the adult self as one that incorporates both life complexity and community interconnectedness into its portrayal – a view that opposes the traditional concept of individuality throughout American literature as being found in Thoreau-like simplicity and isolation. Margaret Morganroth Gullette agrees that Anne Tyler offers readers an atypical and, at the same time, fuller representation of selfhood than most fiction today presents, depicting in her novels what Gullette views as "the highest idea of adulthood we can yet accept from fiction" (*Safe* xxix). Gullette believes that Anne Tyler's novels present a radical perspective on life development, one in which aging is seen as a positive, rather than a negative, process. She argues that Tyler's narratives enable readers to "imagine ourselves, as adults plunked down in narrative, not becoming victims, but *making ourselves beneficiaries of the drift of time*" (*Safe* 163).

Critics who believe that Anne Tyler's fiction challenges and enlarges the reader's sense of self and of life's possibilities in American culture do not find Tyler's characters "passive" (Gilbert 143; Brooks 343) but, rather, active players in their own lives who learn to take responsibility for themselves and others through the course of Tyler's narratives. These scholars do not find Tyler's message to be a fatalistic one denying the power and importance of individual human agency to affect change; neither do they find her endings overly optimistic or "rosy." For instance, novelist Doris Betts believes that Anne Tyler "tries to make her characters earn [their] solutions, step by step" (4), concluding that her "positivism has . . . [a] tough realism" (13) incorporated within the resolutions of her plots. Some theorize that, because Anne Tyler is a comic writer in the classic sense, her writing has been misunderstood and then evaluated as trivial and escapist. Charlotte Templin, for instance, argues that Anne Tyler "is getting praise from those who are attuned to comic art for reasons that have to do with personal makeup and literary taste" (193). She asserts further:

> To the British, Tyler is an interesting writer, one who can offer enjoyment and insight into human life and American society. . . . British reviewers are generally uniformly positive, lacking in the outspoken negative criticism that is a major refrain in the American reviews. The British have a respected tradition – the comedy of manners – in which to place Tyler, and this may be another reason for her favorable reception. (179)

Hilary Mantel posits, too, that it is Tyler's comedy which leads critics astray and brings about charges of "superficiality" because, Mantel believes, these same critics "misunderstand the values of comedy." Further, Mantel feels that Tyler is quintessentially a comic writer, explaining, "Comedy is not a tool in [Tyler's] kit, but a central mechanism; it is not a means to soften pain but an end in itself. And pain is not absent from her planet. Her characters are the resilient survivors of quiet inner disasters" (26).

Of course, comedy has always dealt with serious social issues and painful realities, whether those of marriage or death, racism, class inequities, or the horrors of war, in the novels of Jane Austen, Charles Dickens, Anthony Trollope, Mark

Twain, or contemporary author Kurt Vonnegut, as in Anne Tyler's writing, as well. At the same time, comedy ultimately affirms human life, suggesting the survival of civilization and the possibility of human betterment. Joseph Mathewson believes that such comic ends, however, are out of fashion with today's critics, saying, "These days the few good writers who also dare to be hopeful provide themselves with the safety net of an ultimate worldly cynicism (like John Irving). Miss Tyler does her act without the net" (124). Margaret Morganroth Gullette finds the same bias against the midlife Bildungsroman works she studies (including Tyler's), a bias which she believes favors literature which "describes the lives of those who succumb rather than overcome" (*Safe* 156). Such preferred works as these Gullette labels "decline narratives," providing readers with a message "that decline is a seductive alternative to improvement. . . . the plot has been engineered to bring about defeat" for characters and readers alike (*Safe* 160). Further, she finds in these works a "prejudice that only the privileged can experience normal development, survive the dangerous age [young adulthood], benefit from living longer, and know enough about their inner life to be grateful for aging. If some people have more to overcome to arrive at safe-at-last stories, their stories should be all the more worth telling" (*Safe* 157). Gullette finds the novels of Anne Tyler, Saul Bellow, Margaret Drabble, and John Updike affirm life, "assert[ing] . . . only that one important individual's life is capable of improving over time despite age. They recognize the possibility that something positive may increase. They don't ignore evil: it gets incorporated in the fictional vision, but not as the last word" (*Safe* 150-51).

Thus, we are left with two very different – in fact, diametrically opposed – views of Anne Tyler's novels at the present time. Try as hard as she might to connect with her readers and be clear in her writing, Tyler has been viewed, on the one hand, as offering "imaginary gardens" without "real toads," American poet Marianne Moore's derogatory image for romanticized literature ("Poetry" 1493), and, on the other, as undermining and challenging some of America's most firmly held and fundamental values. She has been seen, at once, as endorsing the status-quo and as promoting a new and radical view of self, family, and the life process, as a whole. As we have seen, some find her characters passive, submitting to whatever life has offered them and refusing to challenge society in any way, whereas others argue that her protagonists stand up, take charge of their lives, and defy society's assumptions about who they are and what they can accomplish in life. Her fictional worlds have been labeled, at once, as we have seen, "deterministic," "fatalistic," and "resigned," as well as "positive," "hopeful," and "empowering."

Of course, all great literature leads to a variety of interpretations, including conflicting ones, and rewards even the same reader with new insights and a deeper understanding over time. However, as Jonathan Culler has said, even the most "traditional text," as well as the much more radical one, "must challenge the reader in some way and lead to a re-reading of the self and the world" (191) if it is to remain valued and stay in print. But this is the very issue under debate: is Anne Tyler a great writer, whether a modern-day Charles Dickens, an Anthony Trollope, or a Jane Austen, helping readers in some way to "re-read" both the self and the world (as Culler has suggested she must to endure), and are her novels worth further critical exploration over the coming years, or should she be designated a mere popularizer and light entertainer whose literary reputation cannot sustain the test of time? As Paul Bail has explained, for all the comparisons made between Tyler and Dickens, Hawthorne, Austen, or Welty, "It remains to be seen whether the critical establishment will preserve Anne Tyler's writing in the coming century or will dismiss it, as has happened in the past to so many well-loved women authors" (21).

Because I value Anne Tyler's fiction, as do Paul Bail, Alice Hall Petry, and many other critics, care about her literary reputation, and want to play a part in making sure that her novels continue to be read and evaluated as seriously as I believe they deserve, I have embarked on this extended study to look more fully at the critical issue of just how Anne Tyler's works ask us to "re-read" ourselves and our culture in new ways. Whether Tyler is a conservative or a liberal is not the main issue here (although I tend to see her as more of the latter than the former). I believe few writers are simply one or the other, however – that the same author may be "conserving" of one thing and not of another, "liberal" about certain issues and not about others, as is the case, certainly, with Victorian author Anthony Trollope.[3] Instead, the main question I would like to address here is how Anne Tyler enables her readers to see themselves and their society in fresh and unexpected ways.

Because Anne Tyler has been so good at portraying popular American culture, I believe she has often been over-identified with that culture and seen as merely reflecting and affirming its values. However, as I will argue in the following chapters, the very structure of Tyler's novels, the narrative trajectories of her plots, and the challenges they present protagonists and readers alike, suggest otherwise. I hope to show how Anne Tyler challenges her protagonists and readers not to rise through the ranks and enter respectable society, as Anthony Trollope did with his reading audience in the nineteenth century, but, instead, encourages them to fall, both materially and socially, in order to develop spiritually. She does not want her characters and her readers to find societal acceptance – which she finds unimportant and misleading – but inner acceptance, instead. She challenges them not to see themselves as their culture's consumers, but as its producers; not as its victims, but as its survivors; not as helpless but as helpful in working out solutions to life problems. Through her narratives, I believe, Anne Tyler encourages an identity which opposes that which American business and advertising so powerfully and persuasively legitimize: an identity not as a spectator and buyer but as a maker, shaper, designer, and doer. Tyler portrays endorsement as coming to her characters not from the outside world (from designer labels or fancy cars, from professional positions or college degrees, as advertising and other media most often suggest), but as coming from inside themselves through constant evaluation and re-evaluation of life choices and goals, as well as through the hard work of determining "what to lose," in Macon Leary's words in *The Accidental Tourist* (310).

What Macon Leary doesn't fully recognize, as yet, but what this novel and others in the Tyler canon finally reveal, is that "choos[ing] what to lose" also means "choosing what to gain." Fairy tale endings may not be possible for Tyler's characters, but real life challenges are shown, instead, as offering them the possibility of personal growth, a sense of accomplishment, and inner satisfaction. Tyler's comic art affirms those characters who refuse to see themselves as life's victims and, instead, make hard choices in their lives. While their decisions concerning what to lose and what to gain may not seem to be ones of major consequence for their society, perhaps, Tyler's works often reveal a greater significance than at first meets the eye. As Virginia Woolf has said of Jane Austen, "What she offers is, apparently, a trifle, yet is composed of something that expands in the reader's mind and endows with the enduring form of life scenes which are outwardly trivial" (qtd. in "Jane" 209). Anne Tyler's works, too, I believe, have this power to present domestic scenes and personal interrelationships in ways that will grow in significance in readers' minds and help them to shape their lives in new ways.

In the following chapters, I will examine how Anne Tyler's quiet domestic dramas gently overturn the conventional expectations and mores of American society. What seems ordinary in her fictional world is often quite extraordinary; her unassuming heroes and heroines come to act in ways which are, at times, surprisingly courageous; their choices, finally, are ones that come to validate life on quite different societal terms than those publicly celebrated in American culture today. While successfully reflecting the contemporary American reality of her readers, Tyler subtly challenges that reality through her sixteen novels, embracing the unexpected and rejecting the familiar in American culture. The following chapter, Chapter Two, will consider the pattern of loss, death, division, and dysfunction in the families Anne Tyler's novels portray. Despite their desire for family stability and perfection, Anne Tyler's protagonists learn to cope with family failure and upheaval – and even contribute to it through their own decisions to depart, divorce, remarry, and disrupt family continuity. In this chapter, I will look at the way her characters find family instability leads unexpectedly to spiritual growth and a newly-discovered sense of well-being.

Chapter Three will trace the downward economic movement many of Anne Tyler's main characters face as they change jobs, experience financial loss, and leave the security of their nuclear families. As they move into trailers, repair ramshackle houses, take on menial jobs, or find themselves in reduced circumstances their pasts have not always prepared them to meet, Tyler's characters frequently discover adventure, interconnect with others, and rise to meet life's challenges.

In Chapter Four, I will look at how Anne Tyler's characters continue to dream of a mythic, genteel past in an unexpectedly topsy-turvy world. Uprooted from long-standing values and traditions, her characters find their lives filled with uncertainty in a turbulent, ever-changing culture. Nevertheless, clinging to the past proves paralyzing and counter-productive. Tyler questions cultural myths of an ideal past and suggests, further, that her characters not only can cope with contemporary life but progress when they do so. The best of her protagonists move from endurance, to adaptability, to embracing change as a means to a better life. Accepting the inevitability of cultural change can lead to personal as well as societal progress in Tyler's novels.

Chapter Five then focuses on the overall arc of decline of Tyler's narrative trajectories – experiences which paradoxically enrich the lives of Anne Tyler's protagonists. As Tyler's men and women grow older, lose their youth or their looks, and "slip-down" or "slip-away" socially, forfeiting more comfortable pasts and dreams of more hopeful futures, they do not find despair and misery, as the culture has promised; instead, they often find their lives enhanced by a sense of upward movement both morally and spiritually. Anne Tyler's novels consciously overturn Disneyesque, fairy tale patterns and promises, forcing protagonists to replace "happy-ever-after" scenarios with ones less brightly colored, ones which require them to make difficult decisions about "what to lose" (AT 310), but also what to gain, ones which reward them in unexpected ways.

Finally, in the last chapter, I will look at how Anne Tyler replaces the mainstream values of late-twentieth and early-twenty-first century American consumer capitalism with her own, quite different, values. While her works reflect the obsessions and dreams, fears and realities, of the contemporary American experience, Tyler nonetheless challenges her society's mores through her protagonists' final choices and unexpected decisions. She offers her middle-class audience a different way to look at their lives – an alternative value system by which to measure their own life progress. Her fiction ultimately reveals the way we fool ourselves – and are fooled by society – into thinking that we have no choices at all – or no good choices, at least. Her fiction empowers readers by confronting them with her protagonists' development and growth as they come to recognize that they actually have made choices in the past, that they are doing so still as they cope with problems in their lives, and that the actions they have taken and will continue to take are affecting the shape of their lives and the nature of their society. In telling her stories, and telling them well, Anne Tyler challenges her readers to re-examine their own lives, their own decisions (those they have taken or those they have avoided), and the society they have thereby been engaged in creating. In these ways, as I will show, Anne Tyler's fiction remakes the world for her protagonists and readers alike.

Notes

Quotations from Anne Tyler's novels are given with the following abbreviations:
AT   *The Accidental Tourist* (1985)
AM   *The Amateur Marriage* (2004)

BWWWG   *Back When We Were Grownups* (2001)
BL   *Breathing Lessons* (1988)
CN   *Celestial Navigation* (1974)
CW   *The Clock Winder* (1972)
DHR   *Dinner at the Homesick Restaurant* (1982)
EP   *Earthly Possessions* (1977)
IMEC   *If Morning Ever Comes* (1964)
LY   *Ladder of Years* (1995)
MP   *Morgan's Passing* (1980)
PP   *A Patchwork Planet* (1998)
SM   *Saint Maybe* (1991)
SFC   *Searching for Caleb* (1975)
SDL   *A Slipping-Down Life* (1970)
TCT   *The Tin Can Tree* (1965)

1.   Robert McPhillips in "The Baltimore Chop," a review of Anne Tyler's *Breathing Lessons*, also argues that Anne Tyler's "fiction belongs to the tradition of the American romance, pioneered by Hawthorne far more than to that of the realistic or naturalist novel" (151).

2.   In an interview with Wendy Lamb, Anne Tyler admitted, "I like every one of my characters; this is very important to me. My mother is shocked by this. She says, 'How can you *like* someone like Jake (the bank robber in *Earthly Possessions*)?' But what I like is a sense of character, however spiky or difficult the person may be" (55).

3.   M. Stanton Evans insists that conservatism and liberalism are not "disparate elements" and believes the two have become "unnatural[ly] separat[ed] . . . because of the way we have been taught our intellectual history" (125-26) – that actually they have a "natural and necessary unity" (125). I will argue that Anne Tyler's novels oppose many of the basic traits of capitalism which, as Garry Wills points out in *Reagan's America: Innocents at Home*, is "an instrument for change, for expansion, driven toward new resources, products, markets. . . . There is nothing less conservative than capitalism, so itchy for the new" (381-82). Tyler is "conservative" in resisting consumer capitalism and in her concern for "the cohesion and continuity of society – what makes people band together and remain together with some satisfaction" within their families, their communities, their society (Wills, *Confessions* 213). Yet these very "conservative" stances are ones most often labeled "liberal" by our society. At the same time, I will argue that Tyler's fiction works to change, open up, and "liberalize" readers' views of their lives, their families, and their communities.

Chapter Two
Growing Through Family Loss

On one point all the critics tend to agree: Anne Tyler's subject is the American family. Immediately, this topic rings up conservative slogans of recent decades, such as "the family that prays together stays together" and the importance of "family values" in American society, as well as advertising messages to "call home," have "family fun" together, or "protect" those you love. But Anne Tyler complicates the issue by insisting on revealing that there are multiple families affecting all our lives. She insists on asking *which* family her characters are to value and hold dear: the nuclear family into which they were born; the families they have developed by marrying or forming an attachment outside the closed nuclear group; or those strangers they interact with on a daily basis and have come to consider family over the years? In *Searching for Caleb*, when Daniel Peck's step-mother, Laura Baum Peck, tells him, "'Always remember, Daniel,' she said, straightening his collar, 'that you must live up to your family's name,'" Tyler's narrator adds, "she never explained what she meant by that. Her darkies broke into hissing laughter on the kitchen stairs and asked each other in whispers, 'What family? What name? *Peck*?' but she never heard them" (51). Anne Tyler asks the hard questions: who, exactly, *is* and *is not* family and how should her characters deal with the often hostile and competing forces of "family" in their lives? Further, Tyler asks whether any family (whatever group that might be) has the right to demand complete constancy and loyalty, as well as whether anyone should remain faithful to family when it goes against his or her nature and best interests.

In Anne Tyler's fiction, we find that family is not a "given" but largely a matter of choice. By the end of each work, Tyler's protagonists have usually lost some family members but gained others, often those they feel constitute a "better" family in which to grow and develop fully as adults. They have done so, in large part, by choosing who to have around them. While their choices may not be ones we would make, most importantly they are ones that they have made for themselves. In losing one family, they usually find they have gained another.

Yet many critics have called Anne Tyler's fiction "deterministic" and have found her characters "doomed" to their nuclear family fates. Mary Ellis Gibson entitled her essay on Tyler "Family as Fate: The Novels of Anne Tyler." While Gibson does not believe Tyler is "either a fatalist or a nihilist" and her characters do continue "attempting to nourish each other" in her works (172), Gibson points out their constant struggle against "the weight of heredity, of fate and responsibility" (168) marking their lives. Grace Farrell in her analysis of *Celestial Navigation* describes, too, how Tyler's characters in this novel are weighed down by loss, "loss that, in one form or another, ultimately violates all domestic units, leaving abandoned survivors" in each family (231). Edward Hoagland in his review of *Breathing Lessons* writes that Anne Tyler's fiction belongs to "the literature of resignation" which accepts whatever life has given us (144), while Mary J. Elkins speaks of Tyler's "deterministic world" in *Dinner at the Homesick Restaurant* where siblings try to help each other through lives which seem everlastingly scarred by family injuries (125). Robert Croft also believes that Tyler's theme is the "contradictory force" of family in her characters' lives. He says:

> On the one hand, family members seek to maintain links with their relatives because the family unit defines an individual's identity, provides security, and creates a vehicle for giving and receiving love. ... At the same time, however, members of a family often experience

> the exact opposite feeling about family. . . . [feeling it necessary] to
> rebel against its restrictiveness and its constant demands. (*Bio* 72)

Critics find that family, whether accepted or rejected, tends to dominate Anne Tyler's characters' lives and psyches – with Tyler continually "probing the dark corners and the sharp edges of family relationships" (Kilgore).

It is John Updike, however, who has most forcefully described Anne Tyler's family-haunted characters in one essay after another. In his review of *Searching for Caleb*, John Updike describes "Miss Tyler's vision" as one in which "heredity looms as destiny, and with the force of a miracle people persist in being themselves" ("Family" 76). In his review of *Earthly Possessions*, he describes "a fundamental American tension . . . between stasis and movement, between home and escape. Home is what we are mired in; Miss Tyler in her darker mode celebrates domestic claustrophobia and private stagnation" ("Loosened" 89). Again, in "On Such a Beautiful Green Little Planet," Updike writes of *Dinner at the Homesick Restaurant* as a "genetic comedy" which "deepens into the tragedy of closeness, of familial limitations that work upon us like Greek fates and condemn us to lives of surrender and secret fury" (107). Her theme is the underside of family, Updike suggests, which Tyler portrays "searchingly and grimly," exposing "the violences, ironies, and estrangements within a household, as the easy wounds given dependent flesh refuse to heal and instead grow into lifelong purposes" ("On Such" 108). What Anne Tyler reveals in *Dinner at the Homesick Restaurant*, Updike believes, is the "bitter *narrowness* of life . . . as the decades accumulate, to claustrophobic and sad effect" ("On Such" 108).

In fact, the word "claustrophobic" would seem to define the condition of the nuclear family for many of Anne Tyler's characters. Ira Moran in *Breathing Lessons* feels "suffocated" by having to care for his father and two sisters, as well as his wife and their two children (166). He tries to imagine what his life might have been like without them:

> Well, if he had put his sister Dorrie in an institution, then – something state-run that wouldn't cost too much. And told his father, "I will no longer provide your support. Weak heart or not, take over this goddam shop of yours and let me get on with my original plan if I can cast my mind back far enough to remember what it was." And made his other sister venture into the world to find employment. "You think we're not *all* scared?" he would ask her. "But we go out anyway and earn our keep, and so will you."
>   But she would die of terror. (*BL* 130)

Ira cannot see a way out of the trap of his family, just as Morgan Gower feels helplessly "oppressed" by his mother and sister crowding in on top of his life with Bonny Gower, then later on top of his life with Emily Meredith (*MP* 35; 287). Tyler's characters come to feel crushed under the burden of their nuclear families, no matter how much they might love them. Twenty-five-year-old Ben Joe Hawkes in *If Morning Ever Comes* rushes home to be of help when his sister Joanne separates from her husband Gary, only to feel "by evening the weight of home settling back on him, making him feel heavy and old and tired" (70). The institution of family also weighs heavily on Duncan Peck, making him "feel desperate" when he thinks of having a child of his own: "The idea of a family – a closed circle locking him in, some unlucky child whom *he* would lock in" (*SFC* 142), seems to Duncan designed to create a cycle of unending misery. He watches as his family, the Baltimore Pecks, wall themselves off from others, "digging the moat a little deeper. They're pointing out all the neighbors' flaws and their slipping dentures and mispronunciations, they're drawing in tighter to keep the enemy out" (*SFC* 88). Family life seems to Emily Meredith, as well, to "make things, oh, so ingrown, so twisted" in *Morgan's Passing* (226), while Jenny Tull in *Dinner at the Homesick Restaurant* feels a similar despair about family. Jenny asks herself, "was this what it came to – that you never could escape? That certain things were doomed to continue, generation after generation?" (209). Anne Tyler's works are filled with "images of crowding and pressure," with characters who feel "pressed, crowded, and claustrophobic" in the very midst of the nuclear family haven, as Margaret Morganroth Gullette has noted in her study of Tyler's family novels (*Safe* 14; 15).

Escape from family is the dream of a majority of Anne Tyler's characters. There is James Green in *The Tin Can Tree* who spent his childhood from the age of four on "like Houdini," fashioning escape after escape from the "dark and heavy" self-righteousness of his religious father and family (258; 256) – only to spend the rest of his life taking care of his brother Ansel "because he couldn't walk out on that one, final member of his family that he hadn't yet deserted" (177). In *The Amateur Marriage*, Lindy Anton deserts her "claustrophobic" family, whom she remembers as "just the five of us in this wretched, tangled knot, inward-turned, stunted, like a trapped fox chewing its own leg off" (300) – staying away for twenty-nine years while her parents raise her son Pagan. Only when she sees a newspaper photograph of her grown son, celebrating his work as a "longtime child and family advocate" (*AM* 276) – the antithesis of Lindy herself, does she begin to attend the occasional Anton family dinner . Mary Tell, too, who has "turned out not to be a believer," is anxious to get away from the "narrow life" she finds her Baptist parents leading in *Celestial Navigation* (63;64), just as Emily Meredith in *Morgan's Passing* plans to escape her "ordinary and pale" (yet eccentric) Quaker family life for a more exciting (and at the same time more mainstream) existence in college (62). Years later her Aunt Janie reminds Emily that she had once told her mother, "'Mama, I do not intend to go to Meeting [at college] . . . and all I want is blue jeans. I'm getting out,' you said, 'I'm going to *join*, get to be part of some big group, not going to be different ever again.' What a funny little thing you were! But of course [your mother] paid you no mind, and rightly so . . . quite rightly so" (*MP* 204). Tyler's families often remain either indifferent to or unchanged by the rebellion of individual members.

Escapes from family often prove difficult or illusory for Anne Tyler's characters. Charlotte Emory in *Earthly Possessions* has spent her childhood agonizing over "two main worries . . . one was that I was not their true daughter, and would be sent away. The other was that I *was* their true daughter and would never, ever manage to escape to the outside world" (15). In spite of her desire to flee, Charlotte finds herself married while still living in the same house "my *mother* was born in," while her "children go to the same school I did and one even has the same teacher" (*EP* 187). Charlotte must be kidnapped before she can find her way into "the outside world" (*EP* 15), but returns to her same overly familiar surroundings at the end of the novel. In *Searching for Caleb*, Margaret Rose Peck does manage to escape the Peck family fortress, running away from her husband Daniel and their six children – only to die in a hotel fire.[4] No successful escape from family seems possible, many Tyler characters come to feel, no matter how desperate they are to elude the fate of family in their lives. Even when Duncan Peck in *Searching for Caleb* leaves home and moves away from Baltimore, the weight of his Peck family history follows him. Periodically, he begins to notice "that he was treading an endless round of days just as his pinched, unimaginative family had done before him" (*SFC* 35). When he starts "to reflect upon the bars of his cage" (*SFC* 35), he works fewer hours, drinks bourbon, and plays solitaire, finally planning "another venture" somewhere where he hopes "Peckness" can no longer catch up with him (*SFC* 35). His relative, Caleb Peck, had seemingly managed to escape long ago, in 1912, after finding that he grew "quieter every year" he remained in Baltimore, living in the Peck family home, carrying on his father's import business (*SFC* 58). When, over sixty years later, in 1973, Caleb's brother Daniel succeeds in tracking him down, he writes asking Caleb to come home to Baltimore; once more, Caleb feels the pull and pall of the Pecks in his life. Reading Daniel's letter, Caleb "rebelled against them all, their niggling, narrow ways, but then some homeliness in the turned-down corners of their mouths would pull at him; then he reached out, and was drowned in their airless warmth and burdened with reminders of all the ways he had disappointed them" (*SFC* 279-80). Caleb accompanies Justine Peck home to Baltimore, only to escape once more, slipping out of his bedroom in the middle of the night before having to meet the entire Peck entourage and disappear into their midst again.

Most of the time, Tyler's characters try to "slip out" of their nuclear families by marrying a family "outsider" different from or completely unknown to their families. Here, again, however, they soon come to feel helplessly overtaken and trapped by events which seem to have simply "befallen" them. As Edward Hoagland says, Tyler's characters "remain bemused or bewildered by the fortuitous quality of most major 'decisions' in their own or others' lives, particularly by how people come to marry whom they do: a month or two of headlong, blind activity leading to years and years of stasis" (141). For example, in *Celestial Navigation*, Mary finds herself married to Guy Tell at sixteen years of age, at a time when she "had never even had a real date" (66). She elopes, determined to disobey her parents, "I thought, I am never going to be like them, I have already broken free," all the while asking, "Why aren't they taking better care of me? . . . [admitting] I kept expecting my parents to follow me and take me back, but they didn't" (*CN* 65-66). Suddenly a teenaged wife and mother, Mary Tell finds herself "*full* of life, with not enough people to pour it into," realizing to her dismay, "My world had turned out narrow after all – different from my parents', but just as narrow" (*CN* 76). Having extricated herself from one headlong, disastrous marriage to Guy Tell, what does Mary do but accept Jeremy Pauling's suggestion that (as Guy has refused her a divorce) they "*pretend*" to be married, confessing that she accepted "because it was all I could think of to do at the time" (*CN* 125; 214).

Other young Tyler heroines "fall" into marriage just as haphazardly and disastrously as Mary Tell. Evie Decker in *A Slipping-Down Life* marries to escape the tedium of life at home before she has even graduated from high school – only to end up alone and pregnant in her father's house a few months later. It is not that Evie has been swept away by passion – not at all. When Evie kisses her husband-to-be, Drum Casey, "they stayed pressed together between kisses, looking out over each other's shoulders like drivers meeting on opposite lanes of a highway" (*SD* 138). Still, they decide to marry because Drum wants a "*change*" as much as Evie wants some excitement in her life (*SD* 130). Having desired some kind of forward movement, Evie finds herself nonetheless disappointed as she rushes forward into marriage, "Things moved too fast. She had wanted a courtship, with double dates and dances and matching shirts, but all she got was three minutes of staring at sleeping houses" before saying, "Oh, well. Why not?" (*SD* 131). Young Jenny Tull, following her first marriage in *Dinner at the Homesick Restaurant*, also admits to having made a reckless mistake, explaining her act by saying, "she'd had no idea (would any unmarried person?) what a serious business she was playing with, how long it lasts, how deep it goes. And now look: the joke was on her. Having got what she was after, she found it was she who'd been got. Talk about calculating! He [her husband Harley Baines] was going to run her life, arrange it perfectly by height and color" [as had her mother Pearl Tull before] (103-04).[5] For many Tyler characters, escape from the nuclear family into marriage proves no escape at all.

In Anne Tyler's fiction, "getting a spouse seems to be a kind of accident" (Gullette, *Safe* 113), no matter how intentional or well-planned the act might have been. Marriage seems to leave a majority of Tyler characters dazed by what has happened to them. The widowed Mrs. Emerson in *The Clock Winder* "couldn't remember which man she had ended up with. It was all the same in the end" (238). In *The Amateur Marriage*, Pauline Barclay Anton looks back at her WWII romance with Michael Anton, admitting it was entirely possible "that she had just wanted a boy of her own to send off to war" (73). Emily Meredith in *Morgan's Passing* chooses Leon Meredith as her husband only to find, "she had locked herself in permanently with someone she couldn't bear" (215). Emily feels she has turned into a fairy tale princess trapped in the wrong fairy tale, imprisoned "in that room with that sewing machine; I feel like someone in a story, some drudge. I feel like the miller's daughter, left to spin gold out of straw" (*MP* 183). In *Searching for Caleb*, Meg Peck, too, finds that her desire for "a normal happy life" away from her bizarre parents has brought her unaccountably into a new and even more strange life surrounded by "*crazy* people" (*SFC* 229). Similarly, Rebecca Davitch's marriage (to a man who dies six years later) leads, incomprehensibly, to her lifelong cohabitation with a perfect stranger, her late father-in-law's elderly brother: "Rebecca had spent more years now with Poppy than with anyone she'd ever known; and she didn't even especially like the man" (*BWWG* 24). In *Earthly Possessions*, Charlotte marries Saul Emory to find herself equally bewildered by what has happened to her life, "I couldn't understand how we'd arrived so soon at the same muddy, tangled, flawed relationship that I had with everyone else" (101-02). She looks around her overstuffed, overcrowded house and finds: "A husband was another encumbrance; I often thought that" (*EP* 37), hating Saul's newly undertaken vocation of the ministry but taking a perverse "pleasure in his distance [as he preaches in the pulpit], in my own dream docility and my private, untouchable deafness" (*EP* 110).[6] Charlotte Emory may feel she has been mysteriously locked into a stultifying marriage, but she will not allow her husband entry into the inner-sanctum of her mind.

Finally, in *Ladder of Years*, Delia Grinstead reads *Captive of Clarion Castle*, feeling that she too has been "captured" by her late father's medical assistant, swept up by a man who simply had "reached. . . . the marrying stage of life" and found her to be the first woman with a castle and a father's riches to offer (*LY* 38). In the same work (one filled with wives fleeing the confinement of their marriages), Ellie Miller reflects on her abandoned marriage, "Funny how men always worry ahead of time that marriage might confine them. . . . Women don't give it a thought. It's afterwards it hits them. Stuck for life! Imprisoned! Trapped forever with a man who won't let you say 'parenting'" (*LY* 228). All of these women feel trapped by marriage and, at the same time, mystified as to how they allowed these liaisons to come about in the first place – not to mention how these relationships ended up being so disappointing, so unsatisfying.

Yet Tyler's men also "fall" into marriage in equally haphazard ways. Michael Anton in *The Amateur Marriage* seems to agree with his ex-wife on one thing alone: "maybe I just wanted a girlfriend. I was young and I wanted a girl and Pauline was the one who was there" (231). Similarly, Ben Joe Hawkes in *If Morning Ever Comes* asks Shelley Domer to come with him to New York on the spur of the moment, then adds, "We could . . . hell, get married," although he has had no thought of this beforehand and the words sound "absurd" even to his own ears (209). Macon Leary in *The Accidental Tourist* reflects that he and Sarah paradoxically "got married *because* we were far apart" (200), causing Macon to resist a second mistaken marriage to Muriel Pritchett by saying, "I'm not ready for this! I don't think I ever will be. I mean I don't think marriage ought to be as common as it is; I really believe it ought to be the exception to the rule; oh, perfect couples could marry, maybe, but who's a perfect couple?" (284). Macon feels that his life has simply been overtaken by forces outside his control for far too long, "He reflected that he had not taken steps very often in his life, come to think of it. Really never. His marriage, his two jobs, his time with Muriel, his return to Sarah – all seemed to have simply befallen him. He couldn't think of a single major act he had managed of his own accord" (*AT* 351).

Tyler's men are as apt to be overtaken and bewildered by their marriages as are her women. Sam Mayhew in *Searching for Caleb* has married Caroline Peck, only to find himself overwhelmed by "Peckness" (even down to the kind of car he drives), while Jeremy Pauling in *Celestial Navigation* comes to feel so dazed by his "cluttered" house and ever-multiplying family (*CN* 156), as well as so diminished by Mary Tell's strength and capabilities, that he stays locked in his studio on the day of their wedding (after years of living together ostensibly as "man and wife"). Similarly, Beck Tull has found that the momentary perfection of his marriage to Pearl has quickly evaporated in her overpowering atmosphere, believing "[Pearl] wore me out. . . . Used up all my good points" (*DHR* 300). Morgan Gower, too, "disappears" upon entering into the Cullen family: marrying Bonny Cullen, moving into her father's house, managing one of the Cullen hardware stores, and living a life that "took away his actual identity while providing him with the time and money to compensate for the loss by playing different roles at his considerable leisure" (Petry, *Understanding* 163). Ultimately, however, this easy Cullen life fills Morgan Gower with despair; as he tells his wife Bonny, "Ah, God. I have to do something about this *life* of mine. . . . It's come to nothing. It's come to nothing" (*MP* 153).

Not only are Tyler's marriages often accidental occurrences which overtake, bewilder, and exhaust her characters, but the children that ensue, willynilly, have the same effect. As Barbara Harrell Carson says of Charlotte Emory in *Earthly Possessions*, "she moves into an engagement and then into marriage, absent of self. And even when her husband brings home a new baby for her to raise, dropping it 'like a stone' into her arms, she is comforted by the thought that she 'had no choice,' that 'everything had been settled for me' (*EP* 155)" (27). Charlotte regards her children as well as her husband as "encumbrances," adding, "(Not to mention their equipment: their sweaters, Band-Aids, stuffed animals, vitamins.) How did I end up with so much, when I had thrown so much away? I looked at my children with the same mixture of love and resentment that I used to feel for my Sleepy Doll" (*EP* 37). Parenthood is such an accidental affair that Charlotte's own mother believed she had been given the wrong child at the hospital, just as Mrs. Emerson in *The Clock Winder* decided that the baby Matthew (her eldest son) was not really her child at all.[7]

The "accident" of pregnancy, followed as it is by the demands of child-raising, also frightens many of Anne Tyler's characters. Maggie Moran in *Breathing Lessons* tells her daughter-in-law Fiona that when her son Jesse (now Fiona's husband) was born, she thought:

> "Wait. Are they going to let me just walk off with him? I don't know beans about babies! I don't have a license to do this. Ira and I are just amateurs." I mean you're given all these lessons for the unimportant things – piano-playing, typing. You're given years and years of lessons in how to balance equations, which Lord knows you will never have to do in normal life. But how about parenthood? Or marriage, either, come to think of it. Before you can drive a car you need a state-approved course of instruction, but driving a car is nothing, nothing, compared to living day in and day out with a husband and raising up a new human being. (182)

Tyler's characters find themselves thrust into parenthood every bit as unprepared as eighteen-year-old Ian Bedloe has been when he takes over his deceased brother and sister-in-law's three children without benefit of marriage (but with the help of his parents) in *Saint Maybe*. While Ian continues to hope that his father won't "let him go through with" this decision he has made to pass up college to raise three children (none of whom he believes is his own blood relative), he ends up embroiled in the responsibilities of child-raising for the next twenty years (*SM* 125).

Before Tyler's characters know it, there are children to be taken care of, children that "clutter" their lives, as Jeremy Pauling finds in *Celestial Navigation* (156). For some, the birth of a baby both brings about and destroys the marriage, at the same time. As Muriel Pritchett tells Macon Leary, "It was having the baby that broke our marriage up. . . . First, we got married on account of the baby and then we got divorced on account of the baby, and in between, the baby was what we argued about" (*AT* 175-76). Evie Decker's marriage in *A Slipping-Down Life* is also broken up, in this case by the impending arrival of a baby – as Evie realizes that Drum Casey will never be the kind of responsible parent she believes she will be, preferring the responsibility of a child to that of both an inert husband and a helpless infant, besides. In *Ladder of Years* Delia Grinstead's marriage outlasts the arrival of three children, but the babies quickly erase its early passion: "But the summer after that they had the baby with them (little Susie, two months old and fussy, fussy, fussy) and in later years the boys, and they had seldom managed even to stretch out on their blanket together, let alone steal back to their cottage" (*LY* 72). While Pauline Anton in *The Amateur Marriage* is afraid to go against conventional wisdom in conversations with her neighborhood friends, she has to admit to herself that she "wasn't so very sure that children really did improve a marriage" (68). Even the most nurturing of Tyler's parents find parenthood overwhelming, at times. While Mary Tell believes herself fulfilled by motherhood, she confesses to Miss Vinton, "But sometimes . . . I feel that every new baby is another rope, tying me down like a tent. I don't have the option to *leave* [Jeremy] any more. I'm forced to depend on him. He's not dependable" (*CN* 142). Devoted caretakers as they are, Emily and Leon Meredith also find parenthood overwhelming, "Somehow, this one small child [Gina] kept both of her parents continually occupied and teetering on the edge of exhaustion. They must be doing something wrong. It didn't look so hard for other people" (*MP* 87). They come to feel that, "from the start, [Gina] seemed to consume them" (*MP* 95).

The responsibilities of childcare often become too much, especially for Tyler's single parents. Lucy Bedloe, thrust on her own again by her second husband's death, tells little Agatha to watch her brother Thomas and infant sister Daphne since she can't afford to hire babysitters:

> "Face the facts, sweetheart: we're in the Department of Reality now."
> Their mother's favorite thing to say. Agatha hated hearing that and
> she would cover her ears like Thomas, but when she took her hands
> away her mother would still be talking: "You think I like having you
> with me every single second? Think I wouldn't rather just leave on
> my own any time I get the notion?" (*SM* 59)

The very children they love can turn into their parents' jailers and adversaries. Single parent Pearl Tull calls her three children "Parasites," adding cruelly, "I wish you'd all die, and let me go free. I wish I'd find you dead in your beds" (*DHR* 53). Pearl admits to being "an angry sort of mother. She'd been continually on edge; she'd felt too burdened, too much alone" (*DHR* 19). Yet, it was trying to be responsible for each of her three children during "all those years when she was the only one, the sole support, the lone tall tree in the pasture just waiting for the lightning to strike" that made her feel so overwhelmed, so "helpless . . . . How scary it is to know that everyone I love depends on me!" (*DHR* 31; 63). Ironically hurting the very children she tries to protect, Pearl says to her eldest son Cody, "I'm afraid I'll do something wrong" (*DHR* 63). Until her death, Pearl remains mystified by her children's distance, the way they seem determined to "shut [her] out" of their lives (*DHR* 125). She believes that "her family has failed. Neither of her sons is happy, and her daughter can't seem to stay married. There is no one to accept the blame for this but Pearl herself, who raised these children single-handed and did make mistakes, oh, a bushel of mistakes" (*DHR* 184-85). Yet Pearl cannot help but feel, "sometimes . . . that it's simply fate, and not a matter for blame at all. She feels that everything has been assigned, has been preordained; everyone must play his role. Certainly she never intended to foster one of those good son/bad son arrangements, but what can you do when one son is consistently good and the other consistently bad? What can the sons do, even?" (*DHR* 184-85). Once more, Anne Tyler's characters feel helplessly caught in the quagmire of family destiny, overtaken by events beyond their control. They feel "stuck" with their families, no matter how negative or destructive those family relationships have proven to be.

In discussing *The Tin Can Tree* and *If Morning Ever Comes*, Alice Hall Petry comments on a "pattern of negative interpersonal dynamics" in those two novels which I believe characterizes the majority of Tyler's families (*Understanding* 24). Petry concludes that "the large number of characters in both novels who are rejected or emotionally damaged by their own families would suggest that, in large measure, Tyler perceives families not as stable, nurturing entities but as potentially serious liabilities" (*Understanding* 27). Anne Tyler's characters not only feel trapped in their families, but most often wounded by them, as well. Parents criticize their children and make them feel unwanted in novel after novel. In *A Patchwork Planet*, Barnaby Gaitlin knows he is the "black sheep" of the Gaitlin family (35), having to tell "the same eternal relatives" on every holiday occasion "that, yes, I'm still a manual laborer; still haven't found my true calling; still haven't heard from my angel yet; maybe next year!" (36). When Barnaby's mother calls him to wish him a better New Year, he decodes her message to mean: *"Hope it's the end of all the trouble you've caused us. . . . Hope at long, long last you're planning to mend your ways; hope you'll meet a decent girl this year and find a job we're not embarrassed to tell the neighbors about"* (*PP* 43-44). Barnaby knows he is a failure in the eyes of his family.

In *A Patchwork Planet* Barnaby Gaitlin is as disappointing to his parents as his brother Jeff is pleasing – a pattern carried out in the good Ezra – bad Cody dyad in *Dinner at the Homesick Restaurant*; the "bypassed" and "displaced" Amanda versus the family's "youngest and smallest and weakest," perhaps more lovable, baby boy Jeremy Pauling in *Celestial Navigation* (41; 17); the dutiful Daniel versus his wayward brother Caleb Peck, whose mother tells the latter, "You have killed your half of your father" in *Searching for Caleb* (55); and even the live Simon who finds he cannot compete with his dead sister Janie Rose Pike in *The Tin Can Tree*, running away because he feels he won't be missed: "I think my mother'd say, '*Who* you say's gone? Oh, *Simon*!' she'd say. 'Him. My goodness. Did you remember to bring the eggs?'" (211). In *The Clock Winder* Elizabeth Abbott, too, is contrasted with her "*sweet and pretty*," newly married and pregnant, totally admirable sister Polly in a letter from her mother which concludes:

> *Honey I just wish you would settle down yourself some, finish at Sandhill College or get married, one. I know you don't like to hear me say that but I just have to tell you what's on my mind. Mrs. Bennett talking the other day said there's always one in every family that causes twice as much worry as all the others, not that you would love them any the less for it, well, I knew what she meant although of course I didn't say so.* (CW 37)

Elizabeth Abbott represents everything that is undesirable to her family. Other Tyler children also offend their parents by their "sheer *sniveliness*" (*TCT* 137); "let[ting] a man down" (*TCT* 256); not "fac[ing] up to things. . . . You always were duckers and dodgers" (*DHR* 33); "not being religious. Reincarnation was the end" (*CW* 62); as well as "leav[ing their mother] all alone . . . [and] driv[ing] everyone else off too," weighing down even fully-grown, adult children with "the feeling that it was they who had failed" (*CW* 50; 248).[8]

"Only" children, too, tend to be perceived as failing their parents. Duncan Peck sees his daughter Meg growing into all he had rejected when he left the Peck family behind: "He knew, for instance, that although Meg was of normal intelligence she had a mind that plodded and toiled, with narrow borders; that she was fiercely anxious for regularity, permanence, order. . . . [before her birth] he had feared all the genetic defects but the obvious one, total Peckness" (*SFC* 145). In the same way Meg's mother Justine has failed her father Sam Mayhew, once again by "chang[ing] into one of those damned Pecks, clannish and secretive with a veiled look in her eyes, some sort of private amusement showing when she watched an outsider. And Sam was an outsider. Not that she was *rude* to him. All the Peck girls had excellent manners. But he knew that he had lost her, all right" (*SFC* 76). Upon Justine's wedding to her cousin Duncan Peck, Sam Mayhew hurls the ultimate rejection at his daughter, "you have been a disappointing daughter in every way, all your life"(*SFC* 103). Whether blunt or subtle in their criticisms, many of Tyler's parents seem intent on inflicting lifelong psychological injuries upon the very children they love.

Yet Tyler's parents are not immune from the barbs of their children, either. Daphne tells Ian Bedloe in *Saint Maybe*, "You think I'm some ninny who wants to do right but keeps goofing. But what you don't see is, I goof on purpose. I'm not like you: King Careful, Mr. Look-Both-Ways. Saint Maybe" (264). Daphne's penetrating analysis is proof positive of what Morgan Gower has found in *Morgan's Passing*: "The trouble with fathering children was, they got to know you so well. You couldn't make the faintest little realignment of the facts around them. They keep staring levelly into your eyes, eternally watchful and critical, forever prepared to pass judgment. They could point to so many places where you had gone permanently, irretrievably wrong" (106). If parents judge their children harshly, the reverse is also true. So Delia Grinstead finds in *Ladder of Years*, as her baby, her "sweet, winsome" fifteen-year-old Carroll, begins "flinching from his mother's hugs and criticizing her clothes and rolling his eyes disgustedly at every word she uttered" (18). Delia increasingly feels "silly and inefficient" under Carroll's "look of utter contempt" (*LY* 23; 25) – a displeased scrutiny felt by other Tyler protagonists, as well, from Morgan Gower to Emily Meredith to Maggie Moran, as they fail to live up to their children's expectations. In *The Amateur Marriage*, even after Pauline and

Michael Anton have raised their runaway daughter Lindy's three-year-old son Pagan into a mature and productive adulthood (despite the trauma of their divorce, followed by Michael's remarriage), Lindy returns twenty-nine years later to berate her one remaining parent, Michael, for "those eternal family excursions!", as well as for her parents' catastrophic character defects: "you were ice and she was glass. . . . Two oddly similar substances, come to think of it – and both of them hell on your children" (300; 304). In response, Michael pleads, "Lindy, show some charity here. We did the best we could. We did our darnedest. We were just . . . unskilled; we never quite got the hang of things. It wasn't for lack of trying" (*AM* 304).

It would seem that Timothy Emerson in *The Clock Winder* has an idea that might work for parents as well as for children caught up in the corrosive dynamics of family interrelationships. Timothy believes in the value of "trading" families:

> [he] imagined a federal law ordering everybody to switch parents at a certain age. Then butter-fingered Elizabeth, her family's cross, could come sustain his mother forever and mend all her possessions, and he could go south and live a happy thoughtless life assisting Reverend Abbott at Sunday vespers. There would be a gigantic migration of children across the country, all cutting the old tangled threads and picking up new ones when they found the right niche, free forever of other people's notions about them. (*CW* 71)

This kind of freedom from the fixed judgments of relations, from "other people's notions about them" (*CW* 71), would be welcomed not just by parents and children, but by many Tyler spouses, as well.

In novel after Tyler novel, husbands and wives injure each other through their "notions" (or perceived notions) of who and what their partners are. In *The Accidental Tourist*, Macon Leary feels he has been put in a "false position" by his wife Sarah, who expects him to be in control, to be responsible in providing and taking care of the family (52), then criticizes him for "trying to slip through life unchanged," being "ossified" (142) in the very role she has demanded he play. He shocks even himself by erupting into anger at Sarah, "don't even start. By God, if that doesn't sum up every single thing that's wrong with being married. 'The trouble with you is, Macon –' and, 'I know you better than you know yourself, Macon –'" (*AT* 321). Other Tyler husbands also feel judged unfairly and unkindly by their spouses. While Bonny Gower tolerates her husband and is amused by his antics in *Morgan's Passing* (145), her attitude towards Morgan is a patronizing one, further diminishing his sense of self-worth. As Bonny admits to Emily Meredith, "think what he could accomplish if he used that brain for sensible things! If he straightened out. If he decided to go straight. . . . just *attending* to things" (144). In the same work, Emily Meredith feels weighed down by her husband Leon Meredith's thinly veiled criticism, as well: "He always makes it seem that everything was my idea, that I'm the one who organized our lives this way, but I'm not. I mean, if he just *sat*, what was I to do?" (*MP* 183). Nonetheless, Leon persists in believing of Emily, nothing "in the world . . . would make her really happy. Unless, perhaps, she could bring the whole solar system into line exactly her way, not a planet disobeying" (*MP* 192).

Tyler's husbands and wives often feel thrust into playing roles in the course of their relationships, roles they did not want in the first place but which, nonetheless, help to drive them apart. Mary Tell is anguished in *Celestial Navigation* to find:

> He [Jeremy] changed. I changed. He gathered some kind of stubborn, hidden strength while I became more easily touched by anything small and vulnerable – changes that each of us caused in the other, but they were exactly the ones that have separated us and that will keep us separate. If he calls me back he will be admitting a weakness. If I return unasked I will be bearing down upon him and plowing him under. If I weren't crying I would laugh. (217)

Despite their love for each other, Mary and Jeremy separate for good. Playing out male and female roles – of strength, on the one hand, and nurturing, on the other –

they lose their sense of individual self-worth. Jeremy knows that he has failed to be Mary's protector, and Mary knows that her mothering ways have smothered Jeremy. They can no longer live together and feel good about themselves.

It is this same sense of self-worth that has been eroded by other Tyler marriages, as well. Maggie Moran in *Breathing Lessons* tells her husband Ira, "you have to make a point of how illogical I am, what a whifflehead I am, how you're so cool and above it all" (33). Their very juxtaposition alongside one another, Maggie feels, furthers both her negative public image and her own private one: "Compared to Ira she looked silly and emotional; anybody would have. Compared to Ira she talked too much and laughed too much and cried too much. Even ate too much! Drank too much! Behaved so sloppily and mawkishly!" (*BL* 74-75). Charlotte Emory in *Earthly Possessions* also feels oppressed by the very proximity of her husband Saul's virtue. She desires to drive Saul off so that "this hopeless powerless feeling would vanish like a fog, if I could just drive him off. I would be free then of his judging gaze that noted all my faults and sins, that widened at learning who I really was. I would be rid of his fine and mannerly presence, eternally showing me up" (*EP* 104). Just as Charlotte Emory feels that her husband sees her as "evil" (*EP* 164), Delia Grinstead in *Ladder of Years* believes that her husband Sam finds her childish, "flighty, unstable, excitable" (206). After all, wasn't "it Sam, for instance, that everybody turned to in times of crisis? He always got to be the reasonable one, the steady and reliable one; she was purely decorative. But how had that come about?" (*LY* 127). Delia Grinstead has come to feel diminshed by Sam, "always so sure he was right," most importantly because she, too, believes, "the fact was, he *was* right, generally" (*LY* 206).

In the midst of being criticized and found wanting by wives, husbands, children, and parents, in the midst of lacerating arguments, family bickering, and tumultuous family gatherings, Tyler's characters most often come to feel quite alone.

Jeremy Pauling can't talk to his own children, who seem to him "visitors from the outside world" (*CN* 158). Daniel Peck, who has been loyal to the Peck family all his life, writes to his renegade brother Caleb, "I am not overly connected to my own descendants, not even to my granddaughter [and traveling companion Justine]. She means well of course but is so different from me . . ." (*SFC* 247). In *Saint Maybe*, Daphne and Ian Bedloe sit uncomfortably together at the dinner table where "most of their conversations felt disjointed, absentminded, like the scattered bits of talk after the main guests have left the room" (248). Barnaby Gaitlin and his father in *A Patchwork Planet* find they "have nothing further to talk about" at Barnaby's thirtieth birthday party after they have exchanged formalities and birthday greetings (68). In *The Amateur Marriage*, Michael Anton feels that he must end his marriage after a thirtieth wedding anniversary dinner where he realizes "all our remember-whens were quarrels," concluding, "It's been hell" (176). Further, Emily and Leon Meredith constantly "miss connections. . . . They started every morning so courteous, so hopeful, but deteriorated rapidly and ended up, at night, sleeping with their backs to each other on the outermost edges of the bed" in *Morgan's Passing* (213).

In *The Tin Can Tree*, as well, Joan Pike feels estranged from her "middle-aged" parents who "weren't sure what they were supposed to do with her; they treated her politely, like a visitor who had dropped in unexpectedly" (*TCT* 32;33), while Peter Emerson in *The Clock Winder* feels "completely on his own" as the youngest of his large family, following in his older brothers' and sisters' footsteps through the now "emptied and echoing" halls of his home, having "given up all attempts at belonging here" (117). Many Tyler characters feel miserable and out of place within their family homes. Duncan Peck speaks for quite a few others when he protests to his family:

> "I've spent eighteen years here growing deader and deader,
> listening to you skate across the surface. Watching you dodge
> around what matters. . . . Can't you say something that *means*
> something?" . . .
> "About what?" said his mother. . . .
> "Don't you want to get to the bottom of things? Talk about
> whether there's a God or not?"
> "But we already know," said his mother. (*SFC* 84)

Duncan Peck has come to feel an outsider in the very heart of his own family, as do
so many of Anne Tyler's characters throughout her sixteen novels.

As Julie Persing Papadimas concludes, "many [Tyler] characters find their
immediate relatives unapproachable and thus feel isolated. In fact, characters suffer
from the greatest degree of isolation when they reach out to their families for
understanding" (45). Ben Joe Hawkes makes a special trip home to help his family
in *If Morning Ever Comes*, but none of his sisters "took any notice of him" (70) and
he ends up feeling unwanted and useless, asking in bewilderment, "Why can't they
all just let *me* take care of them?" (145). Michael Anton in *The Amateur Marriage*
has come to feel "merely a frill. A luxury. A dessert" (296) after twenty-two years
of marriage to his second wife Anna Stuart (while, paradoxically, his divorced wife
Pauline had continued to rely on him to get her car serviced and shovel her walkways
right up to her sudden death in 1987). In *Ladder of Years*, Delia Grinstead, too, feels
"like a tiny gnat, whirring around her family's edges" (23), believing that her
disappearance from the family will merely cause them to say, "Well, at least we can
get things done right, now she's gone" (82). Morgan Gower also feels extraneous to
his family; his wife Bonny has failed even to tell him about one of her pregnancies
in the past, and now he seems to be the last to know of his daughters' impending
marriages (*MP* 97; 99). It is little wonder that Bonny Gower concludes that Morgan
needed attention he did not get from his family, yet she suggests that this need, too,
is a particular character failing on his part: "He only feels he's real when he's in

other people's eyes. . . . Things have to be *viewed.* All alone in the bathroom, he's no one. That's why his family doesn't count. They tend not to see him; you know how families are. So he has to go out and find himself in someone else's line of vision" (*MP* 269). When they are not being criticized by family members, Tyler's characters often find themselves simply tolerated or ignored – becoming completely dispensable, even invisible, they feel.[9]

In such psychologically destructive environments as Tyler's families prove to be, it is no wonder that her characters tend to form negative images of themselves. Charlotte Emory, Delia Grinstead, Elizabeth Abbott, Beck and Cody Tull, Morgan Gower, and Barnaby Gaitling could each join Joanne Hawkes Bentley in *If Morning Ever Comes* in saying, "Got so I couldn't bear my own self. . . . I left" (74).[10] Rebecca Davitch in *Back When We Were Grownups* is not alone in asking, "*How on earth did I get like this? How? How did I ever become this person, who's not really me?*" (20). When Tyler's characters haven't reached the point of actually disliking themselves, they still find it difficult to recognize themselves in the persons they have become. Sometimes they feel, further, that they have simply disappeared, swallowed up by family, to become nothing at all. Mrs. Emerson in *The Clock Winder* believes she has lost herself through her marriage and family; she thinks, "she had never been like herself again. All the rush of life in this house, that had carried her along protesting and making pushing-off gestures with both hands. All the mountains out of molehills, the molehills out of mountains. . . . 'The horrors I've seen taken for granted!'" she exclaims, as she reviews what has become of her life (237). Justine Peck, too, comes to feel lost in her own life. She "awoke one day to wonder how it had happened: what she had mislaid was Justine herself" (*SFC* 258). As Alice Hall Petry has said of *Searching for Caleb*, "A family dynasty, however wealthy or imbued with 'good taste,' is not necessarily conducive to the nurturance of the individual self" (*Understanding* 151) – nor, it would seem, are many of Tyler's smaller, less prestigious, less self-congratulatory family units beyond the Pecks, the Gaitlins, the Cullens, or the Emersons. In Anne Tyler's novels, family life seems especially designed to bring about a diminution or loss of self.

As if these damages are not enough to add to the list of injuries Tyler's families inflict on each other, there are, as well, the deaths, separations, and divorces which disfigure families and cause pain and hardship in the lives of Tyler's characters. In *The Accidental Tourist* and *The Tin Can Tree*, parents are devastated to experience the sudden deaths of their young children. Just the opposite happens in *Saint Maybe* when parents die and leave behind bewildered infants and toddlers. Teenagers and young adults are shocked to lose parents in *Morgan's Passing*, *If Morning Ever Comes*, *A Slipping-Down Life*, *Earthly Possessions*, *The Tin Can Tree*, and *Searching for Caleb*, while mature adults feel bereft, as well, upon the death of a mother or father in *Celestial Navigation*, *Dinner at the Homesick Restaurant*, *Ladder of Years*, *Saint Maybe*, *Earthly Possessions*, and *The Amateur Marriage*. The young, family-oriented Shelley Domer in *If Morning Ever Comes* is shattered to lose both parents and her only sister – her entire family – all at once in a fatal automobile accident.

In work after work, as well, Tyler families experience loss as couples separate: Jeremy Pauling and Mary Tell in *Celestial Navigation*; Beck and Pearl Tull in *Dinner at the Homesick Restaurant*; Joanne Hawkes and Gary Bentley in *If Morning Ever Comes*; Julian Edge and Rose Leary in *The Accidental Tourist*; Leon and Emily Meredith, as well as Morgan and Bonny Gower in *Morgan's Passing*; or Rosemary and Adrian Bly-Brice, Ellie and Joe Miller, and Delia and Sam Grinstead in *Ladder of Years*. Separations turn into divorces in other family units in Tyler's fiction: Pauline and Michael Anton in *The Amateur Marriage*; Fiona and Jesse Moran in *Breathing Lessons*; Mary and Guy Tell in *Celestial Navigation*; Jenny Tull and Harley Baines, followed by Sam Wiley, in *Dinner at the Homesick Restaurant*;

Muriel and Norman Pritchett in *The Accidental Tourist*; Lucy Bedloe and Tom Dulsimore in *Saint Maybe*; and Natalie and Barnaby Gaitlin in *A Patchwork Planet*, to give only a partial listing.

Family instability is inevitable in Anne Tyler's works, no matter how hard families work to hold onto a fixed center. In *Searching for Caleb*, the staid Pecks feel their family "suddenly cracked and flew apart like an old china teacup" (63) when, in 1912, Margaret Rose deserted Daniel and their six children, Caleb Peck disappeared, the family patriarch Justin Peck died, and the family business had to be sold off. Yet they persist as others desert the Peck homestead (Duncan and Justine) or die (Daniel Peck), continuing all the while to cling to the notion of the family's solidity. However, as contemporary novelist Jayne Anne Phillips has said of her own fiction about family:

> Regardless of whether there is a divorce or a death in the family, every family falls apart because their children grow up, the parents die, and they stop living together. Everybody has that experience of first loss, which is just the fact that people grow up. Most children, for some short period of time, have that sense of being wrapped within the family, it may be a dysfunctional family, but there still is that incredible structure that, to children in particular, seems everlasting. And I think when I write about these bonds breaking up, I'm not even so much talking about rootlessness, or what's happening in America, or the good old days versus the bad old days, or the past versus the present. I'm just talking about . . . the way things come to an end, everything comes to an end, and the way . . . human beings deal with loss, move beyond it, are either buried by it or stand on top of it and go on to something else. (154)

This, too, is Anne Tyler's subject – this sense of family hurt, abandonment, loss, debacle and disaster – which must be given into, endured, or triumphed over. As old Missouri tells Joan Pike in *The Tin Can Tree*, "Bravest thing about people, Miss Joan, is how they go on loving mortal beings after finding out there's such a thing as dying" (106). Hurt can overwhelm characters such as Lucy Bedloe in *Saint Maybe*, who takes an overdose of pills after her husband Danny's fatal car crash. Even the optimistic Bee Bedloe, Danny's mother, admits, "'everything's been lost. Isn't it amazing that we keep on going? . . . our oldest son is dead and gone and we'll never see him again and our life's in ruins! . . . We've had such extraordinary troubles,' she said, 'and somehow they've turned us ordinary. . . . We're not a special family anymore'" (*SM* 181). No family proves immune to disaster in Anne Tyler's fiction, no family is allowed to be "special, " even the "ideal, apple-pie" Bedloes, with their "two amiable parents, three good-looking children, a dog, a cat, a scattering of goldfish" (*SM* 4).

And so it would seem, as John Updike has said of *Dinner at the Homesick Restaurant*, that Anne Tyler's characters are condemned to lead "lives of surrender" ("On Such" 107) to families that hurt, constrain, isolate, exhaust, or suffocate them. However, this proves true in Anne Tyler's novels *only* if they continue to cling to what Joseph C. Voelker calls the "family myth" (13). If they agree with Pearl Tull that, "your family's enough for you, isn't it? . . . Aren't we lucky to have each other?", that "we Tulls depend on ourselves, only on each other. We don't look to the rest of the world for any help whatsoever" (*DHR* 48; 94), then Tyler's characters certainly do end up dismayed and disappointed. Such characters include James Green's father in *The Tin Can Tree*, Mrs. Emerson in *The Clock Winder*, the stay-at-home Pecks in *Searching for Caleb*, as well as Pearl Tull in *Dinner at the Homesick Restaurant*. In such works and such families, Anne Tyler reveals what Mary F. Robertson calls "the monster of family self-absorption" (191). As Tyler's families (especially in *Dinner at the Homesick Restaurant*) sit at dinner tables through one dissastisfying, disrupted, agonizing meal after another, those occasions "which are usually the classic expression of family order," Robertson says, turn into ones through which "Tyler shows symbolically the family's inability to thrive when its ideals are hermetic" (196). When Tyler's families try to seal themselves off from others, become everything to each other, their "desire for family purity leads to entropy," as Mary Robertson has concluded in her study of Tyler's fiction (203). Family fortresses built to protect against the outside world – closed off and seemingly self-sufficient – will always fail.

Instead, Anne Tyler's family novels posit that, to survive, to grow, and to thrive, individuals actually "need to establish [their] identity in opposition to family myth" (Voelker 13). In her novels, Tyler shows characters struggling to develop themselves and enlarge their worlds beyond the small, nuclear family unit, thereby "disrupt[ing] the conventional expectations of the family novels . . . and dislodg[ing] the ideology of the enclosed family and the notion that the family is the main forum for making history" (Robertson 186). Tyler's family novels seek to open up the family and, as they do, change our concept of what family is and should be. Mary Robertson argues that what Anne Tyler's family-centered novels actually reveal is "Tyler's refusal to regard the family as the most significant agent of character development and social representation" in her characters' lives (190). Tyler challenges her readers to rethink their ideas about family: its makeup, its effects, and its very centrality as shapers of our lives.

Certainly, Anne Tyler acknowledges that it may be difficult, if not impossible, to leave the nuclear family totally behind. As Frank W. Shelton argues, "one carries [the family's] presence and influence wherever one goes ("Necessary" 181) – and we see instances of this "family carry-over" again and again in Tyler's novels.[10] A dramatic example of this occurs in *Ladder of Years* when Delia Grinstead runs away from her family in Baltimore, coming to the village of Bay Borough (where she knows no one), only to learn later that her mother's family once lived there, that even its streets are named after her mother's relatives, and that the town founder (another deserter like herself, a man named George Bay who left the Union army in the Civil

War) is, in fact, more than a man commemorated by a statue she has passed day after day in the park; he is her own family relation (112). In *Morgan's Passing*, Emily Meredith, too, is amazed to discover, on a trip to her hometown for her great-aunt Mercer's funeral, that her daughter Gina has her "Aunt Mercer's mouth. Emily had never realized" and, further, that her family had made marionettes in the past, ones that, in fact, resemble her own hand-made, "invented" puppets (203; 206). Of course, Emily can't help but feel somewhat deflated by what she has found, "And here she imagined she'd come so far, lived such a different existence!" (*MP* 206).

Caleb Peck, too – the one Peck who got furthest away from Roland Park, Baltimore, disappearing for more than half a century without a word to his family – nevertheless has still not totally escaped "Peckness" in *Searching for Caleb*. As Duncan Peck explains to his wife (and Peck cousin) Justine: "Who do you know who acts more like a Peck? Consider that he has remained alone his whole life long, never let in anybody who wasn't a blood relative. Never got close to White-Eye, never married that waitress, never was a father to Roy" (*SFC* 292). Caleb hasn't escaped "Peckness" anymore than Duncan himself has through his marriage to a Peck (one who, in fact, embodies many of the family's most treasured traits). Yet these characters have all distanced themselves physically from their families, formed relationships with family outsiders, and developed a knowledge of their own skills and abilities beyond the confines of the family unit, either at the outset or by the end of these novels. They are not, finally, imprisoned within the nuclear family unit nor prevented by its members from choosing the shape and direction of their own lives. Family does not define them, although it has influenced their appearance, manners, or actions, to some degree.

What Tyler's novels actually suggest, according to Alice Hall Petry, is that, while we might not have total choice and control over our lives, at the same time "we are not 'doomed' to do anything by virtue of either upbringing or genes"

(*Understanding* 202). Characters might console themselves, as Sarah Leary does, "that after a certain age people just don't have a choice. . . . It's too late for me to change. I've used up too much of my life now" (*AT* 310), or agree with Morgan Gower's sister Brindle that "I've ruined my life . . . and it's far too late to change it" (*MP* 51).[10] Yet Tyler reveals such characters lie to themselves when they suggest they are trapped and fated to continue leading unsatisfying, paralyzed lives. They not only *can* effect change, come to new decisions, and make choices – difficult, often agonizing ones – but they *must* do so if they are to find meaning and fulfillment in the lives they lead. As Macon Leary tells his wife Sarah, his decision to leave her for Muriel Pritchett "wasn't easy. It's not the easy way out, believe me" (*AT* 352). His choice is simply one that is necessary if he is to leave Sarah's stultifying views of him behind and grow into a more vital, open person, with Muriel's encouragement. As Joseph Voelker explains, in Tyler's world, "escape from the personality one's family imposes is always possible" (27); however, as Anne Tyler shows in *The Accidental Tourist*, it is seldom easy. Characters must "choose what to lose," as Macon Leary tells his wife Sarah (*AT* 310), but at the same time choose what to gain from their choices and the persons they wish to include in their lives.

In her fiction, Anne Tyler celebrates survival and growth, from her earliest novels to her most recent ones. Characters never have to be "destroyed by love," any more than Jenny Tull or her siblings have been by their damaged nuclear family in *Dinner at the Homesick Restaurant* (96). As Jenny tells her brother Ezra, "Why, the three of us turned out fine, just fine!" (*DHR* 200) – leading their own independent and satisfying lives as an efficiency expert (Cody), a restaurateur (Ezra), and a pediatrician (Jenny).[11] The strongest of Tyler's characters find they can survive the deaths of their children or parents, their family's scorn and rejection, as well as unexpected pregnancies, runaway children, parental abandonment, or devastating divorces. As Muriel Pritchett proudly tells Macon Leary in *The Accidental Tourist* (while, at the same time, seeking his companionship and encouragement to help sustain her):

> I've *had* to be inventive. It's been scrape and scrounge, nail and knuckle, ever since Norman left me. . . . I've got about fifty jobs, if you count them all up. You could say I'm lucky; I'm good at spotting a chance. Like those lessons at Doggie, Do. . . . Twice now I've paid for an entire Ocean City vacation just by going up and down the beach offering folks these box lunches me and Alexander fixed in our motel room every morning. (189)

But Tyler's characters do not accomplish these miracles of development and survival on their own, anymore than Muriel Pritchett can do so without the many who have given her job opportunities and unexpected chances, including Macon Leary himself. Always they are aided by others, by family outsiders, in finding that "selfhood comes not in isolation but in connectedness" (Carson 24). They may turn their backs on the nuclear family to seek entirely new relationships, bring strangers into the midst of their families, or augment family life through meaningful connections with outsiders; continually they find that blood relations are never enough for building a full life, that other people are necessary to their personal fulfillment.[12]

As we have seen, Tyler's characters most often find (as Anne Jones says of Ben Joe Hawkes in *If Morning Ever Comes*) "their needs badly met at home where habitual ways of relating and an insular view of the family keep them from reality and growth" (3). Ironically, as Tyler's characters discover, "strangers are less apt to respond negatively and abusively than those who love us" (Bennett 66). And so it is understandable that Tyler's characters reach out beyond their families for affirmation and love. As Julie Persing Papadimas explains, "Tyler's characters appear more comfortable with in-laws, friends, acquaintances – even strangers – than with relatives. It is to these outsiders that the characters most often reveal themselves and utter truths" (49). Family is not enough in Tyler's novels, even if, as with Cody

Tull, characters must learn, at first, "to keep things separate – his friends in one half of his life and his family in the other half. His mother hated for Cody to mix with outsiders" (*DHR* 48). It is only with the help of outsiders that Tyler's characters find the ability to grow and thrive. For example, Cody's brother Ezra turns to the house of his friend Josiah, whose mother Mrs. Payson gives Ezra the generous love and warming comfort he lacks at home: "My, I'm just so fond of that boy [Ezra]. . . . Why, he has been like a son to me, always in and out of the house" (*DHR* 77), Mrs. Payson confesses to Ezra's sister Jenny Tull.

Similarly, in *Earthly Possessions*, Charlotte looks to her neighbor Alberta Emory for a more exciting alternative to her own "queer" and "sad" mother (*EP* 65), while Maggie Moran's daughter Daisy "practically lived with the Murphys," finding "perfect Mrs. Murphy [who] headed the PTA and the Bake Sale and (since she didn't work) was free to drive the little girls to every kind of cultural event, and she hosted wonderful slumber parties, with treasure hunts" (*BL* 229) a welcome change from her own embarrassing, imperfect mother (to Maggie Moran's dismay). Elizabeth Abbott, too, finds the Emerson family important to her growth in *The Clock Winder*, as does Morgan Gower with the Merediths (especially Emily); Delia Grinstead with Joel and Noah Miller (and several other townspeople of Bay Borough); Macon Leary with Muriel and Alexander Pritchett; and Michael Anton with Anna Grant Stuart. So, too, Ben Hawkes and his sister Jenny sneak visits to Lili Belle Moseley's (as did their father before them), where Lili's generous nature enables them to see "how closed off [their] family looked" by comparison to Lili's much more warmly inclusive boardinghouse in *If Morning Ever Comes* (138).

Even characters who are afraid of intimacy learn to connect with family outsiders to enrich their lives. Barnaby Gaitlin in *A Patchwork Planet*, who "wish[ed] I could rearrange my life so I'd never have to deal anymore with another human being" (112), helps others through his work with Rent-a-Back, finding significant support in the loyalty of his clients and "the most amazing rush of happiness" (288) in the company of his admiring co-worker Martine. In the same way, Elizabeth Abbott in *The Clock Winder* and Ian Bedloe in *Saint Maybe* overcome their fears about the harm they have done (and might do) other human beings by taking care of someone else's family and finally marrying Matthew Emerson and Rita diCarlo, respectively. At the end of each work, Elizabeth Abbott and Ian Bedloe have been plunged into the ultimate of responsibilities – care for their tiny, newborn children, the most vulnerable beings of all – having been trained for this task by all their earlier instructive, and challenging, relationships.

Some Tyler characters may continue to fear being overly connected to others, yet even these reluctant individuals wind up surrounded by people at the conclusions of their stories. Jeremy Pauling loses Mary Tell and their children, but he continues to live in the midst of his boardinghouse roomers. When he goes shopping with his longtime roomer Miss Vinton, they walk together, looking like any other "elderly couple, together no doubt for centuries, arriving at the end of their dusty and unremarkable lives" (*CN* 276).[15] Ezra Tull, too, remains a bachelor connected to other people in his own special way. Once Ezra confessed to his mother:

> "I'm worried I don't know how to get in touch with people. . . . I'm worried if I come too close, they'll say I'm overstepping. They'll say I'm pushy, or . . . emotional, you know. But if I back off, they might think I don't care. I really, honestly believe I missed some rule that everyone else takes for granted; I must have been absent from school that day. There's this narrow little dividing line I somehow never located." (*DHR* 125)

Fearful of intimacy as Ezra may be, he is beloved first by his friend Josiah's mother and then by neighborhood restaurant owner Mrs. Scarlatti. His relationship with the latter "makes the crucial difference in [Ezra's] . . . ability to grow and be [himself]," Mary F. Robertson explains (194). When Mrs. Scarlatti leaves him the restaurant, "her death clearly releases new energies in him. He soon changes the name from 'Scarlatti's' to 'The Homesick Restaurant,' and he thrives by arranging matters more in his own way" (Robertson 194). Ezra Tull appears several years later in *Saint Maybe*, still unmarried and alone, still respecting other people's privacy, yet surrounded by the many customers who are grateful to be warmed and nourished in his "home away from home" restaurant (created to meet their needs in *Dinner at the Homesick Restaurant* and continuing to provide nourishment and comfort in *The Amateur Marriage*).

Connecting with family outsiders is shown to be necessary for personal growth and social enrichment in Tyler's fiction. As Mary F. Robertson shows so effectively in "Anne Tyler: Medusa Points and Contact Points," "true difference . . . [is found to be] nourishing" and "strangeness [is] . . . the very resource by which to prevent alienation" in Tyler's *Dinner at the Homesick Restaurant, Earthly Possessions*, and *Morgan's Passing* (200; 191). This "strangeness" and "difference" extend to the very smallest of social units, to many of Tyler's most successful couples as well. What Macon Leary comes to value most in Muriel Pritchett in *The Accidental Tourist* is "the pattern of her life; . . . the surprise of her, and also the surprise of himself when he was with her. In the foreign country that was Singleton Street he was an entirely different person. This person had never been suspected of narrowness, never been accused of chilliness; in fact, was mocked for his soft heart. And was anything but orderly" (212). Macon gradually comes "to admire [Muriel]. Had he ever known such a fighter?" (*AT* 279); as he does so, he finds her courage, "her spiky, pugnacious fierceness" (*AT* 230), helps to bring him out of his state of paralysis and futility. Muriel emboldens Macon and expands his possibilities for life, helping him to see "his life as rich and full and astonishing" (285) even after the pointless, fatal shooting of his son Ethan. Muriel enables Macon to feel, "I'm more myself than I've been my whole life long" (249) when in her company. At the end of the novel, when Sarah warns Macon, "[You and Muriel will] be one of those mismatched couples no one invites to parties. No one will know what to make of you" (*AT* 352), Macon agrees. However, he has come to believe "that who you are when you're with somebody" may be the most important thing of all (*AT* 317). Macon likes the person he has become with Muriel.

It is the very strangeness of the other person, offering another distinct approach to life, an alternative perspective, that nourishes and broadens Tyler's characters. In *The Accidental Tourist* this process of cross-fertilization will extend to Julian Edge, Macon's "swinging singles" publisher, who falls in love with Macon's homebody sister Rose Leary. Julian marvels at what has happened to him, saying, "I want to join a real family. God, Macon, isn't it amazing how two separate lives can link up together? I mean two *differentnesses*" (*AT* 206). But Julian will find that he must deal with more than just Rose's "differentness," that this family-oriented person he has married, coupled with his own desire to experience family life, will require him eventually to move into the Leary family brownstone with Rose and her two stay-at-home brothers.[17] Tyler's characters find that the very differences which tempt them into marriage in the first place are the ones which must continuously be negotiated after the marriage, as well – offering, at their best, the possibility of a lifetime of interest and challenge.

This pattern of negotiated difference is repeated in many Tyler novels, as seemingly mismatched couples come together to live out their lives in ways they must constantly review and realign. Thus, the serious Ira and the scatty Maggie Moran in *Breathing Lessons* learn again to value each other and the marriage they have created. What might be viewed by others, as well as by themselves, on occasion, as "bickering," they really find is a process of "discussing . . . [and] compiling our two views of things" (311). Despite their different approaches, Maggie and Ira come to realize, all over again, that they really are "in this together"

(*BL* 323). In *Earthly Possessions* Charlotte has married the boy next door, Saul Emory, only to learn "how very different from me he really was" (*EP* 82). By the novel's end, however, she has learned to appreciate his differences and to relish each "tiny, jarring rearrangement" (200) that must be made to accommodate one another (not to mention the many outsiders they have taken into their home and their lives).

Ruth Spivey, too, learns to see her husband Cody Tull as someone who is "irreplaceable" in her life – to see "how much he matters, there's no one the least bit like him" (218) – but only after she has taken their son Luke and left Cody in *Dinner at the Homesick Restaurant*. While Ruth sees herself as "nothing but a little backwoods Garrett County farm girl, hardly educated" (*DHR* 217), she realizes that Cody is, after all, a handsome, mannerly, well-educated, and successful man. What can she offer him – except, of course, the very difference he seeks to include in his life?[16] Just the reverse occurs when the well-bred, upper-class Barnaby Gaitlin in *A Patchwork Planet* finds himself falling in love with "a Sparrows Point kid, from steelworking stock. Scraped sharp knuckles on the steering wheel; gigantic black nylon jacket that smelled of motor oil" (25). Martine's grit and mettle are just what Barnaby Gaitlin seeks to add to his life.

Mismatched couples are a staple in Anne Tyler's fiction. In *Morgan's Passing*, the quirky, ever-changing Morgan Gower finds in Emily Meredith:

> the single point of stillness. Everyone milled around her while she stood upright at the center. . . . He loved her old-time, small-town manners – her prompt gifts and cards and thank-you notes, her Christmas fruitcake, her unfailing observance of every official occasion. She was the most proper person he had ever met. (224-25)

Emily, in turn, "never lost her surprise at finding herself alongside this bearded man, this completely other person" with his "foreign" mother and sister, the strange and fascinating new son she and Morgan Gower have produced together (270). Similarly,

Matthew Emerson in *The Clock Winder* finds his character counterbalanced by his "wife-to-be" Elizabeth Abbott: "He was slow, thorough, too serious; she provided the lightness for him. What answering glimmers she found in him she nourished along, and then he would surprise her by laughing too and losing that dark, baffled look on his face" (88-89). At the close of *The Clock Winder*, Peter Emerson says, "Maybe they're right. . . . You shouldn't hope for anything from someone that much different from your family [as his new wife P.J. seems to be]." Elizabeth Abbott (now "Gillespie" Emerson) immediately retaliates (speaking, I believe, for Tyler herself): "You should if your family doesn't *have* it" (*CW* 311)! Those very differences from the familiar, from family ways and customs, are the essential ones Tyler finds for opening up her characters and enabling them to develop in unexpected and more fulfilling ways.[18]

Anne Tyler's novels suggest that inclusivity is always better than exclusivity, from the very smallest interpersonal relationships to the very largest. When Tyler's characters learn to be more open, more flexible, more tolerant, when they find themselves able to accommodate difference and thrive on variety, they begin to feel fulfilled with their lives. In *Back When We Were Grownups*, Rebbeca Davitch is surprised to learn from Will Allenby (her old boyfriend) that she once had wanted a large family, ten children, "a big, jolly *crew* of children" (172) – very much the family she has ended up having by marrying Joe Davitch rather than Will Allenby, in fact. Rebecca has not lost herself, as she has thought, in the midst of the jumbled families of her one daughter and three step-daughters, the odd assortment of Davitch relatives forever intruding on her life, not to mention the Davitch "Open Arms" business run out of her own home, turning her life into "a kind of crazy quilt of unrelated incidents – always some other family to consider, some strangers getting married or retired or promoted" (*BWWWG* 107) for whom she must provide celebration parties. Instead, Rebecca finds she takes after the aunt she has always admired, her Aunt Ida, who "was forever opening her doors to other people's offspring." She finds that she has followed Aunt Ida (her mother's sister and complete opposite) in creating her very own "household [that] seemed capable of limitless expansion" (*BWWWG* 60).

Inclusivity is the theme of other Tyler novels, as well. In *Dinner at the Homesick Restaurant*, Jenny Tull finds fulfillment in her third marriage to Joe St. Ambrose, joining his six children to her one daughter Becky. While she cares for children in her practice as a pediatrician, Jenny Tull nevertheless finds even more joy in presiding at home over this "tableful of children" with her husband Joe:

> They were doing well, she decided – even the older ones, who'd acted so wary and hostile when she had first met them.
> Then she had an unsettling thought: it occurred to her that this would have to be her permanent situation. Having taken on these children, straightened their upturned lives and slowly, steadily won their trust, she could not in good conscience let them down. Here she was, forever. "It's lucky we get along," she said to Joe.
> "It's extremely lucky," he said, and he patted her hand and asked for the mustard. (*DHR* 194)

Here is another "household seem[ingly] capable of limitless expansion" (*BWWWG* 60), as are those of Delia Grinstead in the final scenes of *Ladder of Years* and Charlotte Emory in *Earthly Possessions* (another protagonist who slowly finds that "I'm so tangled with other people here [in her home with Saul Emory, their children, their roomers, and her photography customers]"; there Charlotte learns, at last, that she is "more connected than I'd thought" (184)). Joan Pike, too, in *The Tin Can Tree*, finds that "here [where] there was always something going on, and a full family around the supper table" (33) there really is "one family instead of three" (123). She leaves them, then returns the same day, determining to make her home with Miss

Faye and Miss Lucy Potter, Ansel and James Green, as well as the Pikes (her aunt, uncle and cousin Simon), who really are "one family" in their care for one another.

Even in *The Amateur Marriage*, after the mismatched Antons divorce and Michael Anton remarries someone with whom he feels much more compatible (both of them adhere to a strict budget, save grocery coupons, and record gas expenses), he finds he has left neither his family obligations nor his ex-wife Pauline behind. Continuing to help Pauline raise their grandson Pagan, Michael also helps her out in practical ways that make him feel useful (even if Pauline has proved herself a survivor, too, with her new job, many friends, and a string of male admirers to her credit). After Pauline's sudden death, Michael reflects, "He knew that he and she had been unhappy together, but now he couldn't remember why. What were the issues they'd quarreled about? He hadn't been able to name even one" (*AM* 304). Only by distancing himself from Pauline has Michael come to appreciate her sense of humor and her vitality, her emotional engagement with life that he had once found excessive. Shocked by her fatal car crash, he even realizes he feels love for her again. At the end of the novel, walking through their old neighborhood of Elmview Acres, Michael imagines how it would be to see Pauline once more: "Is it you?" she would ask. "It's you! It's really and truly you!" she would cry, and her face would light up with joy. He began to walk faster, hurrying toward the bend" (*AM* 306). Michael's ability to love has been extended through years of separation, pain and loss – the hard lessons of his "amateur marriage" to Pauline – and his family, the Antons, have endured and expanded (including Michael's second wife Anna Stuart). Continuing to meet for large family dinners where they share memories of the past and of Pauline, they are joined, at times, by the runaway Lindy, her school teacher husband, and their two children, at gatherings most often hosted by Pagan Anton and his wife Gina Meredith (daughter of Leon and Emily Meredith of *Morgan's Passing* and now feminist mother of two small Anton children).

As Margaret Morganroth Gullette concludes, "In most of Tyler's characters, plenitude is *not* an instinct; instead, a genuinely austere self crouches beneath the burden of adult requirements. This self regards having things as a painful discipline, the proliferation of family as a mistake to be undone" (*Safe* 113). Yet the more Tyler's characters can learn to embrace (in their homes and in their lives), the more extended their families become, and the more outsiders they are able to welcome to the family dinner table, the greater their potential for happiness is shown to be.[19] Tyler's characters mark their maturation through the delight they learn to take in the differences of others. As Tyler's "characters travel from homes where everything stays the same to homes that admit change, variety and surprise . . . . they move from (false) Eden to (real) earth," Anne G. Jones concludes (13).

What characters lose when they leave behind more narrow, intolerant, exclusive families is more than compensated for by the inner expansion of spirit taking place inside them. The more they choose to stretch to interact effectively and creatively with others, the more they are able to develop their "best selves."[20] And when these best selves are recognized and rewarded in some way, a character's personal growth is assured and sustained in Tyler's fiction. When it is not, Tyler's characters must choose to move on. We see this clearly in *Morgan's Passing* where Morgan Gower turns to the appreciative Emily Meredith because his wife Bonny at best tolerates him, at worst fails to see him at all – as Ben Joe Hawkes has become invisible to everyone in his own home, but not to the attentive, caring Shelley Domer, whom he decides to take with him to New York and marry in *If Morning Ever Comes*. Macon Leary, too, finds he becomes someone much more useful, more resourceful, more interesting, and more flexible – the person he wants to be – with Muriel Pritchett rather than with his wife Sarah (and her unflattering views of him) in *The Accidental Tourist*. Similarly, Rebecca Davitch finds she prefers being the cheerful, creative entertainer Joe Davitch took her to be (even now in widowhood), rather than uniting with Will Allenby and experiencing "that dampening of her spirit; that tamped-down, boxed-in feeling; the sense she had in Will's presence that she was a little too loud and too brightly colored" (*BWWWG* 227).[21]

When protagonists are viewed in ways that enlarge their spirits and affirm their skills and characters -- as Elizabeth Abbott is valued by the Emersons in *The Clock Winder* and Barnaby Gaitlin is trusted and admired for his work with Rent-a-Back clients by Martine, not by his "angel" Sophia, in *A Patchwork Planet* – they can begin to reach out with more confidence to a larger world. Therefore, it is important that they choose carefully the families they have around them. Are their family members people who will close them off, discourage and deflate them, or are they ones who will expand their human potential and affirm their lives' value? Choosing the right people to bring out their own best qualities allows Tyler's characters to lead enriched lives and, in turn, enrich the world they live in. Family, ultimately, does not determine Tyler's characters (unless this is their choice); instead, her most evolved characters determine who their families will be, as well as the kind of people they themselves will become. In this way, they take adult responsibility both for their own lives and for the families they create. Although they may give up and leave behind one family, they quickly find themselves involved with another. In Anne Tyler's novels, "family" is who and what we want it to be – and members are never in short supply.

Notes

4. In *A Patchwork Planet*, another "renegade" relative, Barnaby Gaitlin's Great-Aunt Eunice, also escapes: "[she] left her husband for a stage magician fifteen years her junior. But she came home within a month, because she'd had no idea, she said, what to cook for the magician's dinners" (*PP* 73). She cannot follow through with her own escape plan.

5. Jenny Tull's words are echoed by Duluth Otis over fifty years after her marriage to Daniel in *Breathing Lessons*. She tells him, "if I knew I'd have to put up with you

so long I'd have made a more thoughtful selection when I married" (*BL* 153). The passing years have only served to underscore just how serious this most often youthful, carefree choice of a marriage partner will be.

6.   Charlotte believes that Bible College changed Saul Emory's attitude towards her, making him seem "fond but abstracted – not what you look for in a husband. He'd settled me so quickly into his life; he'd moved on to other projects. I felt like something dragged on a string behind a forgetful child" (*EP* 101).

7.   Emily Meredith is another Tyler mother who cannot believe that her daughter Gina quite belongs to her. Gina is so "joyous," so energetic, that she seems "a changeling. . . . She was the gnome's baby, not theirs" (*MP* 96).

8.   Adult children are weighed down by other emotions than guilt towards their parents. Amos Emory tells Charlotte in *Earthly Possessions* that his mother Alberta (whom Charlotte had so much admired as a child) had "had a tongue like a knife," that all of her sons had "come away from her in shreds" – especially Charlotte's husband Saul who hated Alberta, Amos says, "worse than any of us" (151).

9.   When Delia Grinstead in *Ladder of Years* reads "her physical description [in the newspaper article on her disappearance]: *fair or light-brown hair . . . eyes are blue or gray or perhaps green*," she thinks, "For heaven's sake, hadn't anyone in her family ever looked at her?" (100). She believes she has been invisible to her family.

10.   Jake Simms tells the kidnapped Charlotte Emory and his girlfriend Mindy in *Earthly Possessions*, "I really believe . . . that anytime you see someone running, it's their old, faulty self they're running from. Or other people's *notion* of their faulty self" (157). The woman Luke Tull hitches a ride with in *Dinner at the Homesick Restaurant* (as he makes his "escape" from home) also admits the truth of this idea. She is not really running away from her husband and teenaged daughter at all but, instead, is trying to "leave behind . . . my own poor view of me" (241).

11.   In *If Morning Ever Comes*, Gary Bentley tells Ben Joe Hawkes, "For years now I've been wondering at [your sister] Joanne, wondering where she got her habits. . . . Now, where, I'd think, as I'd wake up and hear her whistling and the blender going and the dishes clattering, *where* did she learn to live like that?" (234). One visit to his wife's home and Gary appreciates the source of her night time activity. Family ways tend to follow Tyler's characters wherever they go and surprise not only others but themselves, as when Maggie Moran suddenly realizes in *Breathing Lessons*, "she'd been so intent on not turning into her mother, she had gone and turned into her father" (75).

12.   In *The Clock Winder*, Mrs. Emerson complains, as well, that it's too late for her to start a new life. She asks herself why her husband had not died earlier, "before I was all used up and worn out? I could have started some sort of new life, back then. I would have had some hope" (18-19).

13.   When Jenny Tull has found herself repeating her mother's pattern of child abuse ("she slammed Becky's face into her Peter Rabbit dinner plate and gave her a bloody nose. She yanked a handful of [Becky's] hair," she finds that "all of her childhood returned to her" *(DHR* 209)). However, Jenny regains control of herself and works to overcome her past to become the kind of loving parent and healer of sick children she has desired to be. Jenny refuses to be locked into her family's damaging patterns, just as her brother Cody strives to be a reliable, hard-working husband/father and her brother Ezra becomes a "nourisher" of others both "sick" of home and "sick" for homes they have never had or can never (as adults) have again.

14.   Julie Persing Papadimas devotes her essay, "America Tyler Style: Surrogate Families and Transiency," to "the theme of surrogate families [which] appears throughout Tyler's novels, emphasizing the inability of nuclear families to provide the love, understanding, and emotional support individuals desire" (49).

15.   Just as Jeremy Pauling runs a boarding house in *Celestial Navigation*, Lili Moseley takes in boarders in *If Morning Ever Comes*, Charlotte and Saul Emory room "sinners" and strays as boarders in their home in *Earthly Possessions*, Joan Pike boards with her aunt and uncle in *The Tin Can Tree*, and Delia Grinstead takes a room in a boarding house in *Ladder of Years*. Boarding houses, Miss Vinton explains, allow for privacy and companionship at the same time. In fact, Miss Vinton believes, "our whole society would be better off living in boarding houses. I mean even families, even married couples. Everyone should have his single room with a door that locks, and then a larger room downstairs where people can mingle or not as they please" (*CN* 141).

16.   Rose Leary, too, will extend her boundaries and enlarge her world through her marriage to Julian Edge, going away from home to help him organize his office files and putting her skills to use beyond the Leary brownstone and its immediate neighborhood.

17.   Of course Ruth Spivey reminds Cody of his "good" brother Ezra in *Dinner at the Homesick Restaurant*. Couples can come together because of the need to incorporate some missing part of home and family into their lives, even as they leave home. In *Searching for Caleb* Duncan marries his cousin Justine to connect the Daniel side of the Peck character with his own Caleb side; and Ben Joe Hawkes carries off "his own little piece of Sandhill transplanted" (*IMEC* 265) when he returns to New York with Shelley Domer by his side. In each case there are large character differences to be negotiated as Cody Tull, Duncan Peck, and Ben Joe

Hawkes enlarge and extend their own personal boundaries through relationships to people quite different from themselves, yet still connected with home.

18. At the funeral in *Breathing Lessons*, Sugar Tilghman asks JoAnn Dermott, "Doesn't it sometimes seem to you like *every* marriage is mixed?" (84). Some of Tyler's other "mixed" relationships appear in *Saint Maybe* where the plain Agatha is married to a dazzlingly handsome man; her easy-going brother Thomas is engaged to a domineering woman; and Ian Bedloe announces that he will marry Rita diCarlo because "I've never met anyone like her" (307).

19. Even in a novel which deals with a couple's shrinking world when the children leave home, openness to others remains important. In *Breathing Lessons*, Ira Moran (who takes care of his father and two sisters) realizes that "Maggie always had to be inviting other people into their lives. She didn't feel a mere husband was enough, he suspected. Two was not a satisfactory number for her. He remembered all the strays she had welcomed over the years . . . " (148). Maggie's inclusiveness may occasionally seem to threaten their marriage, but it is this generosity of spirit that Ira admires in her (just as she loves Ira because he is the kind of man who takes care of his family). The strength of their "twosomeness" depends on their mutual respect for each other's caring nature.

20. Anne Tyler believes that having children extended her creativity and made her a better person. She writes in "Still Just Writing," "It seems to me that since I've had children, I've grown richer and deeper. They may have slowed down my writing for awhile, but when I did write, I had more of a self to speak from" (9). In old age, Michael Anton's only regret in *The Amateur Marriage* is not having developed "more of a self," as well; when he looks back at his life, he "wished he had inhabited more of his life, used it better, filled it further" (302).

21. Rebecca Davitch acknowledges that Joe "had married her for her usefulness," yet comes to understand that, "while she had once believed that she'd been useful only in practical matters, . . . now she saw that her most valuable contribution had been her joyousness – a quality the Davitches sorely lacked." Further, Rebecca recognizes that Joe Davitch had been "just as useful to *her*; no doubt about it," that "he had rescued her from: that ingrown, muted, stagnant, engaged-to-be-engaged routine" she had once had with the stultifying Will Allenby (*BWWWG* 246).

Chapter Three
Rising Through Economic Decline

Just as Anne Tyler asks readers to redefine the successful family, so too she asks them to redefine the successful life. The most important word in respect to both family and lifestyle in her fiction is one that is also very important in mainstream American culture, especially American consumer culture. That word is choice. However, while consumer culture suggests that the most important choices we can make are choices of what to buy – cars, clothing, perfumes, breakfast cereals, hedge trimmers, even stylish houses and pedigree college diplomas – Anne Tyler suggests otherwise. While American consumer culture promises that monetary wealth and what it can buy will make us happy and satisfied, Anne Tyler's characters find happiness and satisfaction elsewhere. Her characters ignore societal messages about success and the "good life" to make other choices in becoming fulfilled adults.

The society they inhabit, of course, is filled with advertising messages tempting them into making continual, costly consumer choices. The Baltimore streets her characters navigate are dotted everywhere with signs tempting them to enter and buy, even in the most run-down sections of town: "here were the Arbeiter Mattress Factory and Madam Sheba, All Questions Answered and Love Problems Cheerfully Solved. . . . the Ace of Spades Sandwich Shop and Fat Boy's Shoeshine. . . . [and further down the street] Syrenia's Hot Pig Bar-B-Q" (*MP* 39). Some of Tyler's characters earn money by working in these Baltimore commercial establishments. Morgan Gower manages the downtown branch of the Cullen Hardware store; Leon Meredith takes a part-time job at a local Texaco gas station;

Anton's Grocery serves the Polish community of East Baltimore; and Leon and Emily Meredith live above the "Crafts Unlimited" shop where Emily works part-time and sells some of her handmade puppets. On another Baltimore street, Ira Moran waits for his wife Maggie in *Breathing Lessons*, standing outside his store beneath its "metal sign swing[ing] in the breeze: SAM'S FRAME SHOP. PICTURE FRAMING. MATTING. YOUR NEEDLEWORK PROFESSIONALLY DISPLAYED" (*BL* 6); and, at the end of the novel, their son Jesse gets another unpromising job (in a string of such uninspiring employment opportunities for unskilled workers) selling motorcycles at Chick's Cycle Shop. Returning from their trip outside Baltimore on the day of Max Gill's funeral, Maggie and Ira are welcomed home by the familiar designators of their neighborhood's many commercial establishments: "Charlie's Fine Liquors. Used-car dealers, one after the other. . . . Dead Man's Fingers Crab House. HAPPY HOUR NITELY, with red and blue neon bubbles fizzing above a neon cocktail glass" (*BL* 298).

Yet, familiar as these messages and the services they offer might be, Tyler's characters seldom are tempted by what the commercial world has to offer them. What they are aware of, most of all, is the huge disparity between the neon, hype, and glitter of these messages and the contrasting realities of their day-to-day existences. When the agoraphobic Junie Moran suddenly "got this urge to visit Harborplace. She had watched on TV when Harborplace first opened and she had somehow come to the conclusion that it was one of the wonders of the world," her brother Ira is reluctant to take her to a place he considers not only "un-Baltimorean," but also merely a "glorified shopping mall" (*BL* 164). Nevertheless, Ira arranges a family outing to encourage Junie's unusual interest in the outside world. As Ira had expected, this excursion "ended in disaster, of course. Junie said everything had looked better on TV, and Ira's father said his heart was flapping in his chest, and then [his other sister] Dorrie somehow got her feelings hurt and started crying and had to be taken home before they'd set foot inside a pavilion" (*BL* 166). Harborplace ads have promised a joy and contentment they cannot deliver, as does so much in contemporary American culture. When Barnaby Gaitlin's mother accuses him of being jealous of his former friend (and adolescent partner in crime) Len Parrish, Barnaby replies, "You call it . . . success, selling off false plantation houses on streets called Foxhound Footway and Stirrup Cup Circle?" (*PP* 78). Fancy names with aristocratic pretensions and "Gone With the Wind" housing facades, as Barnaby recognizes, cannot give people the good life they crave. A majority of Tyler's protagonists understand that the life they want cannot be found in trendy malls, stylish neighborhoods, or plastic veneers. In fact, Tyler's characters find the good life cannot be purchased anywhere, at any price, at all.

Anne Tyler and her characters, in fact, make fun of American advertising culture and its false promises. In *A Slipping-Down Life*, after Evie Decker carves the name "CASEY" into her forehead (to attract the attention of musician Drumstrings Casey), a local real estate agent sends her a newspaper clipping about the incident with this commercial attachment: "Congratulations on your recent achievement. And when it's the *tops* in achievement you want, just think of Sonny Martin, Pulqua County's Biggest Real Estate Agent" (*SDL* 69). Evie Decker's "achievement," of course, is a quite dubious one – as Sonny Martin would have realized if he had looked at more than just Evie's name and photograph in the local newspaper – but, then, of course, so is Sonny Martin's own claim to being "*tops*" in the personally impersonal, falsely up-beat, sales pitch world of consumer America.

Duncan Peck knows this in *Searching for Caleb* and subverts advertising copy's content to comment on real life issues in his own family. When Justine has a birthday, Duncan uses "a bank ad saying WE'RE INCREASING OUR INTEREST" to comment on his wife's growing versatility and their interpersonal development (which has no connection, whatsoever, to any money they might have saved or any interest rate they might have earned – both quite unlikely given their impoverished lifestyle) (*SFC* 165). On another occasion, when Duncan's daughter Meg buys an expensive dress to appear more like her peers, "only because she wanted to look like the other girls for a change, not all homemade and tacked together," Duncan tapes this ad to her closet door: "HAVE YOU EVER HAD/A BAD TIME IN LEVI'S?" (*SFC* 165). Duncan wants Meg to learn that what is important in life is not trying to fit in and impress others, but knowing herself and fulfilling her inner needs. The irrelevance of commercial goods to the search for life satisfaction is commented on by yet another of Duncan Peck's ads. As Meg races to catch her disappearing suitor Arthur, she finds only the family "Ford . . . with a magazine page flapping in the space where the door should have been: WOULDN'T YOU REALLY RATHER HAVE A BUICK?" (*SFC* 173). It is Arthur that Meg wants, and neither a Ford nor a Buick could possibly satisfy her true desires.

Despite the advertising industry's attempt to link material goods to intimacy, love, friendship, security, and happiness, Tyler's characters recognize that mere possessions cannot bring about these ends. The belief that material things are important and can make you happy suggests either shallowness or immaturity in Tyler's fictional world. Adults who take pride in their possessions are unworthy guides and companions in Tyler novels. Barnaby Gaitlin in *A Patchwork Planet* is surrounded by such people in his own family: by his mother in her "A-line skirt, tailored silk shirt, navy leather flats with acorns tied to the toes," a woman who "went after Culture with a vengeance" (68; 67); by both parents who live "in Guilford, in a half-timbered, Tudor-style house with leaded –glass windows" in which the living room waits with "an expectant look, like a stage" (*PP* 67; 68) – parents who give him, as a birthday present, "a gift certificate from some menswear store or other, someplace Ivy League and expensive" (*PP* 69) (and totally out of character for Barnaby himself); and by his brother Jeffrey Paul Gaitlin the Second, with his "four-by-four [car], and a Princeton degree, and a desk half the size of a tennis court on the top floor of the Gaitlin Foundation. None of which I wanted for myself, Lord knows" (*PP* 82), Barnaby admits. His former friend, Len Parrish, appears (especially to Barnaby's mother), "such a winner. Him in his expensive coat and velvety suede gloves," driving "a sleek black Lexus" (*PP* 84; 83), but Barnaby knows better – as he does, as well, about Sophia Maynard, owner of "a silver-gray Saab. I had always thought Saab owners were shallow, but now I saw I might have been mistaken" (*PP* 89). However, it turns out that Barnaby is not wrong about Sophia's "shallowness." He realizes, long before she reveals her lack of faith in him and her misjudgment of his character, what he has known all along, "she was an ordinary, middle-class, middle-aged bank employee with no particular life of her own, and it showed what a sorry state *my* life had come to that I could have imagined otherwise for an instant" (*PP* 58). Barnaby rejects the superficial values of the world in which he has grown up and anyone who seems to share its self-satisfied, myopic vision.[22]

People who succumb to advertisements – driving flashy cars, wearing expensive clothes, and purchasing pretentious houses – reveal not only the shallowness of their values but their immaturity, as well. As Morgan Gower has told Emily Meredith, her daughter Gina is at that teenaged stage of life where such superficial things matter: "she's at that age now; she disapproves of irregularity. She'll like Leon's apartment swimming pool and tennis courts and whatever else. He may even have a sauna bath! Ever thought of that?" (*MP* 289). But Tyler's true heroines and heroes outgrow this youthful stage to adopt "irregular" lives, becoming their own people and attending to what matters most by listening to their own needs and their intuitive responses to the people around them.

Such cultural signifiers of success as Saabs and saunas do not really matter much at all in Tyler's world. When her young characters crave possessions, it is for the love, security, or friendship they seem to offer – certainly not for the objects themselves. In *Dinner at the Homesick Restaurant*, Jenny Tull's stepson Slevin steals Pearl Tull's vacuum cleaner because it reminds him of the one his mother once had (and the place she once occupied in his life). When, as an adolescent, Barnaby Gaitlin broke into neighbors' houses, it was to "read people's private mail. Also photo albums. . . . I sat on the sofa poring over somebody's wedding pictures. And even when I took stuff, it was always personal stuff. This little snow globe once from a nightstand in a girl's bedroom. Another time, a brass egg that stood on scaly claw feet and opened to show a snapshot of an old-fashioned baby inside" (*PP* 9) – revealing Barnaby's deep need for human intimacy and meaningful family relationships.

Similarly, in *Ladder of Years*, Juval Wesley breaks into the most respectable house in Bay Borough (belonging to the owners of its one factory, a furniture factory), even though the occupants are well-known for giving their money away to charity, for not having jewelry and silver in the house, and for having "the only house alarm" in the entire town (*LY* 158). This mishap occurs on the eve of Juval's departure to "join the navy" and begin "a highly promising" specialized, technical military career (*LY* 158). Delia Grinstead's theory that Juval "ruined things so he wouldn't have to leave after all" is promptly dismissed by her employer Mr. Pomfret as unsound, as well as unseemly on the part of a mere secretary (*LY* 158) – yet Delia, of course, is correct. Juval Wesley is not emotionally ready for the new life his intellectual skills have awarded him, anymore than is Ben Joe Hawkes in *If Morning Ever Comes*. Having just begun Columbia law school, Ben Joe uses his sister Joanne's separation as an excuse to rush home to help out – but also to check up on possessions he has left behind in the care of his sister Susannah. His mother scolds him saying, "Ben Joe, . . . there's no reason to get so excited about a few possessions you've already given away. . . . You're too old to be missing things, anyway" (*IMEC* 90). Ben Joe's real need, of course, is not to have his old guitar or his hourglass, but to have the security he can never experience again: the security of his early years when his parents' marriage seemed insoluble, his father was still alive, and "home" seemed something that would last forever.

Very few material possessions matter to Tyler's mature characters – and, as we have seen with some of her younger protagonists, the reasons why they matter are always more important than the objects themselves. Charlotte Emory in *Earthly Possessions* admits, "my only important belonging since I have grown up is a pair of excellent walking shoes" (37). Readers know from the first line of the novel why walking shoes would be so important in Charlotte's life: "The marriage wasn't going well and I decided to leave my husband" (*EP* 3). Charlotte is desperate to walk away from past decisions, from people she has allowed into her life, and from her mother's house – that stale-smelling, decrepit, turreted edifice from which she has never managed to break free (*EP* 12).

Other Tyler protagonists value not walking shoes but good tools as necessary to repair the damage in their lives, secure crumbling structures, and remake their lives in better ways. As Michael Anton explains in *The Amateur Marriage*, "There was something so reassuring about hardware stores. We can help you deal with anything, was the message he drew from them" (299). Hardware store manager Morgan Gower in *Morgan's Passing* clings to the one piece of advice, "the only philosophy [his father] had ever stated outright," after his father's inexplicable suicide: a methodology for "repairing, replacing, maintaining. One step follows another, and if you have completed step two, then step three will surely come to you" (46; 47) – even if this philosophy clearly has failed to carry Morgan's father successfully through life. It still is comforting for Morgan to hold onto his father's words, "'One thing our family has always believed in,' his father used to say, 'is the very best quality tools. You buy the best tools for the job: drop-forged steel, hardwood handles. And then you take good care of them. Everything in its place. Lots of naval jelly'" (*MP* 46). Even if Morgan has become totally ineffectual in his own home, he puts his tools and skills to good use in helping out Leon and Emily Meredith in their tiny apartment.

In *The Accidental Tourist*, as well, Macon Leary values basic repairing skills and attempts to pass them on to Muriel Pritchett's son Alexander, as it's too late to help his own deceased son Ethan. Macon teaches Alexander how to fix a leaky faucet so that the boy will be able to cope better on his own someday and feel the pride that comes from knowing he has "solved the problem" (*AT* 215). At Christmas, Macon gives seven-year-old Alexander a full set of "undersized but real" tools "with solid wooden handles," having "hunted those tools down one by one. . . . and rearranged them in their compartments a dozen times at least" (*AT* 219) prior to the holiday itself.

Macon's sister Rose also has long been recognized for her repairing skills throughout her Dempsey Road neighborhood, skills shared by many of Anne Tyler's resourceful survivors from Duncan Peck in *Searching for Caleb* to Pearl Tull in *Dinner at the Homesick Restaurant* to Elizabeth Abbott in *The Clock Winder*. When the latter receives her first paycheck as Mrs. Emerson's new "handyman," she goes out and buys "a multi-purpose electric drill that would sand, saw, wirebrush, sink screws, stir paint – *anything*" (*CW* 34) – a tool that will allow Elizabeth to feel a sense of accomplishment and become even more useful to Mrs. Emerson (while being seen as nothing but a useless burden by her own parents). At the novel's end, although Elizabeth has become a wife and mother, and the kitchen has become her new territory, nevertheless a "scatter of tools" still occupies pride of place on the counter "beside the breadbox" (*CW* 296). When all else fails, good tools promise to get many of Tyler's characters through their lives.

In addition to walking shoes and a well-stocked toolbox, only those material goods that have acquired particular meanings and associations over the years come to matter to Tyler's protagonists. Old Mrs. Alford in *A Patchwork Planet* wants her grandchildren to see her Christmas tree decorated with ornaments she has carefully preserved over the years, "most of them homemade: construction-paper chains gone faded and brittle with age, pine cones glopped with red poster paint" and, on the top of the tree, "a bent cardboard star covered with aluminum foil, not one point matching any of the others" (*PP* 34; 35). Such decorations obviously have no monetary value but they remind Mrs. Alford of a past when she was young and healthy, at the center of her family, playing an active part in the day-to-day world – a time that has long since passed.

A much younger character, Ben Joe Hawkes, also places value on trivial objects in his life, lying in the bed of his boyhood room looking at the layers of his twenty-five-year past:

> the more recent layers never completely obliterating the earlier ones. Of the first layer only the peeling decals on the closet door remained – rabbits and ducks in polka-dotted clothes, left over from that time when he had been a small child. Then the layer from his early boyhood: a small red shoe bag, still in use, with a different symbol of the Wild West on each pocket, a dusty collection of horse books on the bottom shelf of the bookcase. And after that his later boyhood, most in evidence: a striped masculine wallpaper pattern, brown curtains, a microscope, the *National Geographics*. (*IMEC* 219)

Ben Joe appreciates the fact that the oldest layers have the most meaning, for they are the ones that seem most "bright and vivid and always made him remember things, in striking detail, that had happened years and years before," while the most recent layers appear much more "flat and impersonal" (*IMEC* 219). Yet Ben Joe leaves all these objects, all these layers of his past, behind – as well as the guitar and hourglass he has given his sister Susannah – when he returns to New York City with Shelley Domer at his side.

Emily Meredith in *Morgan's Passing* also decides to leave behind everything her Aunt Junie has offered her, including her deceased Aunt Mercer's jade bar pin, a coffee-table china slipper, three little brass monkeys, and family-made marionettes. She feels everything she saw at Aunt Mercer's house reminded her too much of her youth: "they were too solid, too thickly coated by past events, maybe; she couldn't explain it" (*MP* 203). Arriving in her hometown of Taney, Virginia, for her Aunt Mercer's funeral, Emily is overwhelmed by memories of her dead mother, her Great-Aunt Mercer, her own youth, feeling at times as if "she would like this whole house – the wallpaper patterned with wasp-waisted baskets of flowers, the carpet always rubbed the wrong way, the china high-heeled slipper filled with chalky china roses" (*MP* 198). At times Emily even "imagined moving in. She pictured resuming her life where she'd left off, drinking her morning cocoa from the celery-green glass mug she'd found in a cereal box when she was eight" (*MP* 198).

Yet Emily realizes there is no going back. She can only move forward, taking nothing with her, leaving all these reminders of her past behind, as Justine Peck, "a pack rat" like the rest of the Peck family in *Searching for Caleb* (31), learns to do, as well. Move by move, Justine begins to leave behind all the accumulated paraphernalia (mostly useless) of her past. On their last move, she and Duncan take "only their books and clothes, plus Duncan's spare parts and inventions. . . . They were leaving everything else behind" (*SFC* 307-08).

In fact, Anne Tyler's characters often feel a desperate need to get rid of the "clutter" they have accumulated in their lives in order to determine, at last, what really matters.[23] What is it they really need to hold onto to assure a more satisfying future? Barbara Harrell Carson concludes that Tyler's characters often cast off their possessions "with a blind hope that by simplifying life they can avoid its troubles" ("Complicate" 26) – wishful thinking that always ends in defeat. On one such occasion in *Celestial Navigation*, when Jeremy Pauling feels "pulled in too many directions" by the tumult of his family life with Mary Tell and all their children, he tries in vain to focus his attention merely on a piece of red flannel he needs for his art. Instead, he finds himself drawn into dealing with a newly delivered refrigerator he has won and forgotten to cancel (156). Jeremy protests this new addition, saying, "This house is getting so full. We surely don't *need* another refrigerator. . . . it feels so cluttered. . . . Mary, there are so many *things* in this house" (*CN* 156) – but, once more, Jeremy is forced to retreat to his studio to experience life stripped down only to what he feels (incorrectly, as it turns out) are the essentials of his life, the demands of his art.

In *Ladder of Years*, Delia Grinstead feels awed by Rosemary Bly-Brice who, "according to [her husband] Adrian . . . had abandoned every single one of her possessions when she left. All she took was the black silk jumpsuit she was wearing and a slim black purse tucked under her arm" (*LY* 51) – a pattern Delia will repeat when she disappears on the next family vacation, wearing only a swimsuit and beach wrap upon her arrival in the small town of Bay Borough. Later, Delia writes her mother-in-law that she has left Sam and the children *"because I just like the thought of beginning again from scratch"* (*LY* 139), living in a boarding house room which gave "not the slightest hint that anybody lived here" (*LY* 97), debating every single purchase of a reading lamp, a fan, a dress, or an immersion coil that might weigh down her life. When Mr. Pomfret's detective gives her an abandoned cat found out in the rain, Delia hesitates, saying, "I don't know if I want my life to get that complicated" (*LY* 143) – yet her life quickly becomes much more complex when she becomes housekeeper, nursemaid, and surrogate wife and mother for Joel and Noah Miller a short time later.

Charlotte Emory in *Earthly Possessions* becomes similarly encumbered by her kidnapper Jake Simms and his pregnant girlfriend Mindy when all she has ever wanted, "since October 16, 1948," is "to get rid of all belongings that would weigh me down on a long foot-march" – including, it would seem, her husband, her children, and the boarders she and Saul have taken into their lives (*EP* 36). Charlotte reflects that her "life has been a history of casting off encumbrances, paring down to the bare essentials, stripping for the journey. Possessions make me anxious" (*EP* 37), she says. Yet she has spent her life surrounded by old photographs and dusty photographic equipment, old furniture (her own family's and now her deceased mother-in-law's), and her father's old theatrical clippings and costumes – as well as by the many people who seem to crowd her life.

Tyler's characters often feel hemmed in by the people and objects accumulating around them, much as six-month-old Gina Meredith feels when her paternal grandparents replace her comfortable cardboard box with a brand new crib: "Gina stared all around her at the eyelet ruffles, the decals, the bars. What a shock, she seemed to be saying. How did this imprisonment come about?" Tyler's narrator answers, "it came about inch by inch. These things just wear you down" (*MP* 94-95). In the same novel, Morgan Gower, weighed down and worn out by all the things which confine him in his own home, "felt awed by the Merediths – by their austerity, their certitude, their mapped and charted lives" (*MP* 46) in comparison to his own topsy-turvy existence with Bonny. While the Merediths' apartment seems so clean and bare, his own house is overcrowded, its kitchen cabinets "stuffed with tarnished silver tea services and dusty stemware that no one ever used. Jammed in front of them were ketchup bottles and cereal boxes and scummy plastic salt-and-pepper sets with rice grains in the salt from last summer when everything had stuck to itself" (*MP* 28). Morgan yearns to "clear [the house] out and start over. . . . Or sell it! Sell it and have done with it, buy a plainer, more straightforward place. But Bonny wouldn't hear of it – something to do with capital gains" (*MP* 29). As Barbara Harrell Carson explains, "in almost all [Tyler's] works, she suggests the need for occasional retreats from complexity, to gain a perspective on the labyrinth, to sort the richness from the messiness" ("Complicate" 32) – a retreat which Morgan Gower, in this case, turns into a permanent condition in his new life in Tindell Acres Trailer Park in Tindell, Maryland, with Emily Meredith and their new son.

Ultimately, it is not the possessions that are the problem – although, of course, as Barnaby Gaitlin realizes from his work with aged, often terminally ill, clients at Rent-a-Back, these same possessions really don't have much ultimate value either. As Barnaby reflects:

> Every now and then, in this job, I suddenly understand that you really, truly can't take it with you. I don't think I ordinarily grasped the full implications of that. Just look at all the possessions a dead person leaves behind: every last one, even the most treasured. No luggage is permitted, no carry-on items, not a purse, not a pair of glasses. You spend seven or eight decades acquiring your objects, arranging them, dusting them, insuring them; then you walk out with nothing at all, as bare as the day you arrived. (*PP* 284-85)

Material goods ultimately count for very little, many of Tyler's characters come to feel, in proportion to the time, effort, and money they require.

Yet the major problem with possessions in Tyler's fiction is that they prevent her characters from seeing who and what they really value in their lives. When her protagonists feel a need to discard the clutter, strip their houses bare, and throw out whatever they no longer need, they are really trying to come to grips with who they are, what really matters to them, and how they wish to shape their future lives. In *The Amateur Marriage*, Michael Anton must leave his wife Pauline after thirty years of life together because he doesn't know who he is or what his real feelings and needs are (as opposed to Pauline's suburban ambitions for their lives). He asks his wife-to-be Anna Stuart, "Why don't you choose [some prints for the walls of his barren apartment]?", confessing, "I don't know what I like. I don't have any opinions" (*AM* 214). Characters such as Michael Anton are trying to start over, re-examine past decisions, and learn what their true needs and values might be – although they seldom understand their underlying motives and are prone to discard the necessary and valuable along with the totally superfluous and useless. Delia Grinstead, for example, reads Carson McCullers' short story, "A Tree, A Rock, A Cloud," in her sparsely decorated, boarding house room in *Ladder of Years*, the words "tree," "rock," and "cloud" resonating in her mind as she falls asleep. Yet Delia fails to recognize the relevance of this story about a man seeking to learn to love by "begin[ning] with something less complex [than people]," first with rocks and clouds and trees, to her own life, one she has stripped bare and gradually rebuilt, piece by piece, person by person (*LY* 144). It is not until almost a full year later that Delia recognizes that the very husband, children, and life she has discarded in Baltimore are the essentials she needs for the future (nor have her husband and children been able to appreciate Delia's full value until she has stripped their lives bare of her very presence).

So, too, in *Earthly Possessions* and *Breathing Lessons*, Tyler's protagonists learn that what has been there all along – and seemingly unimportant in the clutter and commotion of daily life, the very marriages and day-to-day occupations of the households they have come to find overly familiar, cluttered, irritating and unsatisfying – is exactly what they need and want to continue to invest their energies in. As Ira Moran finally acknowledges in *Breathing Lessons*, "the true waste was. . . . not his having to support these people but his failure to notice how he loved them" (*BL* 175). Day-to-day cares and accumulating clutter cloud minds and hearts, as well as houses and views, preventing Tyler's characters from seeing into their own souls.

Whatever paraphernalia they have gathered together along their life journeys, Tyler's heroines and heroes are definitely not those who have attained vast worldly goods or great wealth and position – nor are they people, by and large, who have enviable degrees. They are not community leaders nor business executives – not the Cullens (into whose midst Morgan Gower has married); the Merediths (into whose family Emily Meredith has married, and from whom Leon, initially, breaks away); the Gaitlins (except their "black sheep" (*PP* 35) Barnaby); or the Pecks (excluding their runaways, Justine, Duncan, Caleb – and, even, unbeknownst to himself, Daniel). Few of Tyler's main characters have college educations – and only a few, Macon and Sarah Leary (graduates of Princeton and Goucher, respectively); Madame Olita (a graduate of Radcliffe); Jeffrey Gaitlin (a graduate of Princeton); and Thomas Dean Bedloe (a graduate of Cornell) – have name-brand degrees. Ben Joe Hawkes, of course, is in his first semester studying law at Columbia University, but he has failed to win a scholarship to Harvard for his undergraduate work (going to Sandhill College, instead), and his mother refuses to let Ben Joe's father use money he has saved for this purpose to buy Ben Joe a seat in Harvard's classes. It remains uncertain that Ben Joe will complete his law education at Columbia University, as well.

Many of Tyler's other protagonists are college dropouts: Joe and Rebecca Davitch, Elizabeth Abbott, Charlotte Emory, Leon and Emily Meredith, Ian and Claudia Bedloe, and Duncan and Justine Peck – sometimes because of their own disinterest, oftentimes due to family deaths or illnesses which make it necessary for them to undertake other responsibilities. Most of Tyler's characters, such as Maggie and Ira Moran, never made it to college in the first place, even though Ira had always dreamed of becoming a doctor (but has had to take over his father's frame shop, instead) and Maggie had been scheduled to go to Goucher immediately after high school graduation. However, it seems Maggie "wasn't much looking forward to it; it was her mother's idea. Her mother, who had taught English before she married, filled out all the application forms and even wrote Maggie's essay for her. It was very important to her that her children should rise in the world. (Maggie's father installed garage doors and had not had any college at all.)" (*BL* 90).

However, Maggie and her three brothers fail to "rise in the world" by obtaining college educations, just as Ezra Tull disappoints his mother Pearl's ambitions for him (to help vindicate her many sacrifices on behalf of the children and perhaps regain some of her family's former dignity). Jenny Tull echoes her mother when explaining Ezra's dreams and goals to his best friend Josiah:

> "What are you talking about? Ezra's not opening a restaurant."
> "Sure he is."
> "Why would he want to do that? As soon as he pulls himself together he's going off to college, studying to be a teacher."
> "Who says so?" Josiah asked.
> "Well, my mother does. He's got the patience for it, she says. Maybe he'll be a professor, even," Jenny told him. But she wasn't so certain now. "I mean, it's not a lifework, restaurants."
> "Why isn't it?"
> She couldn't answer. (*DHR* 75)

Restaurants, however, will be Ezra's lifework, difficult as it may be for his family, particularly his mother, to accept. Similarly, the Gaitlins (especially, once more, Barnaby's insecure, social-climbing mother) will need to accept that Barnaby will never make them proud of his (still non-existent) college degree the way his Princeton graduate brother Jeff has.

The majority of Tyler's characters have only a high school diploma to their credit, while still others have dropped out of school to play in a band (Jesse Moran and Bertram "Drumstrings" Casey) or to marry (Mary Tell, Meg Peck, Muriel Pritchett, and Evie Decker – even though Evie and Meg do plan to finish high school after their marriages). Some retain a certain respect for education, all the same, as does Mr. Lamb in *Ladder of Years*, who felt that "he himself had not had the opportunity of a college education, though he felt he would have put it to good use" (275), or Mrs. Casey in *A Slipping-Down Life*. The latter defends her high school dropout son Bertram by saying, "We may not be college-educated in our family but we are *law*-abiding, we don't give no cause to complain about us" (*SDL* 122).

Undeniably, college-educated people have greater status in American society. Nevertheless, Tyler suggests they don't always put their educations "to good use," as Mr. Lamb would have done. Ben Joe Hawkes' grandmother complains in *If Morning Ever Comes*:

> "Too much emphasis on brains in this family. What good's it do? Joanne quit after one year of college and the others, excepting Ben Joe, never went. And Ben Joe – look at him. He just kept trying to figure out what that all-fired mind of his was given him for, and first he thought it was for science and then for art and then for philosophy and now what's he got? Just a mish-mash, is all. Just nothing. Won't read a thing now but murder mysteries." (66)

Education may be a means to a life – but it offers no clear program or guarantee of happiness, as Ben Joe Hawkes' confusion about himself, his family, and his future makes clear. *Morgan's Passing* offers another example, as well, that of Morgan Gower's father, an educated man and high school English teacher who, nonetheless, has committed suicide as Morgan is preparing to graduate from high school. Tyler's characters find the basic knowledge they need for life comes from experiences outside the classroom, however strange a message that might seem, as Robert Croft notes (*Companion* 85), for an author who has herself studied at both Duke and Columbia universities.[24]

Those who best come to understand themselves, their abilities, and the world they live in do so through work – work that is often unskilled, menial, manual, or, at times, seemingly superfluous labor (as puppeteers or fortune tellers, for instance). If inherited wealth gives Bonny Cullen an enviable "definiteness. . . . She was so clear about who she was" (*MP* 29), work becomes the most common means for Tyler's characters to ground themselves in reality, determine exactly who they are, and discover, finally, what they value. No one could be more "definite," for instance, than Eleanor Grinstead, the "Iron Mama" Delia both fears and envies in *Ladder of Years*, a woman "who patched her own roof and mowed her own lawn and had reared her one son single-handed in that spotless Calvert Street row house" (31) by doing secretarial work to support herself and her son Sam. Tyler's heroines and heroes are the "makers and doers" (*MP* 84) of American culture, its problem-solvers and hands-on helpers, not its consumers or the corporate executives so valued in American society. While her characters may have internalized the culture's devaluation of their efforts and skills – as does Emily Meredith in *Morgan's Passing*, who considers herself inferior to her "actor" husband from a wealthy background, or Barnaby Gaitlin in *A Patchwork Planet*, who knows he is the embarrassing failure of the well-to-do and respected Gaitlin Foundation family – their resourceful, resilient, working lives offer up the true talents and real contributions which enhance American society. They may be "unknown" – a fate Jesse Moran plans to escape, himself, unlike his humdrum parents with their nondescript, trivial jobs and lives (*BL* 161) – but Ira and Maggie Moran's daily toil (as a shopkeeper and nursing home attendant, respectively) forms the true backbone of Tyler society and is more important and meaningful, she suggests, than the achievements of the glittering few (rock stars, for instance) who win its accolades.[25]

Most of Tyler's characters work, first of all, as does Barnaby Gaitlin, simply because "I need to pay my rent and grocery bill. . . . I'm not looking to get rich" (*PP* 80). They often feel burdened by considerable "financial strain" (*DHR* 83) – a strain which can make Tyler's single-parent mothers, Pearl Tull, Jenny Tull (as a struggling medical student), and Lucy Dean Bedloe, quite desperate. The latter, undereducated and non-skilled, feels trapped into lying about her job experience to support herself and her three small children. Lucy protests, "I'll lose out the minute I tell them the truth. These people just *want* you to lie. They practically *beg* you to lie. 'I've got thirty years' experience,' they want me to say. Even though I'm not but twenty-five" (*SM* 63). Muriel Pritchett, too, in *The Accidental Tourist* has "lain awake, oh, many a night, thinking up ways to earn money" (189) to take care of seven-year-old Alexander and herself.

Newlyweds Evie Decker and her husband in *A Slipping-Down Life* also barely get by as "money came in dribbles – five dollars here, fifteen there," so that "when they were poorest they ate stale saltines and spaghetti in dented tins, reduced for quick sale. They turned out coat pockets and dug between sofa cushions" (*SDL* 161-62) until Evie (without Drum's approval or knowledge) takes a part-time position at the circulation desk of the local library. Emily and Leon Meredith worry about money in the early years of their marriage, as well. Finally, Emily persuades Leon that they should advertise to give plays at children's birthday parties, improvising once more when the only call they get is for a puppet show rather than a play:

> "My daughter's just wild about puppets. She doesn't like plays at all."
> "Well, I'm sorry – " Emily said.
> "Last year I had Peter's Puppets come and she loved them, and all they charged was thirty-two dollars, but now I hear they've moved to – "
> "Thirty-two dollars?" Emily asked.
> "Four dollars a child, for seven guests and Melissa. I felt that was reasonable; don't you?"
> "It was more than reasonable," Emily said. "For a puppet show we get five per child." (*MP* 79)

Emily invents and sews and performs in a variety of ways to help herself and her husband get the money they need to support their meager lifestyle – and their newborn daughter Gina, as well.

Other, older characters also continue to worry about earning enough money to provide for their families. Mr. Pike in *The Tin Can Tree*, laid off from his construction job, must find work where he can, going out to pick tobacco despite his young daughter's death and his wife's depression because "we need the money" (141) to enable the living (himself, his wife, and his son Simon) to go on with their lives. Luray Spivey in *Searching for Caleb*, too, is so "*frazzled* with money worries" (273) that she sends the unbusinesslike Caleb Peck home to take care of her children, then takes over Caleb's job as a short-order cook at the family restaurant in order to bring in more money to meet her family's needs.[26]

No matter how lowly their positions or how great their need for money may be, however, Tyler's characters demand respect. As Alice Hall Petry says of Tyler's black characters in "Bright Books of Life," first and foremost, these background figures in Tyler's fiction (and in American society) gain a "*practical* knowledge" of life through their low-status, seemingly invisible, and unenviable positions (10) – a practical knowledge which gives them not only a sense of their own reality but that of others' lives, as well (their employers' lives, for instance). Alvareen in *The Clock Winder* writes to Elizabeth Abbott that: "*Mrs. Emerson is changing ageing before my eyes and the symptom is parsimonousness. Turning into one of those old ladies that checks on every dime when there's a fortune in the bank. She saves moldy old leftovers and gripes do I take some of the ham for my lunch then goes out and buy herself a Buick*" (173). Alvareen knows her employer's paradoxes and problems better than Mrs. Emerson does herself. Further, Alvareen refuses to become a mere extension of Mrs. Emerson: "*On the phone she was telling about 'my maid is going to drive me up the wall one of these days.' Lady take care who you call yours I wanted to say but held my peace. She is all the time talking like she owns people, my florrist and my pharmacist and my meat man*" (*CW* 173).

Alvareen retains her sense of pride and insists on her own identity: she does *not* belong to the Emersons. Similarly, Clotelia in *A Slipping-Down Life* remains her own person, as well, seeming to Evie always "an indifferent stranger kicking dust puffs with the toe of a cream suede high-heeled boot," dressed in "ski pants and an African cape," (55-56) refusing, over a four-year period, to become a "member of the family" (56) – someone definitely not defined by the Deckers nor by the housework she does for them.

Most of Tyler's characters refuse, as Joseph Voelker says of Jeremy Pauling in *Celestial Navigation*, to allow the world "to define [them] economically" (*Art* 85). Jeremy refuses to be treated simply as a "supplier of the commodity 'art,'" on the one hand, or as fulfilling the "conventional male [role of] . . . provider," on the other (Voelker *Art* 85; 86). While money may be necessary for the lives of Tyler's characters (even that of the retiring and unworldly Jeremy Pauling), those lives can never be reduced merely to services performed or economic functions fulfilled as maids, handymen, carpenters, grocers, puppeteers, nurse's aides, store clerks, or pediatricians (anymore than the value of Jeremy Pauling's art and life can be quantified in such a way). Mrs. Emerson in *The Clock Winder* is correct in saying, "money is essential . . . but not important" (*CW* 59), as all of her children acknowledge, for in Tyler's fiction characters' lives and skills matter in more essential ways than the salaries they earn or their lack of job status in corporate American society.

Work, first and foremost in Tyler's novels, can provide worthwhile self-knowledge and a sense of individual identity. Delia Grinstead in *Ladder of Years* begins to think of herself not as incompetent and useless, but as a woman who "*looks completely self-reliant*" and actually is so as Mr. Pomfret's secretary (123). Similarly, Pauline Anton feels proud to have "moved on" after her divorce, refusing "to waste [her] energy nursing grudges" against her ex-husband (247), nor remain paralyzed by the grief she has felt over her runaway daughter Lindy; instead, she reaches out to others through her part-time work as a receptionist for a group of cardiologists in *The Amateur Marriage*. Barnaby Gaitlin finds his Rent-a-Back labor moves him from a sense of unworthiness and failure to seeing himself as his clients, his co-worker Martine, and his employer Mrs. Dibble do, as *"a man you can trust,"* in *The Patchwork Planet* (288). Rebecca Davitch, too, finds hostessing parties for decades at the "Open Arms" has been more than something her deceased husband Joe thought she would be good at; the work has helped develop her generosity of spirit, enabling her to become the very kind of person she had always wanted to be, a person really good at enabling others (as well as herself) to have "a wonderful time" in *Back When We Were Grownups* (274).

Work brings both a sense of self and a sense of self-worth to other Tyler characters, as well. Emily Meredith in *Morgan's Passing*, so prone to denigrate her own skills while praising her husband Leon's, proves herself to be the truly resourceful marriage partner. She makes many different kinds of puppets, sews costumes for all the shows they put on (from ones about dental hygiene, to ones enacting biblical stories, to a variety of fairy tales, as well), creates the scenery for each show, and plays the parts of many of the puppets – while Leon sits moping and complaining that the work they do is beneath him and inadequate to his acting talents. As Emily becomes more and more confident of her own capabilities, she also becomes less and less satisfied with Leon as her choice of a marriage partner. Evie Decker in *A Slipping-Down Life* also proves to be the more hard-working, reliable partner in her marriage. She looks forward to her new job at the local library: "she pictured herself in a blue smock, calm and competent, going through a set of crisp motions with catalogue drawers" (162).[27] Not only is this work Evie will find satisfying in itself, but it also suggests that she will be able to walk out on Drumstrings Casey and take care of a newborn baby on her own.

Work also is part of what enables Ian Bedloe in *Saint Maybe* to redeem himself from the state of being, he feels, "a hopeless sinner" (110). In addition to raising the three children his brother Danny and sister-in-law Lucy have left behind, Ian apprentices himself to a carpenter, creating furniture that "was fine and smooth and sturdy" (*SM* 315) with his own hands. In creating something of practical value in the world, something he can be proud of, furniture he has honed and shaped himself, Ian begins to re-fashion his own life and find eventual self-acceptance.

Other Tyler protagonists find that no one job can completely absorb their interests or express their personalities. Duncan Peck in *Searching for Caleb*, for instance, has held many different jobs since marrying Justine:

> In the last twenty years he had been, among other things, a goat farmer, a photographer, and a cabinetmaker; he had worked in a pet store, a tobacconist's, a record bar, and a gourmet shop; he had taken census, shorn sheep, and fertilized the lawns of a suburban development on a toy tractor. Almost all these jobs had been enjoyable, but only briefly. He began to grow restless. (34-35)

Duncan advises his daughter Meg *not* to marry the Reverend Arthur Milsom but, instead, to "learn to surf. . . . Join the Foreign Legion" (*SFC* 171), anything to try out different roles and facets of her character, as he has done in his own life. Similarly, Duncan's wife, Justine, advises Red Emma Borden at the Caro Mill Diner to forego restaurant work to pursue her dream of becoming a mailman:

> "Change," said Justine.
> "Beg pardon?"
> "Change. I don't need cards for that. Take the change. Always change."
> "Well – is that my fortune?"
> "Yes, it is," said Justine. "Goodbye, Red Emma! See you soon!" (*SFC* 29)

Elizabeth Abbott gives similar advice to Timothy Emerson in *The Clock Winder* since he says he can no longer "picture a future any more" (as he fears being expelled from medical school for cheating on a test). Elizabeth tells Timothy to "find something else to do. . . . Maybe you should make a *big* switch. Lumberjack? Fur-trapper? Deck-swabber?" (*CW* 95-96; 95), but Timothy fails to take her advice – committing suicide, instead.

Morgan Gower of *Morgan's Passing*, however, is Tyler's most famous example of someone who cannot settle down to just one job (until the novel's end, when Morgan takes on Leon Meredith's identity and a myriad of roles in his occupation as co- puppeteer with Emily). Throughout his adult life, Morgan has tried out many different types of work, from being a gynecologist (delivering Emily and Leon Meredith's Gina) to adopting the personas of a "glassblower . . . and a tugboat captain for the Curtis Bay Towing Company, and a Mohawk Indian high-rise worker" (*MP* 145) – and many, many other occupations, besides. He reads the "want ads" in the local paper, occasionally trying out a position for a few days, especially "those ads with character. (*Driver to chauffeur elderly gentleman, some knowledge of Homer desirable*)" (*MP* 32). By taking on many different occupations, however briefly, Morgan Gower seeks to explore the varying facets of his personality, hoping to gain a clearer understanding of his own needs and identity.

Tyler's characters find work not only provides them with money and a handle on reality – even what might be seen as demeaning, trivializing labor in the tobacco fields, shearing sheep, or fertilizing suburban lawns – but work also helps them better understand themselves and find personal fulfillment.[28] Tyler's artists and artisans take pleasure in using their skills and talents to create something interesting, evocative, useful, or beautiful. Three are photographers (Charlotte Emory, James Green, and Nathaniel Moffat); two are full-time writers (Macon Leary writes travel guides and Adrian Bly-Brice designs newsletters) – and one, Biddy Davitch, publishes a monthly newsletter on diet for the elderly; two others are craftsmen (Ian Bedloe makes furniture and Ira Moran is a frame maker); one is a sculptor (Jeremy Pauling), while Sarah Leary is studying this art, as well; and three others are musicians (Jesse Moran, Bertram Drumstrings Casey, and Caleb Peck). Emily Meredith makes puppets – and she and Leon, then later Morgan Gower, put on shows to delight young children. Emily "loved the moment when a puppet seemed to come to life – usually just after she'd sewed the eyes on. Once made, a puppet had its own distinct personality" (*MP* 84) – as Tyler's characters find expression for their "distinct personalities" through the work they do. Tyler's chefs – from Caleb Peck to Ruth Spivey to Ezra Tull – and nutritionist Biddy Davitch all take pride in the unusual dishes they serve and the nourishing meals they provide. Creating good food, for them, becomes an expression of self – and an act of love.

Other Tyler characters express their creativity and imagination in finding ways to provide livings for themselves. As Muriel Pritchett tells Macon Leary, "I've *had* to be inventive" (*AT* 189), developing a research service, "We-Search Research," for college students as just one of her means of providing for herself and her son Alexander. Susie Grinstead in *Ladder of Years* starts another business, "House in a Box," which also targets university students by offering them start-up kits for their first kitchens or bathrooms. In *A Patchwork Planet*, Mrs. Dibble begins her "Rent-a-Back" service for crippled and elderly clients who cannot afford chauffeurs, maids, gardeners, and handymen but, nonetheless, need affordable help to carry out the many tasks they can no longer manage on their own. Rebecca Davitch's husband Joe began the "Open Arms" business out of the ground floor of his family home, providing celebration parties for retirees, graduates, the newly married, those with wedding anniversaries, and so on, after his father has died unexpectedly (as an uninsured insurance agent). Biddy Davitch in *Back When We Were Grownups*, as well, designs her own nutrition newsletter for a retirement community, *What Kind of Wine Goes With Oatmeal?*, while Adrian Bly-Brice creates another newsletter, entitled *Hurry Up, Please*, for people interested in the subject of time travel. In *The Accidental Tourist*, of course, Macon Leary has turned his own dislike of travel into a livelihood as he creates travel guides for people who hate to fly and be away from home as much as he does. Also, in *Saint Maybe*, Rita diCarlo expresses her ingenuity by developing a unique business as a "Clutter Counselor" to help people such as the Bedloes sort out the necessary and important from the jumbled accretions in their lives. Many of Tyler's characters can take pride not only in earning a living but in using their imaginations to find innovative ways to do so.

These are Tyler's creators, her "makers," while other characters are her "doers" (*MP* 84) – although, of course, some (such as those above) may combine the two categories. Mary Tell works with children at a day-care center, and Maggie Moran takes care of the elderly at the Silver Threads Nursing Home where she has worked since graduating from high school. Some are store clerks (Pearl Tull, Jesse Moran, Serena Gill, Muriel Pritchett, Mrs. Gower, or Daphne Dean Bedloe), while Morgan Gower manages a hardware store, Michael Anton owns a Baltimore grocery, and No-No Davitch owns the Budding Genius flower shop. Others are physicians (Zeb Davitch treats the children of the inner-city poor; Jenny Tull is a Baltimore pediatrician, as well; and Sam Grinstead primarily takes care of elderly patients). Some are teachers, including Sarah Leary, Amanda and Laura Pauling, Doug Bedloe, Peter Emerson, Anna Grant Stuart Anton, and Mr. Decker. Daniel Otis is a retired roofer; P.J. Emerson, Red Emma Borden, and Mabel from *Breathing Lessons* are waitresses; Fiona Moran and Ramsay Grinstead's girlfriend Velma are beauticians; Delia Grinstead and Joan Pike do secretarial work; Pauline Anton is a medical office receptionist; and Horace Lamb in *Ladder of Years* sells storm windows. All draw on their different talents and skills to serve others in a variety of ways, following Daphne Dean Bedloe's advice to Ian in *Saint Maybe* to "use all the life you've got"

(264) and Daniel Otis's words to his nephew Lamont in *Breathing Lessons*, "Spill it! Spill it all, I say! No way *not* to spill it" (170). All are Tyler's "doers," using up their energy and spilling out their lives as they go about performing a variety of community tasks.

Those who are most exemplary in Tyler's fiction attempt to be useful and – consciously and conscientiously – try not to harm others. They are not waiting for success and happiness to arrive (as are Drumstrings Casey, Brindle Morgan, Leon Meredith, Lucy Dean Bedloe, or Jesse Moran) but try to find, as Cody Tull tells his son Luke, a "job [they] enjoy" (*DHR* 223), something that needs to be done, and, at the same time, work they won't "mess up," or where, at least, as Ian Bedloe says, "it was possible to repair the damage" (*SM* 126). Elizabeth Abbott, as well, tries to be of use in *The Clock Winder* without hurting others (as she blames herself for Timothy Emerson's suicide), becoming a companion for the failing and confused Mr. Cunningham and, later, a crafts teacher at a girls' reform school. Justine Peck, as well, puts her intuition to use as a fortune-teller, but only after Duncan assures her: "Just don't say anything that would cause somebody harm. But I don't think people take *bad* advice. They've got intuition too, you know. In fact I'd be surprised if they take any advice at all" (*SFC* 135). Tyler's characters find that not doing harm is as important as exercising their talents and abilities in pleasurable and useful ways.[29]

Most important of all in Tyler's fiction, however, is that work which enables people to interrelate meaningfully with others. Such an occupation might be cooking for other people, as does Biddy Davitch, making exotic canapés and gourmet dishes "as if the food were her only means of communication" (*BWWWG* 14). Caleb Peck also fixes food for others "so seriously and so tenderly that it tasted like a gift" (*SFC* 293), and Ezra Tull fixes his customers meals that are "hot and garlicky and . . . made with love" (*DHR* 119) – both pricing items individually, according to each customer's ability to pay. In addition, Caleb Peck as the "Stringtail Man" joins his fiddle to black musician White-Eye's guitar, playing the blues so that "their two stringed instruments spoke together continuously like old relations recollecting and nodding and agreeing" (*SFC* 268). Their musical conversations reach out to include many others, as well, so that by "the Crash in 1929" the duo "had become a [New Orleans] fixture. Though not famous, they were familiar; and the poorest people were willing to give up a coin in order to keep the world from changing any more than it already had" (*SFC.* 269).

These characters reach out to their fellow human beings through food and music, as other characters reach out to others in the community in more obvious ways. For instance, Mary Tell takes care of young children in a Baltimore nursery school, Karen Anton (now Antonczyk, emphasizing her Polish roots) acts as a legal defender for the local poor, her nephew Pagan Anton has become a "family advocate" for autistic children such as he himself once was (*AM* 276), and Zeb Davitch's pediatric practice reaches out to the poor children of downtown Baltimore. Saul Emory ministers to the impoverished and desperate passing through his hometown of Clarion, Maryland, while Joel Miller acts as principal of Bay Borough's local high school. Maggie Moran, too, feels "valuable and competent" when, at eighteen years of age, she helps the elderly, opening their curtains and moving their water pitchers, attracting groups of patients around her who enjoy the pleasure of her company at the Silver Threads Nursing Home (*BL* 91). Maggie doesn't want to follow the advice of her boyfriend Boris Drumm (a college student outraged by the world's injustices) by becoming a nurse with a respectable degree. She protests, "I don't want to stand at a nursing station filling out forms; I want to deal with folks!" to make their lives more pleasant in hands-on, everyday ways, even if her position isn't one that will give her status in the eyes of the world (or in the eyes of her boyfriend, either) (*BL* 96).

So, too, with Barnaby Gaitlin, who comes from a family of "do-gooders" (also at a distance), founders of the Gaitlin Foundation for the Indigent (*PP* 80), who disdain the "useful purpose" of Barnaby's work with the crippled and elderly because he does it "for a fee" (*PP* 80). Yet Barnaby (like Maggie Moran) develops close personal relationships with his clients and becomes "tangled up in [their] lives" (32). He gets to know his customers' problems and needs, their various likes and dislikes (such as Mr. Cartwright's digestive problems with sauerkraut and Mrs. Cartwright's need for a navy coat that won't show the dirt), as well as their financial situations ("Mrs. Gordoni . . . couldn't afford our fees but needed us so badly (rheumatoid arthritis) that we would doctor her time sheet – write down a mere half hour when we'd been at her house a whole morning" (*PP* 56)). This "good-heartedness" is just what Barnaby's boss Mrs. Dibble feels her customers deserve (despite any loss of profits her business might experience as a result of his kindness): "They love you, Barnaby," Mrs. Dibble told me. . . . It hasn't escaped their notice how you've cared for them all these years. . . . You're my very best worker!" (*PP* 42; 189).

Work such as this enables Tyler's characters both to interrelate in a significant way with others and, at the same time, achieve a satisfying sense of self-worth. As Mary F. Robertson explains in discussing several of Tyler's earlier novels:

> one can best be oneself if one is connected in some significant way with those in the public who are different from oneself. Charlotte's house has a room with an outside door which serves as a photography studio that is open to the public [in *Earthly Possessions*]. Ezra's "homesick" restaurant similarly connotes both the public and private life [in *Dinner at the Homesick Restaurant*]. The Merediths' apartment, into which Morgan eventually moves with Emily, is located above a public crafts-shop with a common hallway [in *Morgan's Passing*]. (200).

Another graphic instance of the way in which working with others enables characters to move beyond the confines of the self occurs in *The Tin Can Tree*. In this novel, Mrs. Pike is so overcome by grief after her daughter's sudden death that she has retreated to her room and stopped sewing clothes for her customers (her business is also one which brings the public into the privacy of the Pike home). While she has become a popular seamstress because of her ability to talk to customers, it is also true that Mrs. Pike needs them for other reasons than the income they provide her. As old Missouri, a lifelong worker herself, tells Joan Pike, "Mrs. Pike is going to have to start working again" (*TCT* 101) in order to be able to re-engage with life once more. In Tyler's fiction, it is clear that working with others benefits both the worker as well as those being helped.

The working lives of Tyler's characters, then, benefit them in many ways, giving them a sense of themselves, opportunities to be creative and inventive, a means to help both themselves and others lead more fulfilled lives, as well as offering different methods of communication beyond human speech. And, of course, there is the most fundamental and basic benefit of all: work gives Tyler's characters a way to earn the money necessary to support themselves and their families. Yet Tyler's hard-working characters most often lead "slipping-down lives" at society's very edge, lives that appear, at times, on the verge of economic ruin. Her heroes and heroines do not move up the social ladder to fulfill the American dream of material success, but, instead, reflect the reality of most American lives since the mid-1970s: lives of economic decline and below median wages for all but a small percent of the population.[30] For the most part, Tyler's novels concern individuals, as Alice Petry says of Tyler's black characters, who have not had "the luxury of falling into the counterproductive lifestyle of those with more opportunities, more education, more money" ("Bright" 11). Such characters include white working people like Ian Bedloe, Muriel Pritchett, Pearl Tull, Ira Moran, or Joan Pike, as well as Tyler's black characters such as Daniel and Duluth Otis or Lafleur and Sulie Boudrault – people who have had to use their wits and their skills to provide for themselves all their lives.

If some characters have known better days and the advantages of a more privileged background (Pearl Tull, Justine and Duncan Peck, Mary Tell, or Barnaby Gaitlin, for instance), they now find themselves, as Maggie Moran acknowledges, "sliding downhill" (*BL* 260). If Maggie's family had once had more stature, now the generations "were descending in every respect, not just in their professions and their educations but in the way they reared their children and the way they ran their households," causing Maggie's mother Mrs. Daley to ask, "How have you let things get so *common*?" (*BL* 260). And the situation may get even worse, financially, for Maggie and Ira Moran, for, as Maggie tells Serena Gill, "they're talking at the nursing home about laying off some of the workers. It's something to do with the new state regulations – they're going to hire on more professionals and lay off people like me" (*BL* 81).

Tyler's world, then, is a financially precarious and difficult one for the majority of her characters. According to Edward Hoagland, Tyler's characters "don't get promotions; they hug what they have. Though once upon a time they did look up the ladder, now they're mainly trying to keep from sliding into a catastrophe such as bankruptcy. . . . Clinging to a low rung of the middle class, they are householders because they have inherited a decaying home, not because they're richer than renters" (140-41). Charlotte Emory's house, for instance, is a "big brown turreted house" which now finds itself stuck between two gas stations in a largely commercial district of Clarion (*EP* 9). Mrs. Emerson, too, lives in a "house [that] had outlived its usefulness. It sat hooded and silent, a brown shingleboard monstrosity close to the road but backed by woods, far enough from downtown Baltimore to escape the ashy smell of the factories" (*CW* 3) – but unable to escape the constant need for repairs.

So, too, with the Cullen family home in which Morgan and Bonny Gower live, a house that now had "started slipping downward, or sideways, or whatever it was that it was doing" (*MP* 30). Jeremy Pauling must rent out rooms in his mother's deteriorating "thin dark three-storey Baltimore rowhouse" located "smack in the middle of the city on a narrow busy street" (*CN* 5). According to his sister Amanda, Jeremy's neighborhood had been "running down, had been for years. Most places had split into apartments and gone over to colored and beatniks, and a few were even boarded up, with city notices plastered across the doors" (*CN* 5). Sam Grinstead in *Ladder of Years* runs his medical practice out of the old Felson family home, trying to renovate its ancient plumbing, remedy its lack of air-conditioning, and repair its out-dated wiring, mildewed shingles, deteriorating plaster, and rotting shutters (now that his father-in-law is dead)– an expense which requires college students Susie and Ramsay to live at home due to reduced "family finances" (18).

Similarly, Rebecca Davitch runs her "Open Arms" business out of "the Davitches' ornate but crumbling nineteenth-century Baltimore row house, with its two high-ceilinged parlors, front and rear, its antiquated backyard kitchen connected to the dining room by an afterthought of a passageway, its elaborate carved moldings and butterfly-parquet floors and seven sculptured marble mantelpieces overhanging seven fireplaces, five of them defunct" (*BWWWG* 22). The mansion's ancient ceilings drop plaster and it requires constant repairs. In addition, their party-giving business had become "very slow these days. Three different people had called to ask [Rebecca] if the Open Arms were in a safe neighborhood, and although she had assured them it was – with reasonable precautions, she said; using normal common sense – they told her they would have to think it over and get back to her" (*BWWWG* 231).[31]

While sliding sideways and downward may be something inevitable (if regrettable) for some, it is often a conscious choice for other Tyler characters who find, as did Edna Pontellier in Kate Chopin's *The Awakening*, "there was with her a feeling of having descended in the social scale, with a corresponding sense of having risen in the spiritual" (132). Macon Leary leaves North Charles Street to live with Muriel Pritchett on Singleton Street, a "street [that] was always backsliding," one that at first had "unnerved him with its poverty and its ugliness" (*AT* 234). Mary Tell, as well, leaves the relative security of Jeremy Pauling's deteriorating Baltimore brownstone for "a tipsy gray shanty with cinderblocks for a doorstep" at the Quamikut Boatyard, a house that "filled [Jeremy] with despair. At each gust of wind outside the cold burst in upon him like little knives from several directions. . . . [seemingly, Mary had chosen] the very *worst* house to live in" (*CN* 260; 265). Duncan and Justine Peck, as well, decide upon carnival life and "a purple trailer in Parvis, Maryland" rather than move back into the security of the Peck family house and business in Roland Park, Baltimore (*SFC* 307). Morgan Gower, too, chooses to leave his wife Bonny (and the aging Cullen family homestead) to embrace a much more precarious life in Tindell Acres Trailer Park as a puppeteer with Emily Meredith.

Anne Tyler's protagonists seldom choose to marry up the social scale – as when Morgan Gower marries Bonny Cullen and Emily marries Leon Meredith, for instance – and, when they do, those marriages usually fail (Morgan and Emily renounce their more socially respectable spouses, choosing to slip down the social ladder and find happiness together). In *The Amateur Marriage*, Michael Anton's marriage to the only slightly more well-heeled Pauline Barclay also fails, although not until many years after Pauline's father has provided them with the down payment on their new house, and they have left Michael's Polish Catholic East Baltimore neighborhood far behind for the modern, post World War II, suburb of Elmview Acres. Many years afterwards, Michael will admit that he feels much more comfortable in Anna Grant Stuart's company, much less afraid of appearing "lower-class" or acknowledging his Polish heritage (214; 211), just as he feels much more relaxed in Anna's "plain white clapboard," old-fashioned house, with "its comfortable air of not trying too hard, not needing to try, taking its own gentility for granted" (210; 211).

One character after another selects a partner on a lower rung of the social ladder than themselves: Mrs. Emerson; her sons, Peter and Matthew Emerson; Macon Leary (with Muriel Pritchett); Pearl and Cody Tull; Barnaby Gaitlin; Evie Decker; and Ben Joe Hawkes (whose mother says of Shelley Domer, "[she] can't help her ancestry, that's for sure" [*IMEC* 93]). Some of these down-scale relationships fail, as well (Evie Decker's with Drumstrings Casey or Pearl's with Beck Tull) or are not completely happy (Mrs. Emerson's and Cody Tull's marriages), but Tyler seems to suggest that characters of lower social class standing often have a great deal to offer their social "betters." Muriel Pritchett challenges Macon Leary to re-engage with life through the example she provides of creativity, resilience, pugnaciousness, and courage. Shelley Domer offers Ben Joe Hawkes compassion born of personal suffering and her quiet interest in his life. Similarly, Barnaby Gaitlin's co-worker Martine presents him with her deep respect for his character, as well as her hard-headed realism and gritty resourcefulness. These are relationships which enable Tyler's protagonists to grow and gain – not monetarily, perhaps, but nonetheless enriching their lives and revitalizing their faith in their own capabilities.

These downward social choices clearly are presented as the right ones for Tyler's characters – for Morgan Gower, for example, who "felt suddenly light-hearted. . . . Everything he looked at seemed luminous and beautiful, and rich with possibilities" (*MP* 311) in his new life with Emily Meredith. Justine and Duncan Peck, too, look forward to "liv[ing] happily ever after" in their new lives as carnival workers; "I know when we're doing something right," Justine confidently announces (*SFC* 307; 308). Their lives may seem to be those of society's "second rate" (as Ian

Bedloe's Church of the Second Chance is mistakenly called) (*SM* 177), but Tyler suggests that these ordinary lives are the very ones that are actually most extraordinary.[32] As Benjamin DeMott says of *Dinner at the Homesick Restaurant*, while adversity injures each of the Tull children, it also brings out the best in their characters. Jenny's "exhuberance," Ezra's "generosity," and Cody's sense of responsibility are all responses to family deprivation, even if they do not recognize the positive ways in which their difficult past has influenced their lives (DeMott 113). When Daniel Peck – formerly a Judge – moves in with Justine and Duncan, helping out by washing their dishes, making his own birthday dinner for all the Peck relatives, baking them a "war cake . . . [which] makes do with considerably less butter and eggs than we would normally use, you see," he then brags, "After all, we're living in reduced circumstances" (*SFC* 202). The Roland-Park Pecks have begun to suspect that Daniel really "*enjoy*[*s*] this life [moving around with Justine and Duncan] – these dismal houses, weird friends, separations from the family, this moving about and fortune telling. [As] If he weren't almost proud of the queer situations he found himself in" (*SFC* 202), discovering new facets of himself and reveling in strange experiences at the end of his life.

It seems that Daniel Peck has changed his view of what is important. He asks his granddaughter Justine to read this statement at a Plankhurst Quaker service: "I used to think that heaven was – palatable? [Justine can't read Daniel's writing.] Palatial. I was told it had pearly gates and was paved with gold. But now I hope they are wrong about that. I would prefer to find that heaven was a small town with a bandstand in the park and a great many trees, and I would know everybody in it . . ." (*SFC* 190). Tyler's characters find that heaven can exist in ordinary, day-to-day experiences – as can heroism, as well (a theme to be examined further in Chapter Five). Elizabeth Abbottt in *The Clock Winder* expresses her amazement in seeing

ordinary people standing in long lines as they wait to cast their votes. Elizabeth
wonders at their quiet patience and steady persistence:

> "There were all these people lined up. Shopkeepers and housewives
> and people, just waiting and waiting. So *responsible*. I bet you
> anything they wait like that every voting day, and put in their single
> votes that hardly matter and go back to their jobs and do the same
> chores over and over. Just on and on. Just plodding along. Just
> getting through till they die. You have to admire that. Don't you?"
> (*CW* 225)

It is these ordinary, workaday lives of tobacco pickers, gardeners, fortune tellers,
sales clerks, puppeteers, nursing home attendants, handymen, waitresses, and cooks
that Tyler affirms through her fiction. These are the people who make things with
their hands, serve tables, clerk at stores, care for the sick and the aged, as well as
stand in long lines to vote – society's laborers who make their communities work by
sharing their talents and going about their daily tasks with considerable willingness,
much dignity, and personal fortitude. Tyler suggests society's real prosperity is to
be found in the richness of these individuals' lives, not in the wages her characters
earn or the profits they generate. The downwardly mobile life may, in fact, be the
one that is more truly successful in Anne Tyler's fiction.

Notes

22.   Mr. Pomfret, Delia Grinstead's boss in *Ladder of Years*, is another character who
        cannot resist buying things. Whenever Delia places an order for an expensive
        gadget he wants from a mail order catalog, the narrator says, "her employer's greed,
        like his huge belly, made Delia feel trim and virtuous" (*LY* 103).

23.   A number of Tyler's characters are attracted to trailers and vans (with their built-in
        features and snug space) because they force choices about what to take and what to
        hold onto. Morgan Gower and Emily Meredith in *Morgan's Passing*, and Justine
        and Duncan Peck in *Searching for Caleb*, end up living in trailers, while Delia
        Grinstead in *Ladder of Years* longs to buy the trailer their roofer Vernon is driving
        (77-79).

24. Tyler seems to suggest that education may offer some job training (as for physicians) but for the most part fails to prepare people for life. Timothy Emerson in *The Clock Winder* offers a good example. Timothy was "thought [to be] . . . a genius" in grade school, then went on and "invented weird gadgets, . . . played chess tournaments, . . . monitored Stravinsky on an oscilloscope that [he] . . . rebuilt [himself]" (*CW* 96), yet he fails at life, committing suicide when he can find no place for himself, no work he desires to do.

25. A few critics would disagree that Tyler affirms ordinary lives. In his review of *Earthly Possessions*, Walter Sullivan says, "in her pursuit of the peculiar, she seems put off by the teachers and preachers and lawyers and businessmen who do their work and live their lives without nourishing eccentricities or trying to make a comic virtue out of failure" (92). While Sullivan wishes that Tyler were more accepting of the solid upper-middle-classes, Daniel Klinghoffer's review of *Breathing Lessons* criticizes Tyler for appearing not to "like the majority of Americans" (137), working-class people such as "the Morans . . . [who are] just too middle-class for her tastes" and to whom he believes she "condescends" (139).

26. Alice Hall Petry has pointed out how important money is for Tyler's characters. She says, "Tyler is fully cognizant of the blunt need for money in the nurturance of the self" – and adds that this is particularly true for Tyler's female characters in order that they be able to stand on their own feet (*Understanding* 91; 95-96).

27. Anne Tyler draws on her own work experience here (as she does elsewhere in her novels). In "Still Just Writing," she recalls, "Before we had children I worked in a library. It was a boring job, but I tend to like doing boring things. I would sit on a stool alphabetizing Russian catalogue cards and listening to other librarians talking around me. It made me think of my adolescence, which was spent listening to the tobacco stringers while I handed tobacco. At night I'd go home from the library and write. I never wrote about what the librarians said, exactly, but having those voices in my ears all day helped me summon up my own characters' voices" (7).

28. Also, for some Tyler characters, accomplishments can help them prove themselves to others and overturn past patterns in their lives. Agatha Dean Bedloe becomes a career woman and wife with no children (the antithesis of her mother), while Delia Grinstead proves to Sam and her children that she is not just an extension of their needs but an effective, valuable human being in her own right. Cody Tull shows his father that he has survived into adulthood without him, becoming a responsible husband and father (unlike Beck) and enjoying more success in his work than Beck ever has (thereby undoing some of the hurt and damage of his father's desertion). Similarly, Pagan Anton's choice of work with autistic children reveals how he is still trying to deal with the effects of his own abandonment by his mother Lindy and

at the same time help heal other emotionally impaired children, as well, in *The Amateur Marriage*.

29. This desire to do no harm can also become paralyzing, Tyler suggests. For example, in *Saint Maybe* Ian Bedloe is so concerned with never damaging people's lives again that it has made him overly afraid. As Daphne Dean Bedloe tells him, he has become "King Careful. Mr. Look-Both-Ways. Saint Maybe" (*SM* 264). To live fully, people will inevitably make mistakes, but Daphne suggests that making errors isn't necessarily bad: "Mess up, I say! . . . Fall flat on your face! Make every mistake you can think of!" (*SM* 264). After all, Tyler makes clear, Ian's big mistake at the outset of the novel has led to his own personal growth, a great deal of love, and positive lives for each of the three children in his care. Clearly, the novel suggests, atonement is possible after mistakes have been made, but Tyler also values the importance, at least, of trying not to hurt others.

30. Margaret Morganroth Gullette says, "in the eighties real wages flattened or actually dropped for all but the top 10%, and hours worked went up for many who still had full-time employment" (*Declining* 230). Mark Weisbrot confirms this decline, extending it back to 1974, arguing that the "the typical wage-or salary-earner has not shared in the gains from economic growth" in America's new global economy, but, in fact, has been adversely affected by these changes ("Globalism for Dummies" 16).

31. See Frank W. Shelton's essay, "Anne Tyler's Houses," for a detailed discussion of decaying houses and domesticity in Tyler's novels up to 1990.

32. In "Still Just Writing," Tyler says, "people have always seemed funny and strange to me, and touching in unexpected ways. . . . It's not a matter of choice [to write about bizarre and eccentric people]; it just seems to me that even the most ordinary person, in real life, will turn out to have something unusual at his center" (12).

Chapter Four
Embracing Cultural Change

While Anne Tyler asks readers to redefine their concepts of the ideal family, as of prosperity and success in American society, she also asks them to resist American cultural myths of an ideal past and an untransformed future. She suggests that societal change not only is inevitable but often can and should be embraced. Her very subject is the unpredictability that Shirley Brice Heath says all serious fiction requires and readers need in order to gain perspective on their own lives (in Franzen 48).[33] The everyday world in which Tyler's protagonists exist is, for the most part, an industrialized, commercialized, ugly, littered, and often frightening one. Their lives are affected by fatal car crashes, out-of-wedlock pregnancies, runaway children, war drafts, random shootings, drug dealing, adulterous liaisons, inexplicable suicides, and the financial anxieties of contemporary society. Nevertheless, Tyler suggests that her characters are wrong to try to cling to the way things once were (or the way they think they once were) and the way they believe they still ought to be. She challenges her characters (and readers) to face the world as it is, welcome the reality of their ever-changing lives, and work for beneficial change.

Tyler's characters believe they are living their lives in the present, yet they yearn for a comforting (if illusory) past. Unable always to distinguish today clearly from yesterday, they find themselves in the place of Morgan Gower, who asks Emily Meredith, "Aren't we all sitting on stacks of past events? And not every level is neatly finished off, right? Sometimes a lower level bleeds into an upper level. Isn't that so?" *(MP* 133). Underlying the existing lives of Tyler's characters are other past, seemingly more perfect, lives (both real and imagined) that "bleed" through and color the present. For instance, Morgan's old house is filled with "pearl pushbutton[s]" for "alerting a non-existent servant [to attend to the needs of those who had rung]. . . . *Mr. Armand. Mrs. Armand. Miss Caroline. Master Keith*" (*MP* 100). Morgan finds himself haunted by the thought:

> that a younger, finer family lived alongside his, gliding through the hallways, calling for tea and hot-water bottles. Evenings, the mother sat by the fire in a white peignoir and read to her children, one on either side of her. A boy, a girl; how tidy. At dinner they discussed great books, and on Sunday they dressed up and went to church. *They* never quarreled. *They* never lost things or forgot things. They rang and waited serenely. They gazed beyond the Gowers with the placid, rapt expressions of theatregoers ignoring some petty disturbance in the row ahead. (*MP* 100)

This past family, with its proper and dignified life, represents for Morgan the values he and his family have failed to uphold in their disorganized, hectic, slatternly modern household. When Morgan's brother-in-law Robert Roberts tries to drown himself in the midst of their family vacation, Morgan admits, "No, plainly what had happened was a comment upon their whole family – on the disarray of their family life" (*MP* 179). It is no wonder that Morgan falls in love with Emily Meredith's "old-time, small-town manners" since her old-fashioned ways make her "the most proper person he had ever met" (*MP* 225).

The seemingly genteel, civilized world of the past both eludes and pursues other Tyler characters, as well. Barnaby Gaitlin in *A Patchwork Planet* has failed to find his guiding angel to help him uphold the Gaitlin family tradition (begun by his great-grandfather), with family legend promising he would then achieve the success and respectability obtained by his male forefathers. Barnaby is painfully aware that he has written no volume of his own to add to the library shelf containing his grandfather's *Light of Heaven*, his father's *A Possible Paranormal Experience*, or his brother Jeff's *A Tradition Repeated,* all detailing encounters with "angels" who have guided these family patriarchs in their work with the Gaitlin Foundation for the Indigent.

In *The Accidental Tourist,* when Macon Leary's marriage has broken apart, his son has been murdered, and his life seems to have become totally unstable, Macon returns to the past – the comfortable home of his deceased grandparents ("two thin, severe, distinguished people in dark clothes [of whom Macon and his siblings had]. . . . approved . . . at once" (66)). In this spacious, old-fashioned, Dempsey Road sanctuary with his sister Rose and brothers Porter and Charles, Macon continues to shelter from the contemporary world, playing the family card game "Vaccination" and eating the perfectly prepared, "*conservative*" baked potatoes of his youth (*AT* 77). Yet, just as Macon once resisted joining his brothers in the secure and familiar world of their grandfather's Bottle Cap factory, he now finds himself reluctant to succumb entirely to their shared past, no matter how upright and safe it still may seem:

> In the portrait on the end wall, the Leary children gazed out with their veiled eyes. It occurred to Macon that they were sitting in much the same positions here this evening: Charles and Porter on either side of him, Rose perched in the foreground. Was there any real change? He felt a jolt of something very close to panic. Here he still was! The same as ever! *What have I gone and done?* he wondered, and he swallowed thickly and looked at his own empty hands. (*AT* 80-81)

Macon may desire at times to travel back in time to the more dignified and stable world of childhood under the care of his grandparents, but vivacious dog trainer Muriel Pritchett, Ethan's unruly dog Edward, and his own discomfiting ambivalence all drag him forward.

The Pecks are another Tyler family with a unique and distinguished history, a family business to take care of, and rituals and manners all their own. Although Grandfather Daniel Peck's life has become a transient one with Justine and Duncan as he searches for his missing brother Caleb, he continues to abhor all personal "dissatisfaction" with tradition and the desire for "*newness*" in people such as his brother Caleb or his nephew Duncan (*SFC* 6). Daniel Peck believes in leading a staid life and following in the path of family members who have gone before. He deplores nonconformity:

> "I can't tell you how many times I've seen it come to pass. A young man goes to a distant city instead of staying close to home, he gets a job, switches friends, widens his circle of acquaintances. Marries a girl from a family no one knows, lives in a house of unusual architecture, names his children foreign names that never were in his family in any preceding generation. He takes to traveling, buys winter homes and summer homes and vacation cottages in godforsaken states like Florida where none of us has ever been. Meanwhile his parents die and all his people just seem to vanish. . . . Then he dies himself, most likely in a very large city where there's nobody to notice . . . and what's it for? What's it all about?" (*SFC* 6).

All the same, Daniel Peck is powerless to keep his own family members in Roland Park, Baltimore, where he feels they belong – and he, too, ends his life abruptly, far away from the Peck family home.

Tyler's novels are filled with characters who cling to vestiges of the past, however quaint or strange they may seem. They write bread-and-butter thank you notes, as they have been trained to do, even the renegade Caleb Peck who writes (following his latest desertion of the Peck family):

November 20, 1973

Dear Justine,

I want to apologize for taking so long to write, but circumstances prevented me up until now.

It was very kind of you to invite me to stay with you. The frankfurters you cooked were delicious, and I shall remember my visit with a great deal of pleasure for a long time to come.

Love,
Caleb Peck (*SFC* 303)

Justine Peck continues to wear a hat (it's a Peck family tradition), as do the Potter sisters in *The Tin Can Tree*:

> The Potter sisters always carried handbags and wore hats and gloves, even if they were only going next door. They were small, round women, in their early sixties probably, and for as long as Joan had known them they had had only one aim in life: they wanted to have swarms of neighborhood children clamoring at their door for cookies, gathering in their yard at the first smell of cinnamon buns. And although no one came ("Children nowadays prefer to buy Nutty Buddies," Miss Faye said), they still went on baking, eating the cookies themselves, growing fat together and comparing notes on their identical heart conditions. (49-50)

So, too, Mrs. Emerson in *The Clock Winder* also clings to old-fashioned ways as the best and proper ones: "She dressed up for everything, even breakfast. She owned no slacks"; she "fight[s] the urge to spend her days in comfortable shoes and forget her chin-strap and let herself go"; and she continues to "take pride in [her] correspondence, [believing] letter-writing is a dying art" (7; 6; 35).

Social proprieties and genteel traditions affect many other Tyler characters, as well, influencing their concepts of how life ought to be lived. In *Dinner at the Homesick Restaurant*, Pearl Tull, at thirty and almost an old maid, had "ridden out of Raleigh triumphant with her new husband and never looked back" (14). After

Beck Tull leaves her and their three children behind, Pearl nevertheless continues to perpetuate the myth of their traditional family life. She writes to her Raleigh relatives, *"We celebrated [my birthday] at home. . . . Beck surprised me with the prettiest necklace"* (*DHR* 11), holding her head high as "every morning . . . [she] went off to Sweeney Bros. [grocery store]. She continued to wear her hat, giving the impression that she had merely dropped in and was helping out as a favor, in a pinch" (*DHR* 15).

Although Pearl worries that her children are "disgracing her" and causing neighbors to question their ideal family life, "sticking potatoes on people's exhaust pipes and letting the air out of tires and shooting at streetlights with BB guns and stealing hubcaps and making off with traffic signs, and moving Mrs. Correlli's madonna to Sonny Boy Brown's kitchen stoop and hanging around the hydrants with girls no better than tramps" (*DHR* 51), she tries to protect them (completely unsuccessfully, of course) from the knowledge of their father's desertion and their family's true failure. Just before her eldest son Cody leaves for college, she acknowledges the obvious, that they are no longer a traditional, intact family, nor have they been for some time:

> "Children, there's something I want to discuss with you. . . ."
> "It's about your father," Pearl said.
> Jenny said, "I'd choose the cafeteria [as a college job for Cody]."
> "You know, my darlings," Pearl told them, "how I always say your father's away on business."
> "But off-campus they might pay more," said Cody, "and every penny counts."
> "At the cafeteria you'd be with your classmates, though," Ezra said.
> "Yes, I thought of that."
> "All those coeds," Jenny said. "Cheerleaders. Girls in their little white bobby sox."
> "Sweater girls," Cody said.

> "There's something I want to explain about your father," Pearl told them.
> "Choose the cafeteria," Ezra said.
> "Children?"
> "The cafeteria," they said.
> And all three gazed at her coolly, out of gray, unblinking, level eyes exactly like her own. (*DHR* 30-31)

For all their apparent lack of concern about their absent father and their seemingly total immersion in the modern co-ed world, the Tull children, too, yearn for a family they can be proud of – a proper, stable, "traditional" family with "a male head" (Town 14) and "a mother who acted like other mothers! . . . gossiping with a little gang of women in the kitchen" (*DHR* 59).

The Tulls have clearly failed as a traditional family and Pearl yearns to understand what went wrong:

> Often, like a child peering over the fence at somebody else's party, she gazes wistfully at other families and wonders what their secret is. They seem so close. Is it that they're more religious? Or stricter, or more lenient? Could it be the fact that they participate in sports? Read books together? Have some common hobby? Recently, she overheard a neighbor woman discussing her plans for Independence Day: her family was having a picnic. Every member – child or grownup – was cooking his or her specialty. Those who were too little to cook were in charge of the paper plates.
> Pearl felt such a wave of longing that her knees went weak. (*DHR* 185)

Others must know the secret to maintaining the ideal American family and more orderly, dignified, proper lives; Pearl Tull admits (quietly, to herself) that she does not.

Many of Anne Tyler's characters beyond the Tull family in *Dinner at the Homesick Restaurant* feel embarrassed to admit that they have failed to live up to society's traditions and achieve cultural "normalcy." Ben Joe Hawkes, in *If Morning*

Ever Comes, knows very well that his father did not have "a dignified passing" (33) but, instead, died of a coronary at his mistress's home (just one of the many family embarrassments that Ben Joe has to contend with and that make him feel ashamed). Charlotte Emory in *Earthly Possessions*, too, is embarrassed by her imperfect parents, her overweight mother and failed father. Consequently, she "worked so hard" to be accepted by her peers at school that she became "secretary of the student body and first runner-up for Homecoming Queen. . . . The one thing I wanted most of all was for people to think that I was normal" (*EP* 54). The motherless Delia Grinstead, too, becomes "Miss Popularity in high school" in her bid for "normalcy" and social acceptance, while her husband Sam Grinstead tries to "*be a rock for my wife and children*" (in the way his own absconded father had never been) (*LY* 115; 125). In *A Slipping-Down Life*, Evie Decker (also the product of a "failed," non-traditional, motherless family) wants "a normal, ordinary wedding, with witnesses who aren't called in off the street" (142) – even if she is only seventeen and eloping with a high school dropout musician at the time.[34]

Meg Peck, too, after years of being embarrassed by her "*extreme. . . . irresponsible. . . . slap-dash*" parents (*SFC* 163-64), yearns for a traditional Peck wedding to the ever-so-responsible and upright Reverend Arthur Milsom:

> Meg would only be happy with a white dress that dipped to a point at the waist, [her Peck grandmother] Sarah Cantleigh's veil, and a bouquet of baby's breath. She wanted to walk down the aisle of the family's church in Baltimore where her mother had been married; she would like to be guarded by rows and rows of aunts and uncles and second cousins, grave Peck eyes approving her choice. (*SFC* 166)

Instead, when Duncan disapproves of Arthur as too ordinary – just "any pale fish in a suit" (*SFC* 172) – Meg elopes and marries Arthur in his own church in Semple, Virginia, without an ancestral veil or a single Peck relative in sight to applaud her choice.

Tyler's characters believe that, if they do the "right" things, adopt proper manners and child-raising techniques, following traditional paths that have been mapped out before them, their lives will turn out well. If Ben Joe Hawkes could just become the patriarch of his family, as the South intended he should be, and "stop . . . those amazing damned things that go on in this family" (*IMEC* 190), all their lives would surely improve.[35] If Maggie Moran could just get Fiona back together with her son Jesse, and have her granddaughter under her own roof again, the Morans could become a traditional American family once more: "people had to be reminded [how they were connected], that was all. The way the world was going now, it was so easy to forget," Maggie believes (*BL* 22). If the Bedloes, too, can just manage to incorporate Lucy and her children gracefully into their midst (even if Lucy is "a little tacky" (*SM* 30), a divorced woman with two children and another on the way that probably wasn't even their son Danny's), they can continue on their sure course as "the Bedloe *family*, Waverly Street's version of the ideal, apple-pie household" with barely a "hitch, [only] a moment of hesitation" (*SM* 4; 8). And if Rebecca Davitch can get her life back into its proper groove, resuming her romance with high school sweetheart Will Allenby, from her hometown of Church Valley High, Virginia, Rebecca could return, at long last, to that time when "everything had matched. There had not been any surprises" (*BWWWG* 41). Society's rules govern for a purpose, many of Tyler's characters tend to feel; flounting tradition only denies them the "clean, simple life [they] would [otherwise] have led" (*BWWWG* 93).

Yet, Anne Tyler calls into question this myth of the calmer, gentler, more traditional, more genteel life of the past. It is as much a fictional creation, she suggests, as are her ministers' eulogies for lives they have barely known and uncomfortable realities they are determined to gloss over. At Max Gill's funeral, Maggie and Ira Moran listen to the minister praising "Max's work for the Furnace Fund," realizing that "he didn't seem to know [Max] personally," that he has portrayed Max as "[nothing more than] . . . a walking business suit, a firm handshake" (*BL* 74), just another man making a brief appearance in an advertising brochure, perhaps.

Another instance of such airbrushing of imperfections, such fictionalizing of individual lives, occurs at Pearl Tull's funeral, as well:

> the minister, who had never met [the Tull children's] mother, delivered a eulogy so vague, so general, so universally applicable that Cody thought of that parlor game where people fill in words at random and then giggle hysterically at the story that results. Pearl Tull, the minister said, was a devoted wife and a loving mother and a pillar of the community. She had lived a long, full life and died in the bosom of her family, who grieved for her but took comfort in knowing that she'd gone to a far finer place. (*DHR* 285)

The minister's words create a make-believe Pearl Tull the family has never known – nor has the reader. Cody Tull sits in the front pew, mentally setting the record straight:

> It slipped the minister's mind, or perhaps he hadn't heard, that she hadn't been anyone's wife for over a third of a century; that she'd been a frantic, angry, sometimes terrifying mother; and that she'd never shown the faintest interest in her community but dwelt in it like a visitor from a superior neighborhood, always wearing her hat when out walking, keeping her doors tightly shut when at home. . . . That she was not at all religious, hadn't set foot in this church for decades; and though in certain wistful moods she might have mentioned the possibility of paradise, Cody didn't take much comfort in the notion of her residing there, fidgeting and finding fault and stirring up dissatisfactions. (*DHR* 285-86)

In truth, Cody believes, Pearl's life had been a "*stunted*" one (*DHR* 285) – the life of a woman so busy trying to appear conventional that she had never really dared to be herself, at all.

Daniel Peck, too, has lived his life trying to play by the rules, remaining loyal to Peck family traditions (at least in word, if not in deed) until the very end. Yet, he finally admits, "in my childhood I was trained to hold things in, you see. But I thought I was holding them until a certain *time*. I assumed that someday, somewhere, I would again be given the opportunity to spend all that saved-up feeling. When will that be?" (*SFC* 250). With his final breath, Daniel Peck admits the cost of his restraint and steadfast loyalty to traditional "Peckness," confessing, "I had certainly hoped for more than *this* out of life" (*SFC* 253).

Another "upright, firm old man," Grandfather Leary, makes his final worldly plans to go to "Lassaque. . . . an island [he had dreamed of] off the coast of Bolivia" because of the people's "reverence for the elderly. . . . the Lassaquans' knowledge doesn't come from books but from living; so they hang on every word from those who have lived the longest" (*AT* 145-46). When he can find no such island in the encyclopedia, Grandfather Leary then turns the attentions of his last days to inventing: "He would sit in his red leather armchair, his suit and white shirt immaculate, his black dress shoes polished to a glare, his carefully kept hands folded in his lap, and he would announce that he'd just finished welding together a motorcycle that would pull a plow" (*AT* 146). Although he imagines he is poor once more, his granddaughter Rose comments, "I honestly believe . . . that he's having the richest and most . . . colorful, really, time of his life. I'll bet even when he was young, he never enjoyed himself this much" (*AT* 147). It is this late-in-life, restless Grandfather Leary who appears to Macon in a dream and challenges him to take action, asking, "You want to sit in this old house and rot, boy? It's time we started digging out! How long are we going to stay fixed here?" (*AT* 148).

Younger characters, too, find that playing by the rules does not lead to the happiness they anticipate. Sam Grinstead in *Ladder of Years* and Cody Tull in *Dinner at the Homesick Restaurant* are determined to be responsible, faithful husbands and fathers (unlike the weak and wayward men who deserted their mothers), but their own marriages develop problems, their wives run away (although they return later), and their children fail to understand their characters or appreciate their sacrifices. In *Searching for Caleb*, Meg Peck rushes into marriage with Arthur Milsom in order to have "a normal happy life," admitting to her parents, "I thought when I got married we would be so – regular" (*SFC* 229; 228). Meg hasn't "want[ed] new experiences" but finds herself, instead, being taught faith healing and "liv[ing] among *crazy* people!" (*SFC* 229). Marriage has catapulted her into an entirely new life quite different from the calm and contented one she had anticipated.

"Normalcy" is a fantasy, Tyler suggests. Attempting to achieve the constancy we attribute to the past, to the "traditional" lives of our ancestors, actually leads to lifelessness and stultification. As Mary T. Robertson suggests, Tyler insists on revealing "history's real randomness and disorder" (203) in her novels – forcing characters such as Ben Joe Hawkes, who has wanted to repeat the conventional patriarchal arrangements of the past, to admit finally, "I can't believe history's going anywhere at all, much less repeating itself" (*IMEC* 239). On closer inspection, the past reveals its secret waywardness, its real life, those rough spots long smoothed over, the true natures of its figures carved in marble.

In *Ladder of Years*, Delia Grinstead finds she is actually related to the man memorialized by the bronze statue she has passed day after day in the town square of Bay Borough. However, even the plaque commemorating his life cannot entirely romanticize George Bay's actions:

> ON THIS SPOT, IN AUGUST 1863,
> GEORGE PENDLE BAY,
> A UNION SOLDIER ENCAMPED OVERNIGHT WITH HIS COMPANY,
> DREAMED THAT A MIGHTY ANGEL APPEARED TO HIM AND SAID,
> "YE ARE SITTING IN THE BARBER'S CHAIR OF INFINITY,"
> WHICH HE INTERPRETED AS INSTRUCTION
> TO ABSENT HIMSELF FROM THE REMAINDER OF THE WAR
> AND STAY ON TO FOUND THIS TOWNSHIP. (*LY* 86-87)

Delia finds that contemporary Bay Borough, too, is less than the "idyllic" retreat she at first had perceived it to be – that it is actually "a town of misfits [such as herself and its founder George Pendle Bay]" and that, in reality, thorny problems prick its pleasant surface: "Rick and Teensy Rackley [a racially mixed couple] were treated very coolly by some of the older citizens; the only two gay men she knew of seemed to walk about with no one but each other; there was talk of serious drug use in the consolidated high school; and Mr. Pomfret's appointment book was crammed with people feuding over property lines and challenging drunk-driving arrests" (*LY* 137; 137-38).

Barnaby Gaitlin in *A Patchwork Planet* joins Delia Grinstead in having had ancestors once visited by angels – ancestors, however, whose lives have also been, perhaps, less than angelic themselves. Grandfather Gaitlin, it seems, "had been visited by one of Creation's dullest angels – a sweet-faced young secretary who arrived for a job interview at a 'perilous moment' in his personal life and instructed him to appreciate his wife and children, after which she vanished" (*PP* 72-73). Barnaby has deconstructed this family legend to reach its essential, underlying, human core: "reading between the lines, I always assumed that what we had here was an instance of attempted sexual harassment in the workplace" (*PP* 73). Barnaby also reassures himself that he is not the only embarrassment to his family by remembering, as well, his "Great-Aunt Eunice . . . [who had] left her husband for a stage magician fifteen years her junior," even if "she came home within a month, because she'd had no idea, she said, what to cook for the magician's dinners" and "was a Gaitlin only by marriage" (*PP* 73).

The staid Peck family, too, has also had its share of deserters: Margaret Rose (Grandfather Daniel Peck's runaway wife) in 1911; Daniel's brother Caleb in 1912; as well as Justine and Duncan Peck in 1953. The latter abhors the Peck family's pretensions to social propriety and superiority. He rants at Justine:

"What's so uncommon about us? We're not famous, we're not society, we haven't been rich since 1930 and we aren't known for brains or beauty. But our ladies wear hats, by God! And we all have perfect manners! We may not ever talk to outsiders about anything more interesting than the weather but at least we do it politely! And we've all been taught that we disapprove of sports cars, golf, women in slacks, chewing gum, the color chartreuse, emotional displays, ranch houses, bridge, mascara, household pets, religious discussions, plastic, politics, nail polish, transparent gems of any color, jewelry shaped like animals, checkered prints. . . . even when we're wearing our ragged old gardening clothes you can peek down our collars and see 'Brooks Brothers' on the label, and our boots are English and meant for riding though none of us has ever sat on a horse. . . ." (*SFC* 88-89)

Still, after her marriage to Duncan, Justine continues "looking backward" (as Madame Olita tells her) towards her seemingly more respectable family past (*SFC* 131), making her little house outside Buskville "a replica of Great-Grandma's house" in Roland Park, Baltimore (*SFC* 110).

While the Antons of *The Amateur Marriage* occupy one of those new, post World War II, suburban Baltimore houses the Pecks have been taught to disdain, and have a much less prestigious family name to uphold, they, too, wrestle with their own issues of respectability, especially the shame they feel about their runaway family member Lindy. As Michael Anton tells the police: "our daughter may be a little bit rebellious . . . a little late getting home some nights, maybe; a little critical of the older generation. But she is not out carousing in bars with a bunch of lowlifes. She isn't some sort of gang moll. She isn't . . . trash, understand?" (120). However, Michael admits to himself that he has felt embarrassed all his life "that something was wrong with the Antons" (*AM* 124), from the time his father died and his older brother Danny's "progressive disease" humiliated him as a teenager in the 1930s, to his military "accident" (getting shot on purpose by a fellow soldier in training during World War II), on through years and years, from the very day of their wedding, of a "ragged and uneven" marriage to Pauline Barclay (*AM* 124). Michael believes "he would always have something to hide. . . . [and] studied his neighbors, hoping for flaws" (*AM* 124). Before their separation, Michael Anton had come to feel that he and Pauline simply were *"putting on an act. You're not really a couple at all. And this is not really a family"* (*AM* 129). Meanwhile, Pauline Anton admits, as well:

> she had lived her life wrong. . . . She had married the wrong man just because that was the track she'd been traveling on and she hadn't known how to get off. . . . She had let the people she loved slip through her fingers – even Michael, whom she did love, it had turned out, wrong man or not. . . . And Lindy. Sometimes it seemed to her that Lindy was the one she'd loved most, although of course a mother loves all her children the same. (*AM* 269)

Why couldn't the Antons just be like "other people's" families, their son George also agonizes, instead of "running away from home or perishing in spectacular crashes. Or showing up after twenty-nine years and wondering where everyone was," as his sister Lindy has done (*AM* 290)?

Tyler's characters are often, as with Charlotte Emory in *Earthly Possessions*, "easily fooled by appearances. Maybe all families, even the most normal-looking, were as queer as ours once you got up close to them" (65), Charlotte concludes, whether they were Emorys, Antons, Emersons, Gaitlins or Pecks. And what is true for individual families is also true for the culture at large. Just as Tyler's private family trees encompass misfits, renegades, snobs, and sexual harassers, the public tree of American history includes its share of miscreants – especially those who enslaved blacks and later advocated, practiced, or scrupulously ignored racial injustice. Underlying the mask of American respectability and civility lies the ugliness of "white superiority" and "black inferiority," of white wealth and leisure acquired at the expense of black labor and poverty. The "pearl pushbutton," privileged past Morgan Gower yearns for in *Morgan's Passing* (100) is one that has depended on the servility of others (most often black) – on the subservient labor still demanded by the prim and proper Peck family, the "helpless" Mrs. Emerson, the small store owner Michael Anton, and young Evie Decker, of whom Clotelia says: "I tell my boyfriend, 'Brewster,' I say, 'you ain't going to believe it, but I know a white girl seventeen years old need a full-time nursemaid. Maid ain't enough. . . . She need a nursemaid'" (*SDL* 122-23).

When Ben Joe Hawkes returns to Sandhill, North Carolina, he finds himself again in "the waiting room [of the rail station] . . . divided in two by a slender post, with half the room reserved for white people and the other half for Negroes. Since times had changed, the wooden letters saying 'White' and 'Colored' had been removed, but the letters had left cleaner places on the wall that spelled out the same words still" (*IMEC* 39). The past layer continues to bleed into the present in Tyler's fiction. Even if "times had changed," Tyler's characters find themselves still living in a world divided by color.

In *Searching for Caleb*, longtime family servants Lafleur and Sulie Boudrault have been angry with the Pecks for years. Lafleur, dead now, "wouldn't have helped out anyway" in the search for Caleb Peck, detective Eli Everjohn determines after looking at Lafleur's defiant expression in a Peck family photograph (*SFC* 233). However, his wife Sulie might have agreed to help, but no one ever asked. With each passing year, Sulie had become more upset by the Pecks' arrogance – the family's failure even to acknowledge her relationship with Caleb or her intelligent presence in their midst. When the Pecks try, finally, "to pension . . . [her] off; didn't she have family somewhere?", Sulie demands they acknowledge her personhood by refusing to leave (*SFC* 233). She "only laughed her cracked, rapid laugh and said, '*Now* you wants to do it. Now you wants,'" with Eli Everjohn seeing what the family apparently cannot or will not: "Oh, she was mad, no question about it" (*SFC* 233-34) at having been used, yet devalued and ignored, by the Pecks all her life.

Sulie takes revenge on them all, retaining her secret of Caleb Peck's where-abouts for over sixty years, all the while patiently waiting to see if the Pecks ever recognize her role in their family long enough to ask her about Caleb:

> "When first Mr. Caleb had left us," she said, "I told Lafleur, 'Lafleur, what do I say?' For I known where he had went to yet I would hate to give him away. 'Lafleur, do I lie?' 'That ain't never going to come up,' he say. 'Them folks don't think you know *nothing*' . . . . I made up my mind I wouldn't tell till they say straight out, 'Sulie, do you know?' And Mrs. Laura I wouldn't give the time of *day* even. I never did. She live forty-six years after Mr. Caleb had went and I never spoken to her once, but I don't fool myself she realize that. 'Sulie is getting so *sullen*,' was what she say. Even that tooken her five or six years to notice good." (*SFC* 234-35)

As Alice Hall Petry has noted, many of Tyler's black characters hold themselves "emotionally aloof from [their] white employers," as Sulie does here (and as Clotelia in *A Slipping-Down Life* and Alvareen in *The Clock Winder* do, as well) ("Bright" 9).

Mrs. Emerson in *The Clock Winder* impulsively fires the black gardener, Richard, for "peeing" on rosebushes he had "watered . . . daily [in one way or another]" since planting them years before (3; 5). She never attempts to cross the racial divide between herself and Richard, or her maid Alvareen; never sees either of them as her fellow human beings with needs, desires, and problems of their own; and reveals her further insensitivity to racial issues by giving "a can of pitted black olives" to Mrs. Bittern who was "collecting food for riot victims" (*CW* 299).

Even those Tyler characters who are much more troubled than Mrs. Emerson by the continuing racial divisions in American society seem helpless to know how to overcome them. Morgan Gower likes to eat lunch at the No Jive Café, where he enjoys their "wonderful" pickles, despite the fact that he is always the only white customer present and the other black patrons "wouldn't talk to him. . . . He'd asked time and time again for an extra [pickle], but they always said no; he'd have to order another hamburger that he didn't even want" (*MP* 43; 42-43). Morgan cannot accept that he is simply not welcome at the No Jive Café. And in *Breathing Lessons*, Alice Hall Petry says, "Maggie and Ira are never sure if Mr. Otis is as mild-mannered and grateful as he seems: the 'haughty, hooded expression' (*BL* 146) caused by his lowered eyelids may indeed have meant he realized Maggie had lied about the [loose] wheel [until she discovered that this irritatingly slow driver was an elderly black man], and Ira even wonders if his inconvenient request to be driven to the Texaco station 'might be Mr. Otis's particularly passive, devilish way of getting even' (*BL* 151)" ("Bright" 11). In *The Amateur Marriage*, too, Michael Anton feels bewildered when he tries to give his former grocery store employee, Eustace, his customary Christmas gift, only to be met at the door one year by Eustace's irate young male relative declaring, "He don't want your envelope! . . . Get away from here with your envelope! . . . Who do you think you are, anyhow, coming round here with your envelopes?" (227). Michael tells his future wife Anna, "I surely didn't mean any harm! I'd been bringing that envelope for years; Eustace always just thanked me politely!" (*AM* 227), unsure now as to whether Eustace also had felt outraged by his Christmas gift and had seen it as a humiliating handout or a mere token gesture on Michael's part. Black and white characters most often remain unintelligible to, or distant from, one another in Tyler's novels, divided by a past of unspeakable racial cruelties and by a present in which whites continue either to ignore or glorify this same shared history as "genteel and civilized," perpetuating past wrongs into present-day lives.[36]

Clearly America's past is not viewed as idyllic in Tyler's works, no matter how bewildering, dangerous, and frightening her characters may find modern society. It is true, contemporary life may seem, at times, as it does to Brother Hope in *A Slipping-Down Life*, totally depraved and disastrous:

"We are gathered here," he said [to his congregation], "as lone survivors on a sinking ship. Only you and I know that ship is sinking. Only you and I seek to find the rotting planks. . . . Today there are women wearing the garb of men, men in stupors from the fumes of alcohol and the taste of foreign mushrooms, dancers dancing obscenities in public and everywhere, on every corner of the earth, sacrifices made to false gods and earthly idols. What next? What next? . . . Our children are no longer safe. . . . Golden nets are cast to reel them into evil and we say, 'It's only music. *We* had music,' we say, but we had the waltz and 'Mairzy Doats.'" (*SDL* 178-79)

Tyler's novels are filled with the sounds of rock music (decried here by Brother Hope), the lure of vulgar advertisements, and the sprawl of America's modern urban wasteland. As Delia Grinstead returns home, she sees "the Baltimore skyline – smokestacks, a spaghetti of ramps and overpasses, monster storage tanks. . . . gray-windowed factories and corrugated-metal warehouses. Everything seemed so industrial – even the new ballpark, with its geometric strutwork and its skeletons of lights" (*LY* 274).

The contemporary landscape is far from attractive – nor is it at all secure and safe. Couples separate and divorce, weddings are halted in the midst of on-going ceremonies (in *The Clock Winder* and *Ladder of Years*), girls become pregnant before they marry (and sometimes have no idea who the father might be, as with Vanessa Linley and her little boy Greggie in *Ladder of Years*). Men and women commit suicide (as do Justine Peck's mother, Morgan Gower's father, and Mrs. Emerson's son Timothy), die in car crashes (as have Danny Bedloe, Pauline Anton, and Joe Davitch), overdose on drugs (Lucy Bedloe and Lindy Anton), and get murdered (Ethan Leary and Bess Pickett). It is no wonder that Sarah Leary despairs of such a world, telling Macon:

"ever since Ethan died I've had to admit that people are basically bad. Evil, Macon. So evil they would take a twelve-year-old boy and shoot him through the skull for no reason. I read a paper now and I

> despair; I've given up watching the news on TV. There's so much wickedness, children setting other children on fire and grown men throwing babies out second-story windows, rape and torture and terrorism, old people beaten and robbed, men in our very own government willing to blow up the world, indifference and greed and instant anger on every street corner. . . . There are times when I haven't been sure I could . . . live in this kind of a world anymore."
> (*AT* 139-40)

Sarah seems to be right; such news bewilders and horrifies with its senseless cruelty, its wanton destructiveness.

As virtually every critic has noted, Tyler's titles often serve to reveal her characters' deep-seated fear of the modern world. Her protagonists find themselves merely "accidental tourists," disoriented and frightened by their surroundings – as terrified, alone, and miserable as Macon Leary fears Muriel Pritchett will be in Paris (and as he has often been himself on his unwilling travels), "wandering helpless, penniless, unable to speak a word of the language" (*AT* 330). In such a world, her protagonists become "celestial navigators," along with Jeremy Pauling, "setting down the few fixed points that he knows, hoping they will guide him as he goes floating through this unfamiliar planet. He keeps his eyes on the horizon while his hands work blind" (*CN* 145). They feel in need of "breathing lessons" to help them survive and cope on such a "patchwork planet" – one that seems as "makeshift and haphazard, clumsily cobbled together, overlapping and crowded and likely to fall into pieces at any moment" as Mrs. Alford's unfinished, quilted version (*PP* 261). Her characters pass through their precarious existences, along with Morgan of *Morgan's Passing*, searching for meaning that is missing from their lives (a search the Pecks focus on their missing family member Caleb in *Searching for Caleb*). Tyler's characters remain unsure of anything, even "if morning [will] ever come," in such a disturbingly haphazard world.[37]

Far from ideal, it is, nevertheless, Tyler suggests, the only chance at life they have. As Poppy tells Rebecca Davitch, "And that's where [your deceased husband Joe] and I differed. . . . Because I was always telling him, 'Look,' I said. 'Face it,' I said. 'There *is* no true life. Your true life is the one you end up with, whatever it may be. You just do the best you can with what you've got,' I said." (*BWWWG* 251-52). Tyler's is a message of comic reassurance: contemporary life can be coped with and its constant changes met, just as they were in the past. There never has been a perfect time, as Michael Anton realizes, even as he shudders to see what has become of Anton's Grocery, now changed into World O'Food:

> He hated that name. He hated the whole chain-supermarket concept, and felt miserable any time he set foot in the place, but somehow his car kept finding its way there. Now he relaxed and gave in to it, listening absently to an interview with a man who had served in France [in World War II]. He had lost both his brothers, three cousins, and his best friend in that war . . . . Imagine the youngsters nowadays accepting such a state of affairs! They would look for someone to sue, Michael thought. (Lindy certainly would.) Somewhere along the way, people in this country had developed the assumption that life should be unvaryingly logical and just. There was no recognition of random bad luck, no allowance for tragedies that couldn't be prevented by folic acid or side air bags or FAA-approved safety seats. (*AM* 300-01)

Bad things will keep happening to people, grocery stores will keep changing (right along with everything else), and people will still have to learn to cope (even if, at times, they will feel with Michael Anton as though they were "the survivor[s] of some natural disaster" (*AM* 304)). As Robert Croft has said, "whether Tyler's characters like it or not, they are all caught up in the process of change merely by being in the flow of time" (*Companion* 57).

However, as Madame Olita tells Justine Peck, "more and more it seems to me that people are resisting change, digging in their heels against it" (*SFC* 128-29).

They try to ward off the new, clinging to the "solidity" of the past, as we have seen
– at best a futile, often stultifying, and (as Tyler's black characters make obvious) an
ignorant and insensitive act. They yearn to escape the present – a desire readily
gratified through commercial American culture. When Brindle Gower's mother
complains, "there's not enough real life on television," Brindle exclaims, "that's the
whole point" (*MP* 48)! Real life is exactly what most people are trying to avoid,
Tyler suggests – and advertisers are eager to help them accomplish this end, even,
as Maggie Moran perceives, in "the hair-spray ads and panty-hose ads" so
"mislead[ing]" in their romantic depictions of life (*BL* 64). Religion, too, may be
used as a form of escape. Dr. Arthur Sisk, of "the mourners' bench" of Saul
Emory's church, is happy to "give [his] life to Christ" (finding himself, otherwise,
on the brink of suicide). As he admits, "well, I liked the way [Saul] put it. I mean,
just to hand my life *over*," which sounds much more attractive to him than hanging
on and soldiering through the modern world (*EP* 144). However, as Charlotte Emory
reminds Dr. Sisk, "you still have income tax and license renewals. . . . Still have bank
statements and dental appointments and erroneous bills. . . . If it were all that easy,
don't you think that I'd long ago have handed *my* life over?" (*EP* 144).

What is needed to survive in this world, Daniel Peck says, is "*stamina* . . . .
[to] endure . . . to fight it out or live it down or sit it through, whatever was required"
to face up to the reality of life (*SFC* 6), and in this assessment he is shown to be at
least partially right. Some of Tyler's characters remain at Daniel's initial (yet, at the
same time, essential) stage of development, telling themselves, as he does, "you
endure, you manage to survive" day after day (*SFC* 159). As Robert Croft concludes:

> for many of [Tyler's] characters one of their main goals is simply to
> endure. In *The Accidental Tourist*, Macon Leary struggles to endure
> the death of his son; in *Breathing Lessons*, Maggie Moran attempts
> to endure the loss of her idea of family; in *Ladder of Years*, Delia
> Grinstead tries to come to grips with her children growing up and

leaving home; and in *Earthly Possessions*, Charlotte Emory must realize that she cannot run away from her own life. Endurance, therefore, is a virtue for Tyler's characters. (*Companion* 88-89)

Alice Hall Petry argues, as well, that Tyler makes clear that her characters "must develop some strategy of endurance" since "change and adversity are inevitable . . . or as Mrs. Scarlatti [in *Dinner at the Homesick Restaurant*] phrases matters, 'Life is a continual shoring up' (99). If one's capacity for 'shoring up' is not part of one's inherited temperament or childhood training, then one can actively cultivate it" (*Understanding* 204; 202).

Pearl Tull, like many other Tyler characters, develops her mending skills to endure and ward off disaster: "She patched a crack, glazed a window, replaced two basement stair treads. She mended a lamp switch and painted the kitchen cupboards. . . . From early in their marriage, from the moment she had realized how often they would be moving, she had concentrated on making each house perfect – airtight and rustproof and waterproof. . . . All she cared about was sealing up the house, as if for a hurricane" (*DHR* 16). Pearl contrasts her carefully acquired skills with the lesser abilities she finds in her children: "Cody lacked the patience, Ezra was inept, Jenny too flighty. It was remarkable, Pearl thought, how people displayed their characters in every little thing they undertook" (*DHR* 16-17).

Emily Meredith also works to build up her character as her own marriage fails in *Morgan's Passing*, increasing her stamina through jogging rather than acquiring house maintenance skills: "I'm in training for some emergency – a forced flight, a national disaster. It's comforting to know that I'm capable of running several miles" (*MP* 234), she tells Morgan. Such characters as Pearl Tull and Emily Meredith join others (Charlotte Emory, Macon Leary, Justine Peck) who, as Julie Persing Papadimas says, "survive changing family structures and transient lifestyles, battling despair with humor as they face hardships and triumph – if only in a small way. As

Miss Vinton states, 'There are other kinds of heroes than the ones who swim through burning oil' (*CN* 127)" (51).

And yet, Tyler implies, while there is heroism in endurance, there is also a danger when characters concentrate simply on building up their survival skills – jogging further and further, repairing more and more tightly, dealing stoically – even humorously – with the hardships that have befallen them. When Macon Leary tells his wife Sarah, "I . . . endure. I'm trying to endure, I'm standing fast, I'm holding steady," she replies, "If you really think that . . . then you're fooling yourself. You're not holding steady; you're ossified" (*AT* 142). Endurance skills may be necessary, even admirable – but they can be taken too far, becoming a substitute for life and leading to the "ossification" from which Sarah Leary recoils. As Robert Croft says, "the best [of Tyler's characters] . . . learn to do more than merely endure, in the process of achieving a greater and deeper understanding and appreciation of life and of themselves" (*Companion* 89).[38]

For Tyler, the next level beyond endurance is adaptability. After Emily Meredith complains that her husband Leon has changed since their marriage, Morgan Gower replies, "of course he's changed. Everybody does; everyone goes bobbing along, in and out of inlets, snagging on pilings, skating down rapids" (*MP* 133). Inevitably people *should* change as they age, Morgan suggests here, as they deal with all the unanticipated inlets, snags, and rapids encountered along life's course. Or, as Rebecca Davitch expresses it when reflecting on her own life's progress, "Oh, life worked out so surprisingly, didn't it?" (*BWWWG* 22). Endurance needs to be augmented by flexibility, Tyler suggests – flexibility that is largely a matter of acquiring an altered perspective. As Madame Olita tells Justine Peck, "you can change your future a great deal. Also your past. . . . Not what's happened, no . . . but what hold it has on you" (*SFC* 129).

Jenny Tull illustrates how important she believes perspective can be in determining the "hold" of events on our lives and our future course in her discussion with her stepson Slevin's teacher:

> "Mr. Davies suggests," said the teacher, " – that's our assistant principal – he suggests that Slevin may be experiencing emotional problems due to the adjustments at home."
> "What adjustments?"
> "He says Slevin's mother abandoned him and Slevin was moved to your household almost immediately thereafter and had to get used to a brand-new mother and sister."
> "Oh, that," said Jenny, waving her hand.
> "Mr. Davies suggests that Slevin might need professional counseling."
> "Nonsense," Jenny said. "What's a little adjustment? . . . Oh, we're all coping! . . . My point is," Jenny said, "I don't see the need to blame adjustment, broken homes, bad parents, that sort of thing. We make our own luck, right? You have to overcome your setbacks. You can't take them too much to heart. I'll explain all that to Slevin. I'll tell him this evening." (*DHR* 195-96)

While Jenny Tull may be overconfident that an evening's chat with Slevin will ensure improved grades and a changed attitude towards school, she knows from her own experience that setbacks can be overcome. She, too, was abandoned by a parent (her father), frightened of her mother, nearly "destroyed by [the latter's] love" (*DHR* 96), yet worked to overcome these and additional problems of being divorced, a single parent, and rejected by the man she loved most. Jenny is a survivor who has done more than simply endure life's setbacks; she has also adjusted and coped, making her own luck by changing her outlook and working "to overcome [her hardships]," as she suggests Slevin needs to do, as well (*DHR* 196).

Adversity is not necessarily destructive. Instead, Tyler suggests, it can offer challenges. As Justine Peck tells her daughter Meg (as they prepare to move to yet another house and another school in a new location), "teaching you to adapt is the best education [your father and I] could give you!" (*SFC* 21). Again, Justine is speaking from firsthand knowledge as she, too, has had to learn to overcome her desire to be settled and her tendency to look back to the family past in Roland Park as ideal, becoming more adaptable in her life. With each passing year of their marriage, Duncan admires his wife's increasing flexibility: "But where was the child Justine had been? There was nothing hesitant about her now. She had become fast-moving, kaleidoscopic. There was a sort of dash to everything she did that surprised and fascinated him. . . . And she moved so easily from town to town! Oh, at first, of course, she was always a little reluctant. . . . 'Oh, well,' she always said in the end. 'We'll move. We'll just move, what's wrong with that?'" (*SFC* 145-46). When she encourages Meg to accept the unexpected challenges of her marriage to Arthur Milsom, Justine is trying to pass along her own strategy for adjusting and coping: "Meggie darling . . . look at it this way. Imagine you were handed a stack of instructions. Things that you should undertake. Blind errands, peculiar invitations . . . things you're supposed to go through, and come out different on the other side" (*SFC* 229). Adjusting is clearly a means of character development and personal growth in Anne Tyler's novels, enabling her characters to "come out different [and better] on the other side."[39]

However, as Duncan Peck points out, adaptability, too, has a dangerous undercurrent (as endurance has, as well): "That's what you're going to tell your daughter? [Duncan asks Justine.] . . . Just accept whatever comes along? Endure? Adapt? . . . And how would people end up if they all did that?" (*SFC* 229). Just as ossification is the negative side of endurance, so passivity is the downside of adaptability. In "Still Just Writing," Anne Tyler alludes to this problem when she pays tribute to her father (an obvious model for adaptability not only in her own life but in the creation of some of her most admirable characters). When her father's lifetime ambition to work for the American Friends Service Committee in the Gaza

Strip was interrupted by her mother's illness, he returned to the United States and, Tyler explains:

> had simply to hang in suspended animation for four months while my mother was whisked in and out of hospitals. However, I believe he was as pleased with life as he always is. He whistled Mozart and puttered around insulating our windows. He went on long walks collecting firewood. He strolled over to the meetinghouse and gave a talk on the plight of the Arab refugees. . . . It seems to me that the way my father lives (infinitely adapting, and looking around him with a smile to say, 'Oh! So *this* is where I am!') is also the way to slip gracefully through a choppy life of writing novels, painting the dining room ceiling, and presiding at slumber parties. ("Still" 10-11)

And yet, Tyler adds, "there's a danger to it: I could wind up as passive as a piece of wood on a wave. But I try to walk a middle line" ("Still" 11).

In *Earthly Possessions*, Charlotte Emory has become no more than such a floating stick of wood in the current of life, unable to take concrete action in her own affairs, drifting from day to day, to the point where she welcomes being kidnapped by Jake Simms as an alternative to having to take responsibility for her own actions. Her brother-in-law Amos has told her that Saul (Charlotte's husband and his brother) has been awed by "the way you coast along, no faith, all capability, your . . . *sparseness*," but Charlotte knows better, admitting, "I was numb, and observed my life as calmly as a woman made of ice [even if] . . . Amos thought I was strong and brave" (*EP* 149; 175). When Amos tells her, "you sail through the house like a moon, you're strong enough for all of them," she confesses, "I should have argued. (I should have laughed.) But all I said was, 'No . . . ' and paused" (*EP* 175). Charlotte understands that her drifting, her adaptability, has become not a strength but a weakness, not life but lifelessness. Neither endurance nor adaptability seems sufficient for a full and well-lived life. They must be supplemented still further, Tyler suggests, by receptivity to the new – to change and to on-going life.[40]

When Justine Peck tells fortunes, she tells her clients, "change. . . . Take the change. Always change" (*SFC* 29). She has learned to welcome life's challenges, not see them simply as inevitable, endurable, at best manageable. In *The Accidental Tourist*, publisher Julian Edge agrees. He argues with Macon Leary after Macon balks at writing a new travel book on the U.S., complaining:

> "But it really seems to me I just did the U.S." . . . A kind of fatigue fell over [Macon]. These endlessly recurring trips, Boston and Atlanta and Chicago . . . He let his head drop back on the couch.
> Julian said, "Things are changing every minute, Macon. Change! It's what keeps us in the black. How far do you think we'd get selling out-of-date guidebooks?" (*AT* 90)

Life's adventure, Tyler suggests, exists in the very surprises, challenges, twists and turns her characters find so daunting and upsetting. Even the patriarchal, controlling Ben Joe Hawkes comes to acknowledge this in *If Morning Ever Comes* as he and Shelley Domer embark on their journey to New York and a new life together. He admits, "what future was ever a certainty?" (*IMEC* 265) as he begins the next unknowable stage of his life, realizing that nothing will ever stay the way he would like it, "still and obedient" as a photographic image or a disembodied figure in a dream (*IMEC* 266). Instead, life races on like a "train [that] went rattling along its tracks" (*IMEC* 266), taking Ben Joe Hawkes and Shelley Domer with it, changing their lives forever. Even that apparently most old-fashioned of individuals in Tyler's novels, Emily Meredith's Great-Aunt Mercer, it seems, had been receptive to change, "donat[ing] her remains to the cause of medical science" (*MP* 195) as her parting gift to on-going life.[41]

Change can be the very source of life, its promise and adventure. While not all cultural upheaval is welcome or good, such changes can be progressive, Tyler insists – the means by which we can relieve suffering (finding new medical cures, for instance), improve human relationships, and build better societies. As Ezra Tull says of fast food restaurants, "It's getting like a collective farm. . . . All these chain places that everyone comes to for breakfast, lunch, sometimes supper . . . like a commune or a kibbutz or something. Pretty soon we won't have private kitchens at all; you just drop by your local Gino's or McDonald's," admitting to his sister Jenny, "I kind of like it" (*DHR* 198). Of course, this is the way Ezra sees his own "Homesick Restaurant," as a contribution to the community, a place where lonely people are welcome, where they will be nourished both physically and emotionally, in a public place which offers them a welcome alternative to the tensions, problems, or isolation of home.

Tyler's novels show people coming together in a variety of ways to cope with their feelings of fear and alienation, creating small, new communities through which they offer solace and help to one another. In *Saint Maybe*, Reverend Emmett (formerly "an Episcopalian seminarian and the son of an Episcopalian minister") has created a new church, the Church of the Second Chance, where, Ian Bedloe tells his parents, "you have to really do something practical to atone for your, shall we call them, sins. And if you agree to that, they'll pitch in. You can sign up on a bulletin board – the hours you need help, the hours you've got free to help others," adding that this new kind of church is one "that makes sense to me" (142; 127).

"Pitching in," helping one another out, doing some small good to make up for past hurt and damage caused – this, Tyler suggests, is the way societies can change for the better – in little, practical ways, through the individual efforts of ordinary people taking positive action to help themselves and others. In *Breathing Lessons*, Maggie Moran has worked all her life at the Silver Threads Nursing Home, enjoying the company of the elderly and making their final days more pleasurable. So, too, Barnaby Gaitlin in *A Patchwork Planet* enjoys working with the elderly and with handicapped clients at Rent-a-Back, taking an interest in their lives and feeling useful as he performs work for them that they can no longer accomplish themselves.

Rebecca Davitch, too, runs the Open Arms business in her home in *Back When We Were Grownups*, helping people celebrate the memorable events of their lives, while Emily Meredith and Morgan Gower entertain children with their puppet shows and Justine and Duncan Peck help to bring Habit Forming Entertainment carnivals (and a little more joy) to people in communities surrounding Baltimore. Elizabeth Abbott teaches crafts at a reform school for girls in *The Clock Winder*; Shelley Domer of *If Morning Ever Comes* works at a nursery school for the children of working mothers; Pagan Anton teaches music to autistic children, while his Aunt Karen acts as a legal advocate for the poor in *The Amateur Marriage*. All of these young people seek to develop their own characters and evolve into more responsible and caring adults as they help others more helpless or needy than themselves.

Other Tyler characters volunteer their time, in addition to paid work they do (as does Ian Bedloe in his work with the Church of the Second Chance). In *Ladder of Years*, Delia Grinstead tutors students with difficulties at Bay Borough's high school, while her mother-in-law Eleanor works with Meals on Wheels, teaches typing at the Home for Wayward Girls twice a week, and gives to charity, writing to advise Delia, "*Lately I've been most dissatisfied with Goodwill but continue to feel that Retarded Citizens is a worthwhile organization*" (135). The retired teacher Doug Bedloe helps Middle Eastern students who have moved onto Waverly Street in *Saint Maybe* as they try to cope with American culture. He assists them as they attempt to set up aerials for shortwave radios and wire radio speakers in their new home until, "before long he was more or less hanging out there. They always had some hare-brained project going, something he could assist with or (more often) advise them not to attempt" (*SM* 165).

In all these various types of community engagement, as Mary F. Robertson explains, it is the "ability to open oneself to the disorder and uncertainty that strangers bring into one's life; . . . the ability to be enriched by these strangers, even to be derailed by them, without trying to erase their radical difference from oneself" that leads to positive human interaction, to personal and social well-being, in Tyler's novels (191). As he helps the foreign students out, Doug Bedloe feels capable and useful once more (despite old age and retirement), learning from their adventurousness and openness, their willingness to engage with whatever is new and different, their "considerat[ion] about dropping whatever unpronounceable names they'd been christened with. Or not christened, maybe," becoming "Fred, Ray, John, John Two, and Ollie" to accommodate American culture (*SM* 163; 165).

The benefit of this relationship is clearly mutual for both Doug Bedloe and the foreign students he befriends, just as Alice Hall Petry shows that Macon Leary, too, over time and through the persistent overtures of Muriel Pritchett, "must come to admit that one can depend on the good graces of others to help one handle life's difficulties" (*Understanding* 226). As Macon tells Sarah (thinking about Muriel's neighbors on Singleton Street "scrubbing their stoops, tinkering with their cars, splashing under fire hydrants," saying what Sarah never thought him capable of believing), "it's kind of . . . heartening, isn't it? How most human beings do try. How they try to be as responsible and kind as they can manage" (*AT* 350). Such small acts of responsibility and kindness as those which take place on Muriel's Singleton Street and Doug Bedloe's Waverly Street form an essential pattern of Tyler's novels. For, she admits, "as the outside world grows less dependable, I keep buttressing my inside world, where people go on meaning well and surprising other people with little touches of grace" ("Still" 15)

It is this kind of small, positive human interaction that Tyler's novels value. In an age of distance learning, on-line communities, broad political agendas, and global economies, Tyler emphasizes the importance of individual agency and the value of small personal actions of "grace." At the same time, she shows how these small initiatives are capable of leading to large, new, permanent, and positive changes in American society, as well – how they can work to overturn traditional restrictions of race, class, and sex which have narrowed possibilities for both individual and community life. In Tyler's depiction of her less hierarchical, more flexible, open, tolerant, and elastic families, as Mary F. Robertson explains, Tyler shows how "a respect for the difference of 'significant others' in such disorderly family structures can liberate us . . . in a practical way" (202).

One such family is Rebecca Davitch's in *Back When We Were Grownups* – a family that includes three step-daughters and one natural daughter; an Arab son-in-law; the longtime gay male companion of one step-daughter; and grandchildren who include a part-Arab grandson and a part-black granddaughter. Rebecca herself married a divorced man (Joe Davitch); has a step-daughter (No No) who marries a divorced man in the course of the novel; and a natural daughter (Min Foo), married three times (and divorced twice). Rebecca feels inadequate to such a complex and diverse family, the result merely, she feels, of having married a man totally different from herself (whom she subsequently lost only six years later). She thinks, "Joe Davitch had been full of enthusiasms, even as a grown man. He'd been large in spirit and in frame, exuberant and outgoing, booming-voiced, quick to laugh, given to flinging out both hands in a gesture of wholehearted welcome. Really it was Joe who had had the open arms" (*BWWWG* 23). Joe had been equal to such a family – and their "Open Arms" party-giving, Rebecca feels – but "she [herself] had turned into the wrong person" (*BWWWG* 3) by virtue of this accidental marriage.

However, by the novel's end, Rebecca acknowledges that she, too, has grown "large in spirit . . . exuberant and outgoing" in the midst of such a family (*BWWWG* 23). Rebecca comes to feel, further, that she has become the *right* kind of person, the person she was intended to be, surrounded by her large, diverse, and ever-growing family – a woman who truly "had . . . open arms" (*BWWWG* 23). Her private transformation shapes her public commitment to elasticity, tolerance, and inclusivity

– the "Open Arms" a microcosm of on-going, positive transformation to greater tolerance and diversity, an ability to celebrate the lives of those different from ourselves, so beneficial to American culture as a whole.

Such inclusive, extended, open-ended families as Rebecca Davitch's abound in Tyler's novels, from Joan Pike's extended family made up of Pike relatives, the Green brothers, and the Potter sisters in *The Tin Can Tree* to Charlotte Emory's boarding-house inhabitants in *Earthly Possessions*. Charlotte concludes her narrative by explaining:

> There is somebody new in Mama's old room: a drunk from the mourners' bench who used to be an opera singer. His name is Mr. Bentham. On good days his voice is beautiful. And Miss Feather is with us the same as always, though Dr. Sisk has moved away. He married a woman from the church last July and lives in a ranch house on the other side of town. . . . Selinda [her daughter] still floats in and out of our lives, and no one has yet come for [their foster child] Jiggs. . . . And I still wheel my camera around, recording upside-down people in unexpected costumes. (*EP* 199-200)

Of the latter, she adds, "I've come to believe that their borrowed medals may tell more truths than they hide" (*EP* 200). Charlotte has developed a new appreciation of those around her; a genuine acceptance of their differences as enriching her life; and, at last, a commitment to the well being of the extended family she and Saul have created together.

Tyler affirms such inclusive families, including that of the Tulls at the end of *Dinner at the Homesick Restaurant*. When Beck Tull returns for his former wife's funeral and attends the family dinner at his son Ezra's Homesick Restaurant, he is amazed to count fourteen people at the dinner table (the fifteenth, Slevin, has gone off to college). Beck pronounces it "a crew. A whole crew. . . . it looks like this is one of those great big, jolly, noisy, rambling . . . why, *families*! . . . A clan, I'm talking about. . . . Like something on TV. Lots of cousins and uncles, jokes, reunions

–" (*DHR* 293-94). Although Cody immediately retaliates, telling his father, "It's not the way it appears. . . . we're in particles, torn apart, torn all over the place, and our mother was a witch" (*DHR* 294), he is the one who later holds onto Beck's "elbow and led him [back] toward the others," feeling himself being "pull[ed] toward them" as he encourages his father to return to the table and "finish" their family dinner (*DHR* 303; 302).

Tyler shows clearly that the larger and more diverse the Tull family has grown by taking strangers into its midst, the more its members have benefited. This is no longer Pearl Tull's narrow, house-bound, "suffocating" nuclear family world (*DHR* 59); it has been enriched by the presence of outsiders of different social class backgrounds and varied life experiences. Its diversity has led to a new richness, a broadening effect, that allows even its most bitter member, the one most haunted by the past, Cody Tull, to rewrite his family history and his mother's life in a more forgiving way at the end of the novel: "it brought back all the outings of his boyhood – the drives, the picnics, the autumn hikes, the wildflower walks in the spring. . . . He remembered his mother's upright form along the grasses, her hair lit gold, her small hands smoothing her bouquet" (*DHR* 303). Such private transformations as Cody's and the Tull family's point towards larger societal transformations as individuals learn to become more tolerant, open-minded, and forgiving of those who are different from themselves.[42]

As Margaret Morganroth Gullette has argued in *Safe at Last in the Middle Years*, Anne Tyler's novels, in fact, affirm many of the cultural changes taking place in American society over the last several decades. While her characters may still, at times, long for what they believe was a more idyllic past, they have actually benefited, Tyler reveals, from America's growing cultural diversity as well as from the new "divorce laws and the sexual revolution [which] have expanded the choices and attitudes open to adults, and the feminist revolution those open to women"

(Gullette, *Safe* 26). These changes allow Tyler's women and men to form more wholesome partnerships in her novels, as well as extend their own individual capabilities. In *The Accidental Tourist*, for example, when Muriel Pritchett tells Macon Leary she has quit her job at Meow-Bow, a "sudden weight . . . fell on [Macon]" (277); yet Muriel quickly assures him, "don't you know Muriel can always take care of herself? . . . Don't you know she could find another job tomorrow, if she wanted?" (279).

So, too, Ian Bedloe in *Saint Maybe* is attracted to Rita DiCarlo, the neighborhood Clutter Counselor, because she "seem[ed] so invulnerable. That may have been why he had married her. He had seen her as someone who couldn't be harmed" (*SM* 331). And even if Michael Anton in *The Amateur Marriage* continues to enjoy doing chores for his ex-wife Pauline, he has also divorced her because he felt "that he would suffocate if he couldn't get away" from her incessant emotional scenes and constant demands (212), choosing to remarry the much more "self-sufficient" (*AM* 218) Anna Stuart. Michael believes he can enjoy the same kind of "adult" love with Anna that she shares with her daughter, a love without "scenes or sulks or silent treatments . . . just a cheerful, courteous, mutually respectful relationship" (*AM* 219). So, too, in *A Patchwork Planet*, Barnaby Gaitlin's co-worker Martine matches him both in resourcefulness at work and care for their Rent-a-Back clients. Laboring side by side, toting their individual cartons, Martine demands both equal responsibility and her male co-worker's respect:

> "Better let me go first," [Barnaby] said when we reached the ladder, but Martine said, "What: you think I can't handle it?"
> "Fine," I told her. "After you." And then had the satisfaction of watching her pretend it was no big deal when sixty pounds of Christmas tree hit her in the chest as she got halfway down. (*PP* 30)

Barnaby watches with ever-increasing admiration at the novel's end as "Martine walked back into the kitchen, dusting off her hands, and she picked up another

carton. I said, 'Martine?' and she said, 'What?,' and I said, 'Haply I think on thee.'
. . . I could tell she knew what I meant" (*PP* 288).

Tyler's men feel a weight has been lifted from their shoulders when their
female partners join them in carrying a load once foisted on them alone. They love
women who are handymen, plumbers, and fixers, as much "makers and doers" (*MP*
84) as they are themselves. However, when the work and love are not mutually
shared, Tyler's women often initiate break-ups – as do Evie Decker, Mary Tell, Delia
Grinstead, Sarah Leary, Emily Meredith, Elizabeth Abbott [with Dommie Whitehill]
and Jenny Tull [with Harley Baines]. Responsibility and care must be mutual for
Tyler's relationships to grow and thrive.

As Mary F. Robertson concludes, "Tyler never uses gender stereotypes; [her]
men can be nurturing as well as [her] women" (196). Ezra Tull is one of Tyler's
nurturing males, expressing his love and care through the food he prepares. So, too,
is Ian Bedloe as he takes on the role of single parent for Daphne, Thomas, and
Agatha. While Ian's father Doug Bedloe has only changed a diaper once in his life,
Ian learns to combine the roles of diaper changer and breadwinner, at the same time.
Ian Bedloe grows, as do so many of Tyler's characters, from simply enduring the
hardships that have befallen him, to adjusting to the changes they have made in his
life, at last growing to love his three small charges and the new life they have given
him. He has become less afraid of life, embracing new challenges (marriage to Rita
and his small son Joshua) in partnership with a sensual, resourceful woman at the
novel's end.

In *Saint Maybe* Ian Bedloe's life has been changed forever by all the strangers
who have disrupted his "normal" life's course and invaded the Bedloe family
compound: the lower-class Lucy; her three small children; followed by Rita diCarlo,
whose "widowed mother was forever dropping by, and Rita's various aunts and
cousins and a whole battalion of woman friends" (*SM* 310).[43] Yet these assorted

strangers have actually enhanced his life, Ian realizes, enabling him to discover its real excitement, beauty, and possibility. While it may be true, as Ian says, that "people changed other people's lives every day of the year. There was no call to make such a fuss about it" (*SM* 337), Anne Tyler does, in fact, "make [such] a fuss." As her characters become more open and receptive to each other and to life, Tyler emphasizes the way in which they create more positive relationships for themselves, as well as a more happy and harmonious society overall. "Change. . . .Take the change. Always change" (*SFC* 29), Anne Tyler challenges readers idealizing an American past that never was, encouraging them to take personal responsibility towards building the more civilized and gracious society they want it to become.

Notes

33. Jonathan Franzen comments that the biggest group of readers coping with change is that of the "millions of American women whose lives do not resemble the lives they might have projected from their mothers'" (48).

34. In *Breathing Lessons* Maggie Moran's high school friend, Serena Gill, hides her embarrassment over "her scandalous mother, Anita, who wore bright red, skin-tight toreador pants and worked in a bar," questing for "normalcy" by dating "sunny innocents like Max [Gill] . . . covet[ing] everydayness, more than she ever let on"; once Serena whispers to Maggie, "I will *never* be like [my mother, Anita], I tell you" (63; 69).

35. In Jorie Lueloff's "Authoress Explains Why Women Dominate in South," Anne Tyler comments on *If Morning Ever Comes*, "the most Southern thing about Ben Joe . . . is his inability to realize that time is changing. This is a very typical Southern fault. People were trying to live on the surface – the way it's supposed to be" (22).

36. Edward Hoagland criticizes Tyler's treatment of racial issues in her novels as inadequate, saying "she is not unblinking. Her books contain scarcely a hint of the abscesses of racial friction that eat at the very neighborhoods she is devoting her working life to picturing" (144).

37. Joseph C. Voelker in *Art and the Accidental in Anne Tyler* finds that her characters have become more resilient and less afraid by *Breathing Lessons*. "Anne Tyler's

earlier protagonists operated at a greater, and a more fearful, distance from the random and dangerous worlds around them," Voelker concludes (177).

38.   Anne Tyler has told Marguerite Michaels, "I'm very interested in day-to-day endurance. And I'm very interested in space around people. The real heroes in my books are first the ones who manage to endure and second the ones who somehow are able to grant other people the privacy of the space around them and yet still produce some warmth" (43). Some critics feel that endurance is her characters' only coping mechanism. Susan Gilbert, for instance, believes that "the solution [Tyler promotes to society's problems] is in endurance," not change (144).

39.   Daniel Peck combines both endurance and adaptability in his own unique way: "He lived in his own tiny, circular world within [Justine and Duncan's] larger one. While they moved up and down the eastern seaboard, made their unaccountable decisions, took up their strange acquaintances and then lost them and forgot them, Daniel Peck buttoned his collarless shirt and fastened his pearl-gray suspenders and surveyed his white, impassive face in the bedroom mirror. He wound his gold watch. He tidied his bed. He transformed even his journeys, the most uncertain part of his life, into models of order and routine and predictability" (*SFC* 160).

40.   In *Celestial Navigation* the agoraphobic Jeremy Pauling also prides himself on keeping up with change (at least from a distance): "He had been seeing girls with bushes for years, in magazines and TV commercials and on the sidewalk before the bay window. He had probably seen more from that window than Mary saw on all her trips to stores and schools and obstetricians. He had observed the world steadily swelling and involuting, developing new twists and whorls and clusters like some complicated cell mass. . . . But he had kept up with things. He knew what was going on in the world. Mary underestimated him" (162).

41.   Tyler's vision is, at once, a conservative one (emphasizing small, individual acts to bolster community and family well-being) as well as a liberal one (advocating greater social as well as personal tolerance, cultural diversity and inclusivity, including changes such as those brought about, for women and men, alike, by the sexual revolution).

42.   In Still Just Writing," Tyler alludes to the way her own life was transformed by her marriage to an Iranian (a child psychologist who wrote novels in Persian), as well as by the presence of his relatives in her life (4; 8-9).

Chapter Five

Leaning Into The Reality of Life

Fantasies about a more perfect past are not the only ones that prevent Tyler's characters from facing up to the realities of their lives. There are other fantasies, as well, purveyed by the novels they take with them on vacation, the movies they watch, the lyrics they sing, and the fairy tales they read their children (and were told in their own youth). These make-believe worlds often prove stronger than the reality of her characters' everyday lives – more attractive than dealing with their humdrum jobs, clogged drains, sick children, sagging shutters, and aging relatives. Yet these plots of perfect romance and heroic adventure are the very ones Anne Tyler's novels seek to subvert and help readers resist in their own lives.

Tyler's female characters seem particularly susceptible to love stories with happy-ever-after endings. In *Ladder of Years*, Delia Grinstead remembers that her primary concern before marriage had been "that Sam would die before she got to be his wife. *Groom Slain on Wedding Eve*, the papers would read, or *Tragic Accident En Route to Nuptials*, and Delia would miss her chance for perfect happiness" (278). Ezra Tull comes to understand that his mother also had dreamed of such "perfect happiness" in her own life, even if "nothing had come of it. Nothing came of anything. She married a salesman for the Tanner Corporation and he left her and never came back" (*DHR* 268-69). Nevertheless, when reading his ailing mother's girlhood diaries aloud, Ezra finds Pearl Tull "had imagined a perfectly wonderful plot [for herself] – a significance to every chance meeting, the possibility of whirlwind courtships, grand white weddings, flawless bliss forever after" (*DHR* 268).

Denied such "flawless bliss" herself, Pearl Tull feels angry when she sees young couples as naive and confident as she once had been at the outset of her marriage to Beck Tull. She confesses to her oldest son Cody:

> "sometimes I stand there watching them and I see they believe they're completely special, the first, the only people ever to feel the way they're feeling. They believe they'll live happily ever after, that all the other marriages going on around them – those ordinary, worn-down, flattened-in arrangements – why, those are nothing like what *they'll* have. They'll never settle for so little. And it makes me mad. I can't help it, Cody. I know it's selfish, but I can't help it. I want to ask them, 'Who do you think you are, anyhow? Do you imagine you're unique? Do you really suppose I was always this difficult old woman?'" (*DHR* 141)

The problem, as both Pearl Tull and Delia Grinstead find, is that "real life continues past the end" of the happy-ever-after fairy tale closings they had imagined for themselves (*LY* 28), with most marriages evolving into the very "worn-down, flattened-in arrangements" (*DHR* 141) Pearl Tull describes here.

Rebecca Davitch, whose marriage lasted only six years (cut short by her husband Joe's sudden death), knows with certainty that no marriage ever ends happily, whether couples separate or stay together, whether they fight continually or never exchange a cross word, whether they stay in love or become stalwart enemies. Rebecca watches her daughters blithely marry, divorce, come together with new partners, and remarry, thinking, "Oh, none of the others [in her family] considered how every engagement on earth would have to end up, Rebecca thought. They glided right over 'till death us do part'" (*BWWWG* 16). Similarly, Maggie Moran in *Breathing Lessons* sits listening to "True Love" being played at Max Gill's funeral, recalling the wedding of her best friend Serena to a then young and healthy Max, remembering "Grace Kelly and Bing Crosby singing 'True Love' in a movie. They'd been perched on a yacht or a sailboat or something. Both of them were dead, too, come to think of it" (*BL* 67). Overwhelmed by memories of her youth and of high school days spent in happier circumstances with her fellow mourners at Max's funeral, Maggie realizes, "No one, she thought, had suspected back then that it would all turn out to be so serious" (*BL* 116). However, Max Gill's funeral is a most serious occasion, even if its solemnity starkly contrasts with Serena's ridiculous, sentimental attempt to reenact her wedding (minus Max, of course).

At Serena's request, Maggie sings "Love Is a Many Splendored Thing" at the funeral service, as she had done (along with her then husband-to-be Ira) for Serena and Max's wedding ceremony many years ago. Now Maggie knows that, if love is "splendored," such "splendor" at its best includes: the pain of ultimate parting; the loss of the one person whom you can comfortably "tell about the trivia"; and the end of the only relationship in which you can feel you are "in this together," as Serena says of her bond with Max (*BL* 323). All those trying but necessary little tasks of daily life continue on, as well, but now the surviving partner must deal with them alone. Warned by Serena decades ago "that marriage was not a Rock Hudson-Doris Day movie" (*BL* 54), Maggie finds herself still wondering during the funeral, "Why did popular songs always focus on romantic love? Why this preoccupation with first meetings, sad partings, honeyed kisses, heartbreak, when life was also full of children's births and trips to the shore and longtime jokes with friends? . . . Then besides the songs there were the magazine stories and the novels and the movies . . . " (*BL* 64). Romantic love, Maggie has discovered, includes so much other life besides, and never "end[s] like a fairy tale"; it "continues past the [happy-ever-after] end" (*LY* 28) to embrace births and deaths, quarrels and celebrations, weeding the garden and moving to new locations, languid afternoons and frightening accidents.

And yet Tyler's female characters persist in dreaming of romance -- often equating it with being rescued from a life of misery, drudgery, and poverty. In *Dinner at the Homesick Restaurant*, when Josiah Payson kisses Jenny Tull, she at first is aghast at his "error" in understanding the nature of their relationship. However, Jenny then begins to find herself tempted by what Josiah must see as "their gentle little 'romance' . . . as seamless as the Widow Payson's fairy tale existence. She longed for it; she wished it were true. She ached, with something like nostalgia, for a contented life with his mother in her snug house, for an innocent, protective marriage" (*DHR* 79). Marrying Josiah Payson would offer Jenny a sweet, uncomplicated husband; a new and more kind mother; and "snug" protection from life's harsh realities (to which her difficult family life has already subjected her). However, Pearl Tull interrupts their romantic kiss, quickly putting an end to this particular dream of Jenny's.

Delia Grinstead proves just as susceptible to fantasies of rescue and protection as Jenny Tull, although Delia has been married since she was eighteen and is now several decades beyond Jenny in both age and life experience. At forty, Delia continues to read romance novels, feeling envious of heroines who are carried off by "wealthy heroes. . . . the men came complete with castles and a staff of devoted servants. Never again would the women they married need to give a thought to the grinding gears of daily life – the leaky basement, the faulty oven, the missing car keys. It sounded wonderful" (*LY* 29). Having accused Sam Grinstead of marrying her for her father's medical practice, to "inherit all his patients and his nice old comfortable house" (*LY* 39), Delia Grinstead finally acknowledges to her sister Linda at the end of *Ladder of Years*, "I schemed to marry him, too. I sat behind that desk [in her father's medical office] just pining for someone to walk in and save me" (309-10). Not only that, but, having left Sam and the children behind for a life on her own in Bay Borough, she still "expected Sam to come fetch her" (*LY* 126), rescuing her by taking her back to Baltimore and placing Delia under his protective wing once more (however damaged it might have been by both the recent onset of his heart condition and several decades of failure to live up to Delia's expectations of him as hero and savior).

Even Ben Joe Hawkes's seventy-eight-year-old grandmother continues to indulge in fantasies of rescue and protection from the problems of her life. Having dreamed as a girl that Jamie Dower might "someday . . . save her life. . . . Pull me out of the water or something" (*IMEC* 161), she mourns his death by saying, "I wish I'd of married Jamie Dower. . . . If I'd of married Jamie . . . I would of had a different family. On account of different genes mingling. They wouldn't all have gone and done queer things . . . " (*IMEC* 185-186). Jamie Dower could have given Gram the life that ought to have been hers – problem-free and happy-ever-after – or so she fantasizes right up until the day of his death in *If Morning Ever Comes*.

Usually Tyler's heroines deny the significance of their own deeds (choosing a marriage partner, taking on a new job, running away from a husband), thinking of themselves as passive even when they are taking action and making choices. Most often they continue to see themselves as maidens in distress who are in need of being rescued. When Charlotte Emory in *Earthly Possessions* finds herself kidnapped by bank robber Jake Simms and held at gunpoint on a wild journey heading towards Florida, she feels not fear and anxiety but gratitude for being "rescued" from her hateful life. Charlotte sees herself as so passive that she feels paralyzed, believing herself incapable of taking action on her own behalf.

At the same time, paradoxically, Charlotte has always dreamed of being an adventurer herself. Years ago, upon finding a photograph of a young, impoverished girl, she felt envy because this child had "grown up on wheels, stayed footloose and unreliable and remained on wheels, and had long ago left these parts" (even though the photograph turns out to be that of her own burdensome, stay-at-home mother) (*EP* 173). Charlotte believes the girl in the photograph is her mother's "true daughter," exchanged for Charlotte after birth in the hospital, and feels betrayed: "It should have been my life. It *was* my life, and she was living it while I was living hers, married to her true husband, caring for her true children, burdened by her true mother" (*EP* 172; 173). Charlotte longs to embark on the hero quest of the adventuring "true daughter," just as old Miss Feather (one of the boarders in Charlotte Emory's household) asks Charlotte to photograph her for her great-nieces, "swathed in a black velvet opera cape, holding a silver pistol that was actually a table lighter" (*EP* 176). In *Earthly Possessions*, Charlotte Emory and Miss Feather both dream of other, more exciting, more dangerous and adventurous lives that are diametrically opposed to the lackluster lives they seem to be leading.

Tyler's male characters dream heroic dreams, as well. Ira Moran in *Breathing Lessons* had hoped by mid-life to have made a name for himself in medical research (not simply have framed needlework and family photos year after year). So, too, Beck Tull kept hoping to impress his now deceased wife Pearl with his exploits, telling his son Cody, "Crazy, isn't it? I do believe that all these years, anytime I had any success, I've kind of, like, held it up in my imagination for your mother to admire. Just take a look at *this*, Pearl, I'd be thinking. Oh, what will I do now she's gone?" (*DHR* 302). Morgan Gower in *Morgan's Passing*, as well, embarks on the hero quest through his many costumes and roles – "his Klondike costume. . . . his Daniel Boone outfit" (*MP* 36), "swooping around in a velvet cape with a red satin lining and a feathered hat. . . . [at other times wearing] ostrich plumes" (*MP* 143), and posing as Toulouse-Lautrec, a Pimlico jockey, or a Washington politician. Tyler's teenaged boys, too, dream of glamour and fame, of becoming idolized rock stars in the cases of Drumstrings Casey in *A Slipping-Down Life* and Jesse Moran in *Breathing Lessons*. Even the modest, cautious Ian Bedloe in *Saint Maybe* had had "moments when he believed that someday, somehow, he was going to end up famous" (*SM* 5).

Ian's dream of fame quickly gives way to another fantasy (as life begins to enmesh him in its plot intricacies, its missteps and misunderstandings): "[Ian] ached, all at once, for a blameless life. He decided that if [his girlfriend] Cicely turned out not to be pregnant, *they* would start living like that. Their outings would become as wholesome as those pictures in the cigarette ads: healthy young people laughing toothily in large, impersonal groups, popping popcorn, taking sleigh rides" (*SM* 109). Ian would like to be saintly and innocent and pure, but as soon as Cicely gets her period, he advises her "to go on the pill now" (*SM* 109-10). The dream of innocence, purity, flawlessness in themselves or in others is one that Tyler's young heroes and heroines – from Ben Joe Hawkes in *If Morning Ever Comes* to Joan Pike in the *Tin Can Tree* or Meg Peck in *Searching for Caleb* – are expected to relinquish along with their youth.

Yet dreams of perfect lives and perfect happiness, of heroism and romance, continue to haunt Tyler's characters. They often feel, with Emily Meredith of *Morgan's Passing*, that they have wandered into the wrong part of the plot and become trapped there as "some drudge. . . . the miller's daughter, left to spin gold out of straw" (183). Emily gives puppet shows with her husband Leon, recognizing that her marriage is failing and watching as the:

> fairytales [they perform] fell into fragments, every line a splinter. When Cinderella danced with the Prince, their cloth bodies clung together, but the hands inside them shrank away. Emily believed that the audience could guess this. She was certain of it. Leon said that was ridiculous. They were making more money than they ever had before; they had to turn down invitations. Things were going wonderfully, Leon said. (*MP* 193)

The romance is over for Emily – but the fairy tales she and Leon produce continue on, conveying the same "happy-ever-after" myths their own marriage refutes. Charlotte Emory, Maggie Moran, Justine Pike, and Delia Grinstead would all agree with Rebecca Davitch's assessment of her own inverted fairy tale life in *Back When We Were Grownups*: "Once upon a time, there was a woman who discovered she had turned into the wrong person" (3).

Tyler's characters fantasize about changing the plot and "getting it right." As Barnaby Gaitlin tells Maud May in *A Patchwork Planet*, perhaps God might be willing sometime to explain "how to do things right. That's what I'm going to ask about when I get to heaven myself: how to do things right" (266). For Barnaby Gaitlin knows full well that he has failed to follow the script correctly, that he's *"close to thirty years old and all but homeless, doing my own daughter more harm than good. Living in a world where everybody's old or sick or handicapped. Where my only friend, just about, is a girl [Martine] – and even her I lie to"* (*PP* 40). Barnaby Gaitlin would like, somehow, sometime, to "do things right" for a change, just as Ian Bedloe in *Saint Maybe* (upon hearing of Lucy Dean Bedloe's death from an overdose of pills) pleads, *"Can't we just back up and start over? Couldn't I have one more chance?"* (90). Many years later, after he has undertaken to do penance for "causing" Danny and Lucy Bedloe's deaths by caring for their three children, Ian complains to Reverend Emmett that he, too, has lost his way and become trapped in the wrong plot, doing the wrong things, "I'm wasting the only life I have! I have one single life in this universe and I'm not using it!" (*SM* 213). Yet Reverend Emmett insists, "Well, of course you're using it. . . . This *is* your life. . . . Lean into it, Ian. . . . Accept that, and lean into it. This is the only life you'll have" (*SM* 213-14). All the same, it remains difficult for Ian Bedloe and the majority of Tyler's characters to accept "the only life" they'll ever have – difficult, as well, simply to "lean into" the flow of their lives, the flow of time.

Cody Tull would like to change his story, as well, lamenting, "if only Einstein were right and time were a kind of river you could choose to step into at any place along the shore" (*DHR* 223). As Caren Town explains:

> Cody would like to "step into" his past life at the moment he chooses and make it all right again; he wants to intervene and change the plot. . . . Somehow, Cody hopes, recounting the past will make it – and him – whole; if he can just get the story right it will all make sense. . . . [just as] Cody also tries to rewrite the story . . . by stealing his brother Ezra's girlfriend Ruth and marrying her. (15)

Somehow the actual life Cody is living has become his secondary life; the imaginary, whole, and perfect life he desires has become his primary obsession, his daily reality.

What is real and what is imaginary become distorted for Tyler's characters. They confuse romances and fairy tales with life itself, leading to a distancing from the actuality of their lives. As Morgan Gower admits:

> "I tend to think . . . that nothing real has ever happened to me, but when I look back I see that I'm wrong. My father died, I married, my wife and I raised seven human beings. My daughters had the usual number of accidents and tragedies; they grew up and married and gave birth, and some divorced. My sister has undergone *two* divorces, or terminations of marriage, at least, and my mother is aging, and her memory isn't what it ought to be . . . but somehow it's as if this were all a story, just something that happened to somebody else. It's as if I'm watching from outside, mildly curious, thinking, So this is what kind of life it is, eh? You would suppose it wasn't really mine. You would suppose I'd planned on having other chances – second and third tries, the best two out of three. I can't seem to take it all seriously." (*MP* 210-11)

Morgan Gower knows that this is his life – and a very full one, at that – and yet he sees it all at one remove, putting on costumes and fantasizing about heroic adventures he might have undertaken, alternative personas he might have assumed. He can't take his own life "seriously."

Aileen Chris Shafer discusses the role of fairy tales and myths in *Morgan's Passing*, concluding that "the cultural myths and stereotypes embedded in these tales appear to foster expectations and goals for the principal characters in [the novel], Morgan and Emily" (126). Shafer argues, "Tyler has demonstrated the need for romance and myth in people's lives, yet, like [Emily's] puppets, these characters are caught by roles in fairy tales that hold sway over their behavior" (137). Morgan Gower fantasizes about being an adventurer, a hero, a prince – Emily Meredith about being married to one. It is not until the end of the novel that Emily and Morgan can both take pleasure in the fairy tales they perform with their puppets as well as delight in their own real, daily lives, as well.

In this novel, as in her others, Anne Tyler resists fairy tale endings to insist that her characters face up to reality. Emily Meredith is not allowed a fairy tale ending to her story, but, instead, finds happiness with "the Beast" (the older, quirky, bearded Morgan Gower) instead of the handsome, rich and clever "prince" (Leon Meredith) she chose as a college freshman. Emily's subconscious had already suggested a more realistic version of "The Beauty and the Beast" when she and Leon performed it earlier in the novel:

> "Just one thing puzzles me," said Mrs. Tibbett.
> "What's that?"
> "Well, the Beast. He never changed to a prince."
> Leon glanced over at Emily.
> "Prince?" Emily said.
> "You had her living happily ever after with the Beast. But *that's* not how it is; he changes; she says she loves him and he changes to a prince."
> "Oh," Emily said. It all came back to her now. She couldn't think how she'd forgotten. "Well. . . ." she said.
> "But I guess that would take too many puppets."
> "No," Emily said, "it's just that we use a more authentic version."
> "Oh, I see," Mrs. Tibbett said. (*MP* 82-83)

Tyler insists on presenting "more authentic versions" of life in her novels than those that fairy tales and romances convey. It is not that her characters must "lean into life" by accepting whatever happens to them as inevitable, unchangeable, right, and true. However, Tyler suggests that they need, with Morgan Gower and Emily Meredith, to resist "happy-ever-after endings" and redefine their concepts of heroism, adventure, happiness, and love in more realistic and fulfilling ways. They must "lean into [the reality of] life"(*SM* 213) – not linger forever in impossible dreams that can never be fulfilled.

"Real life" seems peculiarly "plotless," as Ezra Tull discovers in *Dinner at the Homesick Restaurant* when reading aloud his mother's diaries, whereas "in novels, events led up to something" (268). Macon Leary in *The Accidental Tourist* finds, as well, that "in movies and such, people who made important changes in their lives accomplished them and were done with it" (*AT* 303). Life itself, Macon learns, is quite a bit more messy and difficult to outline, analyze, or predict. Its plot possibilities are much more numerous, intricate, and tricky than our favorite stories have led us to expect. Romances and fairy tales may entertain children, Tyler suggests, but the familiarity of their plot patterns becomes boring after a while. Yet these are the plot patterns we have been led to expect and which overshadow our own stories, making our lives seem "plotless," haphazard and uneventful by comparison.

In *Celestial Navigation*, after Mary Tell has left Jeremy Pauling, she reads to her children "the same old fairytales over and over. . . . I could tell these stories in my sleep. 'Another, now another,' the children say. Don't they ever get tired?" (222). Mary Tell relates the tales she reads out loud to the life she has actually led, concluding:

> I understand that from the outside I seem to have been leading a fairly dramatic life, involving elopements and love children and men stretching in a nearly unbroken series behind me, but the fact is that when you proceed through these experiences day by day they are not really so earth-shaking. All events, except childbirth, can be reduced to a heap of trivia in the end. When I die I expect I will be noticing a water ring someone left on the coffee table, or a spiral of steam

rising from a whistling teapot. I will be sure to miss the moment of my passing. (*CN* 223)

Life's drama is much more elusive and subtle than fairy tales suggest and is filled with the trivia that can distract or mislead us (for who is to say what will prove truly trivial and what not?). Fairy tales, in fact, may have so desensitized us to ordinary life that we find ourselves unable to appreciate the complexities or identify the very highlights of our own plots.[43]

Further, Mary Tell has also learned that fairy tales oversimplify and falsify life in other ways:

> Rapunzel. The Princess and the Pea. Rumpelstiltskin. My voice grows croaky. My mind runs ahead of the words. I play silent games with the tired old plots, I like to ponder the endings beyond the endings. How about Rapunzel, are we sure she was really happy ever after? Maybe the prince stopped loving her now that her hair was short. Maybe the Genuine Princess was a great disappointment to her husband, being so quick to find the faults and so forthright about pointing them out. And after Rumpelstiltskin was defeated the miller's daughter lived in sorrow forever, for the king kept nagging her to spin more gold and she could never, never manage it again. (*CN* 223)

Life is not a fairy tale – although it can be richer and more interesting and satisfying, Tyler suggests. Nor does marriage offer an escape from life – nor love conquer all. Life, Tyler insists, brings "endings beyond the [fairy tale] endings" (*CN* 223) that have colored and distorted our vision since childhood, creating expectations of banquets and castles, princes and princesses, heroic adventures and "happy ever after" romances.

Most of all, Tyler's characters have been led to expect an eternal, unchanging, make-believe world where, Barbara Harrell Carson explains, they could "evade the human involvement in time . . . [and] bypass the changes, losses and painful growth inherent in real life" (26). In the realistic world of Tyler's fiction, however, the passage of time (rather than cruel kings or fearful dragons much more easily conquered) becomes the true adversary – "the cruellest of invisible presences" wreaking havoc on their lives (Updike, "On Such," 109). It is this relentless force that seems to rob them of everything they value, their most cherished dreams, causing Delia Grinstead to "wonder how humans could bear to live in a world where the passage of time held so much power" (*LY* 213). Even young Ian Bedloe (upon learning of his new sister-in-law Lucy's pregnancy) feels a deep regret, "Couldn't [his brother Danny] have let her stay as she was? Did everything have to keep marching forward all the time?" (*SM* 21). Tyler's answer, of course, is "yes." There is no timeless world outside the pages of fairy tales. Yet Tyler's characters find themselves shocked by the presence of time in their lives.

For most of Tyler's characters, time seems to move too fast and too brutally, rearranging intact lives and destroying hopes and dreams. For Maggie Moran, Max Gill's premature death from cancer "was so terribly sad, [his funeral] the kind of day when you realized that everyone eventually got lost from everyone else" (*BL* 22-23). As Alice Hall Petry explains, Max's death becomes "a symbol for Maggie of a phenomenon she herself is experiencing: the feeling that time is out of her control, that it is accelerating – and that as a result, years have slipped by without her realizing it. . . . And she becomes frantic when she feels that her car's odometer is out of synchronization with the highway's mileage test. 'Slow down!' she commands Ira. 'We're losing! We're too far ahead!' (*BL* 25)" (*Understanding* 248).

Time seems to have accelerated for other Tyler characters, as well. Sam Grinstead bemoans the passage of time, finding himself "too far ahead" (*BL* 25), as Maggie Moran has done, telling his wife Delia, "now that I'm nearing the end of [my life], I seem to be going too fast to stop and change. I'm just . . . *skidding* to the end of it" *LY* 307). Delia, too, "had a sense of time slipping away from her" (*LY* 48), adding to her frustration over the current malaise of her marriage. Eighty-year-old Michael Anton walks down St. Cassian Street, where he grew up in the Polish community of East Baltimore in *The Amateur Marriage*, amazed to find much of the street "boarded up now, dead or dying. The original Anton's Grocery had a padlock on the door and graffiti sprayed across the front" (*303*). He remembers all those who are gone – old neighbors, his deceased parents, his brother Danny, his ex-wife Pauline – and concludes, "in the end, everyone dropped away, and someday it would be Michael's turn even if he half fancied that he would go on forever" (*AM* 304).

It is this passing life that Jeremy Pauling tries to capture through his sculptures in *Celestial Navigation*, even if (as Miss Vinton says) it "is nothing *but* motion and passes too swiftly for us to observe with the naked eye" (145). Because time passes so quickly, Cody Tull admits, "time is my obsession: not to waste it, not to lose it" (*DHR* 223), while Ira Moran, also, has become preoccupied with time's wastage: "For the past several months now, Ira had been noticing the human race's wastefulness. People were squandering their lives, it seemed to him. They were splurging their energies on petty jealousies or vain ambitions or long-standing, bitter grudges. . . . Didn't he know well enough all he himself had wasted?" (*BL* 125). So, too, in the same novel, Daniel Otis's nephew Lamont scolds him, "You been married fifty-some years to that woman . . . and half of those years the two of you been in a snit about something. . . . Even worse than children. . . . Children at least got the time to spare, but you two are old and coming to the end of your lives. Pretty soon one or the other of you going to die and the one that's left behind will say, 'Why did I act so ugly?'" (*BL* 169). Time seems to move too fast, either slipping away or being snatched from the grasp of Tyler characters who would like to stop it altogether and live "happily ever after."

However, time also defeats other Tyler protagonists by seeming to trap them in place and hold them stationary so that they cannot make necessary changes or accomplish what they need to do. When her daughter-in-law Fiona and her granddaughter Leroy have disappeared from Maggie Moran's life once more at the end of *Breathing Lessons*, "Maggie had a sudden view of her life as circular. It forever repeated itself, and it was entirely lacking in hope" (315). So, too, Mary Tell finds in *Celestial Navigation*, "sad people are the only real ones. They can tell you the truth about things: they have always known that there is no one you can depend upon forever and no change in your life, however great, that can keep you from being in the end what you were in the beginning: lost and lonely, sitting on an oilcloth watching the rest of the world do the butterfly stroke" (85). Sometimes time seems simply to have come full circle, trapping characters in a lost and hopeless state as they watch the rest of the world pass them by.[44]

Even when time seems to travel in a linear fashion, it can move as painfully slowly as it can speed by quickly. Jeremy Pauling's view of time changes after he and Mary Tell start to live together. Now he marvels that he had once "felt . . . that his life was running out too quickly, and that he should have something more to show for it. Was that what caused *all* major events in the world? He had felt compelled to take desperate steps before it was too late, but now it seemed that life would stretch on forever and grow more tangled and noisy every day. There had been no need for such a plunge [as becoming involved with Mary]" (*CN* 170-71). Charlotte Emory, too, finds herself "trapped, no escape [after her father's heart attack and her return home]. My mother couldn't even sit him up without me there to help. I saw my life rolling out in front of me like an endless, mildewed rug" (*EP* 56). Another young woman, Evie Decker, also finds her life at home passing unbearably slowly. She thinks, "if every evening lasted this long, how much time would it take to get her whole life lived? Centuries. She pictured herself growing older and fatter in this airless dark house, turning into a spinster with a pouched face and a zipper of lines across her upper lip, caring for her father until he died and she had no one left but cats or parakeets" (*SDL* 127). Evie's fear of eternal spinsterhood propels her forward into a reckless marriage with Drumstrings Casey.

Whether it seems to move too quickly or too slowly, in a circular or a linear fashion, closing them in or disappearing out of sight over the horizon, time seems to have what Alice Hall Petry calls "the unique capacity to destroy" (*Understanding* 247). Tyler's protagonists tend to look mainly at the negative impact of time on their lives (while ignoring whatever gains they make through its passage). For example, when Maggie hears false rumors of Ira Moran's death in an army training accident following her high school graduation, she finds herself startled to discover "that her generation was part of the stream of time. Just like the others ahead of them, they would grow up and grow old and die. Already there was a younger generation prodding them from behind" (*BL* 95). Maggie begins to feel powerless and vulnerable, caught in this relentless flow of time that will soon render her generation, not to mention herself, insignificant and obsolete. Growing up and growing old come to seem part of the "slipping-down" life of decline and decay for Tyler's characters – rather than an adventure to be enjoyed at every stage of their lives.

They are shocked to discover that the life process is not at all as it has been made to seem in fairytales and romances. Each phase of life proves far more difficult, disappointing, and frightening than they have been led to anticipate, its "happy-ever-after" endings elusive and fleeting, at best. While many of Tyler's characters grow and develop over time, gaining from each stage of the life process, they often feel helpless and dismayed by their experiences in the immediate – particularly in the earliest periods of their lives. Childhood especially seems to trap Tyler's characters in plots they cannot control where time already appears as a foe needing to be defeated. In *Dinner at the Homesick Restaurant*, Jenny Tull spends much of her youth frightened and anorexic (as her own daughter later will be, as well), afraid of "her mother . . . [whom she sees as] a dangerous person – hot-breathed and full of rage and unpredictable" (70). Over and over, Jenny dreams "what she had always dreamed: her mother laughed a witch's shrieking laugh; dragged Jenny out of hiding as the Nazis tramped up the stairs; accused her of sins and crimes that had never crossed Jenny's mind. Her mother told her, in an informative and considerate tone of voice, that she was raising Jenny to eat her" (*DHR* 70). It is no wonder that a photo of Jenny as an emaciated, frightened young girl makes her appear to her stepson Slevin (preoccupied with his own mother's desertion and his sense of misery and betrayal) to be "a . . . concentration camp person, a victim, Anne Frank! It's terrible! It's so sad!" (*DHR* 203). Jenny's brother Cody views his childhood similarly. As he tells his father Beck on the day of their mother's funeral, "We were kids, we were only kids, we had no way of protecting ourselves. We looked to you for help," but Beck had "turned his back on [them]," leaving them to their own devices (*DHR* 300). While their brother Ezra looks back on his youth differently, he too remembers how "he'd felt defenseless as a child. . . . He had trusted his mother to be everything for him. When she cut a finger with a paring knife, he had felt defeated by her incompetence. How could he depend on such a person? Why had she let him down so?" (*DHR* 261).

In Tyler's world, childhood is filled with feelings of fear and vulnerability, not happiness and innocence, as characters develop (as do the Tull children) the very qualities of resilience and flexibility – even enthusiasm for life's challenges – that will benefit them later in life. In *Back When We Were Grownups*, Rebecca Davitch recognizes that young Peter is frightened and tries to make him feel especially welcome at the engagement party for his father Barry and her youngest stepdaughter NoNo. Rebecca offers Peter a special, welcoming toast (now that she has rescued him from a suicidal plunge into the river):

> "*Next, a toast to Peter!*
> *Someone new in our family!*

> *Nothing could be sweeter."* . . .
> But Peter said, *"I'm* not in your family." . . . I've already got
> a family!" . . . [he] started running. . . .
> "Stop him," Zeb said suddenly.
> Everybody looked at him.
> "He's going toward where the river bends! He's headed for
> the water," Zeb said. (*BWWWG* 19-20)

That night, Rebecca dreams of riding on a train with a young boy who "belonged to her without question," even if she had no son – a boy who had her hair, eyes, and nose, but "most familiar of all was some quality in his expression, something hopeful and wistful, some sense he felt a little bit outside of things. Didn't she know that feeling!" (*BWWWG* 21). It is only at the end of the novel that Rebecca realizes this boy is Peter – that their kinship is not simply their reluctant membership in the Davitch family but their shared sense of being outsiders, of feeling shy and awkward and misplaced in time (even if, by the novel's close, they have both developed further and found a niche for their unique talents in this diverse and noisy clan).

Childhood vulnerability draws other Tyler adults, too, into sympathy with young children's lives. Ian Bedloe in *Saint Maybe* empathizes with his deceased brother's not-so-adorable children:

> [Thomas] had the nuzzling, desperate manner of a small dog starved
> for attention, which unfortunately lessened his appeal; while Agatha,
> who managed to act both sullen and ingratiating, came across as sly.
> Ian had seen how grownups (even his mother, even his earth-mother
> sister) turned narrow-eyed in Agatha's presence. It seemed that only
> Ian knew how these children felt: how scary they found every waking
> minute.
>   Why, being a child at all was scary! Wasn't that what
> grownups' nightmares so often reflected – the nightmare of running
> but getting nowhere, the nightmare of the test you hadn't studied for
> or the play you hadn't rehearsed? Powerlessness, outsiderness.
> Murmurs over your head about something everyone knows but you.
> (115)

This same sense of the helplessness of children which draws Ian into caring for Thomas, Agatha, and the infant Daphne, and Pauline and Michael Anton into caring for their abandoned, autistic grandson Pagan, even if he appeared "like blotting paper . . . absorbing all that came his way and giving nothing back" (*AM* 159), also makes it difficult for Caleb Peck in *Searching for Caleb* to nurture Luray and Roy Spivey's tiny twins. When Luray sends him to take care of the children, Caleb acknowledges that "he had never been good with children. The sight of them made him wretched; he was so sorry for humans in the state of childhood that he couldn't stand to be near them. When one of the babies cried his insides knotted up and he felt bleak and hopeless. So he tended them as if from a distance, holding himself aloof" (275).

Childhood also seems a wretched time (although for very different reasons) to Duncan Peck in *Searching for Caleb*. Duncan argues, "all our misery comes from the length of our childhood. . . . Everything arises from boredom, right? Irritation, loneliness, violence, stupidity – all from boredom. Now. Why are we bored? Because the human childhood is so durned lengthy, that's why. Because it takes us so durned long to get grown. Years. Years and years just hanging around waiting. Why, after that just *anything* would be an anticlimax" (*SFC* 169-70). Childhood is a test of endurance and coping that must be passed – one that can make adult life seem quite tepid by comparison.

In *The Tin Can Tree*, James Green also empathizes with the Pike children's desire to grow up and put their youth behind them. Young Simon Pike wanted to "smoke cigars, take tap-dance lessons, buy his own Woolworth's, and grow sideburns. [His younger sister] Janie Rose . . . asked her mother weekly, 'Do you think it's time I should be thinking of getting married?' And then she would smile hopefully, showing two front teeth so new that they still had scalloped edges, and everyone would laugh at her" (*TCT* 209). James doesn't laugh, however, for he understands the Pike children's longing for adulthood as a time when they at last will begin to enjoy themselves and develop more control over their lives: "[James] couldn't remember that being a child was so much fun" (*TCT* 209).

In *The Tin Can Tree*, Joan Pike, too, has continued living with her aunt and uncle for four years because of her love for her young niece and nephew, not simply her growing attraction to James Green. Joan remembers how she once had been the only person who could comfort her niece: "When Janie Rose's hamster ran away, and Janie Rose stayed an hour in the bathroom shouting that it wasn't important, brushing her teeth over and over with scalding hot water that she didn't even notice and crying into the sink, Joan was the only one who could make her come away" (*TCT* 33). Following Janie Rose's death, as Joan leaves town on a bus to return to her parents' home, she is reminded of her nephew Simon's past helplessness and his continuing need for her guidance when she sees a blind man being led across the road, "that slow, trusting way he let himself be guided forward, with his hands folded gently in front of him," remembering that this "was like Simon during the first year she'd lived there, when he was six and still had to be awakened at night and taken to the bathroom so he wouldn't wet his bed. He had gone just that obediently, but with his eyes closed and the shadows of some dream still flickering across his face" (*TCT* 231). Joan decides then to turn back, realizing that Simon now has been made to feel more helpless than ever before. Dark, new shadows cast by his sister's fatal accident and his mother's withdrawal from life have made Simon feel even more vulnerable to discover, "Oh, Lord, people *break* so easy" (*TCT* 193) – (and so senselessly, as well, as Macon and Sarah Leary have also found when their son Ethan's life suddenly ends at age eleven, "murdered in a Burger Bonanza his second night at camp" in *The Accidental Tourist* (18)).

If childhood seems an endurance test of powerlessness, fearfulness, or boredom, young adulthood presents its share of difficulties, as well. This time of life is filled with constant decision-making, stress, and uncertainty. In *Breathing*

Lessons, Maggie and Ira Moran look back on their newlywed stage as a time when they were really, as Maggie says, just "children. . . . Like infants. We were hardly older than [their daughter] Daisy is now; just imagine. And thought nothing of deciding then and there who we'd spend the next sixty years with" (*BL* 118). Ira agrees, remembering, "We were scared to death, is what it was. . . . We were trying to act like grownups but we didn't know if we could pull it off" (*BL* 119). In *Dinner at the Homesick Restaurant*, Jenny Tull also plunges into her first marriage with Harley Baines, wanting to have an adventure, a break in her routine, desiring "the *angularity* of the situation – the mighty leap into space with someone she hardly knew. Wasn't that what a marriage ought to be? Like one of those movie-style disasters – shipwrecks or earthquakes or enemy prisons – where strangers, trapped in close quarters by circumstance, show their real strengths and weaknesses" (89). Already, in young adulthood, Jenny has felt "her life . . . narrowing. She could predict so easily the successive stages of medical school, internship, and residency. She had looked in a mirror, not so long ago, and realized all at once that the clear, fragile skin around her eyes would someday develop lines. She was going to grow old like anyone else" (*DHR* 89). Leaping over the predictability of her life and the destructiveness of time into the adventure of marriage, Jenny does, in fact, shipwreck, awaking to find herself suddenly on her own with a small daughter to raise.

In *Breathing Lessons*, Maggie's high school friend Serena also feels pressured into marriage by time, as well, but, unlike Jenny Tull, feels her life has become so stressfully unpredictable that she needs to marry Max Gill to find some relief: "It's just *time* to marry, that's all," she said [to Maggie]. "I'm so tired of dating! I'm so tired of keeping up a good front! I want to sit on the couch with a regular, normal husband and watch TV for a thousand years. It's going to be like getting out of a girdle; that's exactly how I picture it" (*BL* 109). Serena's life after marriage, however, proves to be much less relaxing and comfortable than she has anticipated – another stage of life's adventure, not the "happy ending" she foresees going on forever and forever (as is the case for Pauline and Michael Anton in *The Amateur Marriage*, as well, thrust as they have been into an early, mismatched marriage by the unsettling circumstances of World War II).

On the other hand, Elizabeth Abbott of *The Clock Winder* finds it hard to picture any future, contented or otherwise, thinking, "maybe, at twenty-three, she had passed her peak and started the long slope downhill" (145). After Timothy Emerson's suicide, Elizabeth becomes even more paralyzed by life, afraid of doing harm to others since she feels she has somehow provoked Timothy's rash act. Agreeing to take care of the elderly Mr. Cunningham, she feels "she was fighting for herself as well [as for his life] – for her picture of herself as someone who was being of use, and who would never cause an old man harm" (*CW* 185).

Youth, according to Margaret Morganroth Gullette, constitutes "the dangerous age" when "characters fear that for some reason they don't understand, they can't create a self-chosen, more self-confident, happier future – they can't progress in the life course as they must and want to" (*Safe* 6; 15). Even when they rush forward into marriage, jobs, and different lives, they often feel "makeshift, amateur" (*BL* 119) in their attempts to become adults (as, of course, they are). Tyler devotes entire novels to protagonists at this difficult age of young adulthood (*The Clock Winder, A Slipping-Down Life, The Tin Can Tree, If Morning Ever Comes,* and *A Patchwork Planet*) while large sections of other works (*The Amateur Marriage, Saint Maybe, Dinner at the Homesick Restaurant, Searching for Caleb, Morgan's Passing, Celestial Navigation, Earthly Possessions*) examine the anxieties and difficulties of this adult-apprenticeship stage of life, as well.

Five other Tyler novels focus primarily on the mid-life years: *The Accidental Tourist, Breathing Lessons, Back When We Were Grownups, Earthly Possessions,* and *Ladder of Years* (while the stories of Morgan Gower in *Morgan's Passing*, the middle-aged Cody, Jenny, and Ezra Tull in *Dinner at the Homesick Restaurant*, the mid-life Pauline and Michael Anton in *The Amateur Marriage*, and the middle-aged Justine and Duncan Peck in *Searching for Caleb* also deal with this stage of life, as well). This period proves, too, to be one of difficulty and disillusionment for Tyler's characters because, as Alice Hall Petry explains, middle age "signifies the loss of youthful promises and dreams" (*Understanding* 246). At fifty-three, Rebecca Davitch cannot help but wonder, "*How on earth did I get like this? How? How did I ever become this person who's not really me?*" (*BWWWG* 20), as she compares herself to the person she had hoped to be, and should have become, if she had married her first love, Will Allenby: "I used to be much more introspective [she tells Will]. I don't know what became of that! Sometimes I hear you talk about the old days, about the way we lived our lives then and the subjects that used to interest us, and I think, Oh, yes, that was back when we were grownups" (*BWWWG* 188). At fifty-three, Rebecca has lost this serious, "grownup self" she had dreamed of becoming as a history major in college, just as the middle-aged Ira and Maggie Moran in *Breathing Lessons* feel they have lost themselves, as well. Ira looks at the disappointing way his life has turned out and feels, "just as sad as [his wife] Maggie was, and for just the same reasons. He was lonely and tired and lacking in hope and his son had not turned out well and his daughter didn't think much of him, and he still couldn't figure where he had gone wrong" (*BL* 280). In *Ladder of Years*, Delia Grinstead, too, feels that she has become "a sad, tired, anxious, forty-year-old woman who hadn't had a champagne brunch in decades. And her husband was even older, by a good fifteen years, and just this past February he had suffered a bout of severe chest pain. Angina, they said in the emergency room. And now she was terrified" (*LY* 18). All of them long for the more important, fulfilled, happy, and perfect lives they had imagined for themselves when young – although sometimes they find themselves wondering, as does the usually affable Ezra Tull, worried that a lump in his groin could be cancer, "if there were any point to life" at all (*DHR* 258).

Tyler's mid-life characters are shocked to find themselves aging. As Morgan Gower says, "Forty-five feels older than I'd thought it would" (*MP* 102), as it does to his wife Bonny, as well. Bonny suddenly finds herself "reclassified" as uninteresting when lifeguards no longer look at her as she passes them by: "I felt so sad. I felt I'd had something taken away from me that I was so certain of, I hadn't even noticed I had it. I didn't know it would happen to me too, just like to anyone else" (*MP* 175). This is the way Maggie Moran feels in mid-life, that "they're taking things away from me" (*BL* 81), yet (unlike Bonny Gower) she had never thought of others (her former high school classmates, gathered together at Max Gill's funeral, for instance) as going through the same transformation as herself. She notices, for instance, that the Barley twins still wear their hair in the same style as in high school, but now "the backs of their necks were scrawny as chicken necks and their fussy pink ruffles gave them a Minnie Pearl look" (*BL* 66). When Maggie (with her voice cracking on the high notes she had once managed with ease) sings a duet with Durwood Clegg, she almost laughs to see him "shift[ing] back and forth like those trick portraits that change expression according to where you're standing: the old lady-killer Durwood meaningfully lingering on *darling, you're all that I'm living for*, with his eyebrows quirked, but then the present-day, shabby Durwood [appeared] searching for the next stanza on Maggie's shampoo coupon, which he held at arm's length, with his forehead wrinkled, as he tried to make out the words" (*BL* 70-71).

As Maggie looks around the funeral gathering, she is astounded to see:

> a semicircle of graying men and women, and there was something so worn down about them, so benign and unassuming, that she felt at that moment they were as close to her as family. She wondered how she could have failed to realize that they would have been aging along with her all these years, going through more or less the same stages

– rearing their children and saying goodbye to them, marveling at the wrinkles they discovered in the mirror, watching their parents turn fragile and uncertain. Somehow, she had pictured them still fretting over Prom Night. (*BL* 87)

Mid-life has caught them all by surprise. They are aging in spite of themselves.[45]

If Maggie's former classmates appear tired and care-worn in middle-age, perhaps it is because they have found, as Margaret Morganroth Gullette says, "once you get started taking care, those who need care seem to proliferate demandingly" (*Safe* 110). There are aging parents to be looked after (Pearl Tull, Mother Anton, Mr. Moran, and Mrs. Gower) or grandparents to look out for (Grandfather Leary and Daniel Peck), as well as miscellaneous others to be watched over (Brindle Gower, Ira Moran's two sisters, or Poppy in *Back When We Were Grownups*) – and, especially, there are the incessant demands of children who require constant attention. The still unmarried Elizabeth Abbott feels awe when she thinks about parenting at all. She exclaims:

> "Isn't it amazing how hard people work to raise their children? Human beings are born so helpless, and stay helpless so long. For every grownup you see, you know there must have been at least one person who had the patience to lug them about, and feed them, and walk them nights and keep them out of danger for years and years, without a break. Teaching them how to fit into civilization and how to talk back and forth with other people, taking them to zoos and parades and educational events, telling them all those nursery rhymes and word-of-mouth fairy tales. Isn't that surprising? People you wouldn't trust your purse with five minutes, maybe, but still they put in years and years of time tending their children along and they don't even make a fuss about it." (*CW* 274)

Parenting is time-consuming, challenging, painstaking work. Having raised his brother's three children already, Ian Bedloe warns his wife Rita (before their son is born): "I had both my parents helping, and still it wasn't easy. A lot of it was just plain boring. Just providing a warm body, just *being* there; anyone could have done it. And then other parts were terrifying. Kids get into so much! They start to matter so much. Some days I felt like a fireman or a lifeguard or something – all that tedium, broken up by little spurts of high drama" (*SM* 312).

Justine Peck and Delia Grinstead both feel terrified that they will die and no longer be able to protect their children from harm, while Pauline and Michael Anton cannot prevent their daughter Lindy from running away or keep her off drugs (although they do take in her son Pagan and raise him successfully into adulthood, as they have their two other children, Karen and George, as well). Macon and Sarah Leary, along with Mr. and Mrs. Pike, also find themselves helpless to keep their children out of harm's way. Ethan Leary's dog Edward and Janie Rose's tin can tree serve as on-going reminders that you can never completely "place every last bit [of a child] in a hole in the ground" (*TCT* 133), no matter how hard grieving parents, and those who comfort them, might try. As old Missouri says of Mrs. Pike, "Sure she's sad. Going to go right on being that way, always a little sad to the end of her days" (*TCT* 105). However, even before she has finished mourning Janie Rose, Mrs. Pike finds she needs to start worrying about losing her son Simon, as well. So, too, Macon Leary, growing to care more and more for Muriel Pritchett's son Alexander, comes to feel, "his life had regained all its old perils. He was forced to worry once again about nuclear war and the future of the planet. He often had the same secret, guilty thought that had once come to him after Ethan was born: *From this time on I can never be completely happy*," although Macon also admits, "not that he was before, of course" (*AT* 258).[46]

However, even when children do grow up safe and healthy, leaving home to get on with their own lives, Tyler's parents often still feel sad and upset. Justine Peck realizes that she has managed to raise her daughter Meg into adulthood "without dying after all; she was freed from her fears. But at night she woke up shaky and sad, and she pressed her face against Duncan's chest and said, 'I'm not necessary any more,'" feeling not at all comforted by his reply, "To me you are" (*SFC* 188). Maggie Moran also finds that "neither one [of her children, Daisy or Jesse] had any further need of her" (*BL* 35), feeling as lost as does Morgan Gower when his daughters turn away from him to develop interests and lives of their own. Morgan reminds his wife Bonny how "I'd warn them to look both ways, not to run with scissors, never to play with ropes or knives or sharp sticks. 'Relax,' you'd say. Remember? But now look; it's as if they died after all. Those funny little roly-poly toddlers . . . they're dead, aren't they? They did die. I was right all along. It's just that it happened more slowly than I'd foreseen" (*MP* 100). Delia Grinstead, too, has lost her three small children to time's passing, acknowledging, "those were the children she longed for" (*LY* 134) and not the three "semistrangers" from whom she now feels oddly detached, "not only [because she] had . . . lost her central importance to them but [because] they, in fact, had become just a little bit less overwhelmingly all-important to her" (*LY* 211). Tyler's parents feel lost when the children to whom they have devoted so much of their lives grow up and grow away from them – even if they themselves are in the process of changing and developing beyond this stage, as well.

When Pearl Tull reflects on this "empty nest" period of her life, she is amazed to realize that this has been the longest phase of all, that her life has been "empty far longer than full. So much of herself had been invested in those children, who could believe how briefly they'd been with her?" (*DHR* 21). For the years when they had been little, she had kept a night light burning in the hall, then later just a bathroom light, and then none at all, so that it seemed "their growing up amounted, therefore, to a gradual dimming of the light at her bedroom door, as if they took some radiance with them as they moved away from her" (*DHR* 21). In those days she had been, as Pearl tells her eldest son Cody, "the center of your worlds! I was everything to you!

It was Mother this and Mother that, and 'Where's Mother? Where's she gone to?' and the moment you came in from school, 'Mother? Are you home?'" (*DHR* 141). And then they had left her behind.

Suddenly, the parenting stage of life is over – but there seem so many other losses to be endured in mid-life, as well. In *Breathing Lessons*, Sissy Parton's husband Michael laments, "I tell you, first I went to all my kids' school plays, and no sooner was I done with those than we start on this [going to funerals]" (*BL* 83). Friends die, aunts and uncles die, even children sometimes die, while parents desert Tyler's characters just, it seems, when they are needed most. After her father's death, Delia Grinstead thinks, "Didn't it often happen, she thought, that aged parents die exactly at the moment when other people (your husband, your adolescent children) have stopped being thrilled to see you coming? But a parent is always thrilled, always dwells so lovingly on your face as you are speaking. One of life's many ironies" (*LY* 129). And for those in mid-life with no spouses and children (grown or otherwise) still to comfort them, the death of a parent can be even more devastating. After Pearl Tull has died, Cody wonders what his brother Ezra will do: "What would he fill his life with now? He had been his mother's eyes. Lately, he had been her hands and feet as well. Now that she was gone he would come home every night and . . . do what? What would he do? Just sit on the couch by himself, Cody pictured; or lie on his bed, fully dressed, staring into the swarming, brownish air above his bed" (*DHR* 287).

For most Tyler characters, however, mid-life remains a time when their lives seem overly full (if still disappointing), a time when they find themselves "willy-nilly pressed in the middle" (Gullette, *Safe* 110), juggling the demands of jobs, at-home children, burgeoning grandchildren, ailing parents, and other aging or needy relatives (despite the funerals they also find themselves attending more and more frequently now). For the most part, they have little time to think much about the next stage of life, when they will become infirm and crippled themselves (although those who work with the aged believe that this next stage has even more shocks and losses to be endured than in mid-life). While Ira Moran fears that he won't "live forever," Maggie "worried she *would* live forever – maybe because of all she'd seen at the [nursing] home" where she works (*BL* 20).

In *A Patchwork Planet*, Gene Rankin decides to leave Rent-a-Back after only three weeks of employment there, complaining: "Seems every time I turn around, I find myself munching cookies in some old lady's parlor . . . and from there it's only a step or two to the ungrateful daughter stories and the crying jags and the offers of a grown son's empty bedroom." Although his boss Mrs. Dibble tells Gene he will "get used to it," Barnaby Gaitlin knows better: "she just said that because she didn't want to train another employee. You never get used to it" (*PP* 32). While Barnaby loves his Rent-a-Back clients, he too finds "this job could get me down sometimes. People's pathetic fake [Christmas] trees and fake cheer; their muffled-sounding, overheated-smelling houses; their grandchildren whizzing through on their way to someplace better" (*PP* 40). For Barnaby, there seems no way to disguise that aging is a sad and serious, as well as a most often painful, business. He feels skeptical about the wisdom and tranquility that are said to come with the last stage of life.[47]

As Missouri expresses it so aptly in *The Tin Can Tree*, "growing old surely do damage a person" (104).[48] Pearl Tull gradually goes blind (despite the fact that she "intended to do no such thing" (*DHR* 5)), Mother Anton has a stroke in *The Amateur Marriage*, while Grandfather Leary, Mr. Cunningham, and Mrs. Gower become confused in old age. As Elizabeth Abbott reads a story to her virtually bedridden patient, paraphrasing the plot for him as she goes along, Mr. Cunningham begins to confuse his own story with the one Elizabeth is reading him:

> "Then [the protagonist, an outlaw] has about a page and a half
> of bad mood, wondering why people will never allow him to go

straight and lead a peaceful life. Let's see. But they don't know he's
thinking that, they offer him a sheriff's badge."

"I don't want the responsibility," said Mr. Cunningham.

Elizabeth glanced over at him and turned another page. "He
has to be argued into it, there's quite a stretch of arguing. Then – "

"I couldn't be expected to take on that kind of burden," Mr.
Cunningham said.

"Well, it would be quite a job. But this is only a story. We're
reading a story now."

"*Oh* yes. I knew that [Mr. Cunningham says]." (*CW* 184-85)

Sadly, even in his befuddled state, Mr. Cunningham knows his adventures are over
now. However, he remains sharp enough to recognize the burdensome nature of
heroism as well as the privilege of old age – its lessened responsibilities.

While Mr. Cunningham's confusion (as well as his startlingly penetrating
intelligence) can make readers laugh, Barbara A. Bennett points out that "beneath the
surface humor, Tyler makes a serious point about the tragedy of aging" (63). Just as
Mr. Cunningham tries to save face by saying that he understands that Elizabeth is just
reading him a story, so, too, Daniel Peck tries to maintain his self-respect despite the
difficulties caused by his increasing deafness. As they prepare to move to another
house in a new town, Justine tells Grandfather Peck:

> "Check your room, Grandfather," [Justine] called. "Turn off
> the lights. Will you help Meg find the cat? Tell her we're just about
> to leave."
> "Knees?"
> "And don't forget your hearing aid."
> "They don't get better *that* fast, the cold has sunk into the
> sockets," her grandfather said. "Ask me again tomorrow. Thank you
> very much." (*SFC* 21)

If Daniel Peck "continues to respond to conversations as if he understands them
entirely," those who love him, "recognizing his need for dignity, refrain from
correcting his errors," Barbara Bennett explains (63).

Aging brings deafness, blindness, fear and confusion to some, as well as "constant pain" (*LY* 230/221) to others (Nathaniel Moffat in *Ladder of Years*, Poppy in *Back When We Were Grownups*, and Bee Bedloe in *Saint Maybe*). It debilitates characters physically and threatens their sense of well-being and self-respect, as well. Yet, as they attempt to go on with their daily lives as routinely as possible, continuing to hold their heads high, Tyler suggests their true heroism, their courage and determination. In *Saint Maybe*, Ian Bedloe comes to understand too late that "his mother's staunch sprightliness had been braver than he had appreciated in his youth. (Last summer, laid up for a week with a wrenched back, he had suddenly wondered how Bee had endured the chronic pain of her arthritis all those years. He suspected that had taken a good deal more strength than the brief, flashy acts of valor you see in the movies.)" (*SM* 323).

Tyler's elderly characters try to maintain their independence as long as possible, frightened of being put in nursing homes in their final years. When Jamie Dower returns to Sandhill, North Carolina, at eighty-four to enter the "home for the aged," it is only because he is "going to die there," as planned, in the town where he was born (*IMEC* 43). On the very day of Jamie Dower's death, Ben Joe Hawkes takes his Gram to the Sandhill Home for the Aged to visit her old friend (at her insistence), but before they arrive, Gram pleads with Ben Joe, "You're going to stay right by me, aren't you, Benjy? . . . I do hate going to the home for the aged, for fear I can't get out again. They might mistake me, you know. When I said I wasn't a patient, they might think I was just planning to escape" (*IMEC* 163). For the elderly, nursing homes often represent the sad indignity of old age, the finality of life's close in death.

This is true for Daniel Peck in *Searching for Caleb*, as well. When Duncan bets his grandfather Daniel Peck a bottle of bourbon that Daniel's brother Caleb is "sitting in an old folks' home this very minute watching *The Dating Game*,"

Grandfather Peck shouts, "'I've stood a lot from you, Duncan,' he said, 'but not this. *I do not have a brother in an old folks' home*'" (208). When in fact Caleb is discovered to be living in the Evergreen County Home for the Elderly in Box Hill, Louisiana, less than three months later, Daniel says of his eighty-eight-year-old, younger brother, "Why! . . . Why, Caleb must be *old*!" (*SFC* 244). As Alice Hall Petry says, before the two brothers can be reunited, Daniel dies of a heart attack "rather than face his brother and the passage of time that he represents" (*Understanding* 140). Daniel Peck has continued to deny the reality of his own life course, dreaming of heaven as a small town where no one "would ever die or move away or age or alter" (*SFC* 190), in the way both he and Caleb have done, of course. While he has endured many difficulties with stoicism and courage, Daniel has also persisted foolishly in trying to make life conform to his Peckish need for a regularity, propriety, and security it can never provide.[49]

Nathaniel Moffat in *Ladder of Years* seems, at first, to have accepted old age much more realistically than Daniel Peck. He has entered "Senior City" outside Bay Borough as soon as it becomes painful to walk, after his legs start to "give out on" him at the end of the day and he can no longer climb the stairs of his home without difficulty (*LY* 193). Nat jokes that the inmates of Senior City are "organized. . . . Like files in a filing cabinet. . . . on the vertical. Feebler we get, higher up we live. . . . Everybody hopes to die before they're sent to Four" (*LY* 193). When Delia visits him for the first time, she acknowledges that it "was like visiting a war zone" (*LY* 189). Nevertheless, Nat finds being there "preferable to burdening your children," even if "the whole setup . . . [seems to him] uncomfortably . . . symbolic" (*LY* 193). As Nat explains to Delia, "'See, I've always pictured life as one of those ladders you find on playground sliding boards – a sort of ladder of years where you climb higher and higher, and then, *oops*!, you fall over the edge and others move up behind you. I keep asking myself: couldn't Thelma [his deceased wife] have found us a place with a few more levels to it?'" (*LY* 193-94). Nat may call Senior City the "House of the Living Dead" (*LY* 196), but he seems to have accepted the necessity of moving out of his home and adjusted to living there quite well.

Yet Nathaniel Moffat, too, has also tried to escape the reality of old age as much as Daniel Peck and Gram Hawkes with their horror of nursing homes. While at Senior City, Nat marries a woman half his age (Binky, a divorcee who works in the gift shop) and fathers a son, understanding too late that he has been indulging in "a time trip. . . . [trying] to travel backwards . . . and live everything all over again" (*LY* 322). Nat admits to Delia and her family that this act is the

> "most irresponsible thing I've ever done in my life. . . . What could
> I have been thinking of? . . . I believe I thought it was my chance to
> be a good father, finally. I know it was, or why else did I assume it
> was a girl? All my others were girls, you see. I must have thought I
> could do the whole thing over again, properly this time. But I'm just
> as short-tempered with James as I ever was with my daughters. Just
> as rigid, just as exacting." (*LY* 321)

Too late, Nat has realized that he is actually an old man who will soon die and that "Binky's the one who's left with the consequences" (*LY* 322). Listening to Nat, Delia understands that her flight from her family in Baltimore, from her aging children and husband, "had *all* been a time trip – all this past year and a half. Unlike Nat's, though, hers had been a time trip that worked" (*LY* 326).

Some "time trips" prove disastrous, such as Serena's desire in *Breathing Lessons* to have "a kind of rerun [of her wedding on the occasion of her husband's funeral], like people sometimes have on their golden anniversaries" (*BL* 57).[50] However, Serena can no more repeat her wedding without the groom than Mrs. Pike can halt time in *The Tin Can Tree* by "stop[ping] all the clocks in her home" to succeed in "remov[ing] herself from that world of pain and change that took her daughter's life" (Petry, *Understanding* 40). It is unrealistic to try to stop the passage of time, to try to stop the aging process or deny the fact of death, to attempt to "turn [time] back again," as Cody Tull would like to do, and "change this or that, undo what you have done" (*DHR* 256). Nevertheless, some time trips, such as Delia Grinstead's in *Ladder of Years*, do turn out successfully. So, too, does Rebecca Davitch's as she watches her son-in-law Hakim's videotape (made from Davitch home movies from 1954-1967 – his present to Poppy for his hundredth birthday). She sees that she had been an uncertain, pudgy "interloper" into the Davitch family, as she had remembered (*BWWWG* 265) – but, at the same time, she discovers that she had also been much happier then than she would recall later: "on the screen, Rebecca's face appeared, merry and open and sunlit, and she saw that she really had been having a wonderful time" (*BWWWG* 274). The videotape forces Rebecca to acknowledge that her memory has been fallible; she has not understood herself or the broadening, enriching, worthwhile life she has lived at all well.

Pearl Tull, too, is successful in her quest to go back in time as she listens to her son Ezra reading her girlhood diaries aloud, searching for some clue to the meaning of her life, some connection between her past self and the woman she has become. After Ezra reads her diary entry for February 6, 1910, Pearl tells him, "there's no need to read any more" (*DHR* 277). Although she has asked for the hymn, "We'll Understand It All By And By" to be sung at her funeral, Pearl is shown here to have found some understanding of her life before its end, as Ezra reads:

> "*Early this morning . . . I went out behind the house to weed. Was kneeling in the dirt by the stable with my pinafore a mess and the perspiration rolling down my back, wiped my face on my sleeve, reached for the trowel, and all at once thought, Why I believe that at just this moment I am absolutely happy. . . . The Bedloe girl's piano scales were floating out her window . . . and a bottle fly was buzzing in the grass, and I saw that I was kneeling on such a beautiful green little planet. I don't care what else might come about. I had had this moment. It belongs to me.*" (*DHR* 277)

Life itself is the gift to be appreciated, Pearl has found, the secret to be valued, the connection between past and present time. The journey may be filled with disappointment and pain, speed along too quickly or crawl too sluggishly, become frightening or bewildering along the way, and yet it is the very adventure we crave. While life offers no happy endings and constant, irritating twists and turns in plots we had never anticipated experiencing, it also contains, Pearl discovers, its perfect, joyous moments. There is the possibility, too, over time, of healing, change, and growth – right up to the point of death, as Pearl learns here, as well.[51]

Tyler's strongest characters discover that the life process and the passage of time offer personal redemption, not simply loss and destruction. As Anne Jones finds, "in time, [Tyler's] novels suggest, lies the possibility of moving into . . . a kind of maturity that accompanies acknowledgment of and submission to the real" (13). As they learn to "lean into [the reality of life]" (*SM* 213), rather than into their "happy-ever-after" expectations born of too many romantic songs, movies, novels, and fairy tales, Tyler's characters begin to enjoy life's challenges and its rewards. When Ira Moran plays solitaire at the end of *Breathing Lessons*, Maggie appreciates that "he had arrived at the interesting part of the game by now, she saw. He had passed that early, superficial stage when any number of moves seemed possible, and now his choices were narrower and he had to show real skill and judgment" (327). Their life together has followed the course of Ira's solitaire game, becoming more, not less, interesting as they have aged and as their choices have become more restricted, Maggie begins to understand. Now they, too, need greater skill and sounder judgment than they have ever needed before. However, Maggie finds this thought invigorating, rather than discouraging, enabling her to feel "a little stir of something that came over her like a flush, a sort of inner buoyancy, and she lifted her face to kiss the warm blade of [Ira's] cheekbone" (*BL* 327). So, too, Delia Grinstead at the end of *Ladder of Years* recognizes that mid-life is not simply a time of loss.

While it is true that there is "no hope of admiring gazes anymore, no chance of unremitting adoration. Nothing left [for her and Sam] to show but their plain, true, homely, interior selves," Delia also finds that these selves "were actually much richer anyhow" than the naïve, untested ones of their youth (*LY* 324). Maggie Moran and Delia Grinstead grow to appreciate life's reality through their experiences, rather than continue to pine for the perfect families and happy endings that romantic fiction had promised.

While it remains true, as Muriel Pritchett tells Macon Leary in *The Accidental Tourist*, "*We're all scarred. You are not the only one*" (201), life continues to prove surprisingly interesting and exciting, all the same. Although Macon still misses Ethan (and will go on doing so), time has helped to restore rather than destroy his passion for life. At the end of the novel, Macon looks forward to life with Muriel and her son Alexander, feeling an "inner rush, a racing forward. The real adventure, [Macon] thought, is the flow of time; it's as much adventure as anyone could wish" (*AT* 342). At eighty, too, Michael Anton wishes "he had inhabited more of his life, used it better, filled it fuller" (*AM* 302) – been a better father and worked out his problems with Pauline, whom he realizes he has loved, but only after years of safe separation and his remarriage to Anna Stuart. However, the elderly Michael has a dream in which a woman who resembles the Good Witch from *The Wizard of Oz* appears to warn him, "don't ever look back, if you want to see your home again" (*AM* 298). Life must be lived forward, and as fully as possible, Michael is still learning. Similarly, in *Back When We Were Grownups*, Rebecca Davitch realizes that she still mourns her husband, yet recognizes, too, that her life's adventure has not ended with Joe's death. She continues to look forward to the future, long after the challenge of raising their four daughters on her own is over, knowing "there were still so many happenings yet to be hoped for in her life" (*BWWWG* 274) – although marriage to Will Allenby will not be one of them. Even death itself, Ezra Tull admits, can be viewed "as a kind of adventure, something new that he hadn't yet experienced" (*DHR* 273) – another life event to be faced with as much grace and spirit as possible.

Sometimes all that is needed to appreciate life's rich challenges is a change of perspective. Morgan Gower admits, "Often I fall into despair. . . . I think, in ten thousand years, what will all this amount to? Our planet will have vanished by then. What's the point? I think, and I board the wrong bus. But when I'm happy, it's for no clearer reason" (*MP* 210). Daniel Otis's story about his dog Bessie, which he tells the Morans in *Breathing Lessons*, contains a similar moral about the importance of perspective in life. Bessie "assumed her ball was lost forever simply because it was blocked by a chairback: a lot of us, muses Mr. Otis, have 'blind . . . spots' (*BL* 171) which make us fail to appreciate what we have *not* lost" (Petry, "Bright" 11). A change of focus is often required for Tyler's characters to appreciate what they still have and what life can still offer them. Thus, Daniel Otis acknowledges that his marriage is far from perfect. Yet, if his nephew Lamont chooses to focus on all its negative aspects, Daniel chooses to view it differently: "And anyhow, just look at the times we had. Maybe that's what I'll end up thinking. 'My, we surely did have us a time. We were a real knock-down, drag-out, heart-and-soul type of couple,' I'll say. Something to reflect on in the nursing home'" (*BL* 170).

Tyler's characters always have a choice of perspective on their past, as well as their present and future lives, as Madame Olita explains to Justine Peck (*SFC* 129). If they believe, with James Green in *The Tin Can Tree*, that flawed relationships can never be changed, they may learn to see that nothing in life remains fixed forever: "[James] had thought that of all the mixed-up, many-sided things in the world, his dislike of his father was one complete and pure emotion and that that alone could send words enough swarming to his mouth. Yet his father stood before him like a small, battered bird" (252), shocking James into silence because of his age and hesitancy – a man James can no longer hate with simple intensity. As life experiences intervene, characters such as James find their outlook inevitably changing. They grow and learn and develop – life's true challenge. This is what has happened, also, to Charlotte Emory after her trip at gunpoint with bank robber Jake Simms. Charlotte finds that her stay-at-home period has been the true adventure in her life (not her whirlwind trip south with Jake Simms). She and her husband Saul, Charlotte recognizes now, "have been traveling for years, traveled all our lives, we are traveling still. We couldn't stay in one place if we tried" (*EP* 200). It is their life together in Clarion that is truly challenging – not her kidnapping adventure. As Tyler's characters mature through their experiences, they often find that the life process itself is one that enlarges – not limits – their interests and enjoyment.

In *Back When We Were Grownups*, Tyler presents a sustained and powerful view of life's joy in the midst of loss and sorrow. In this work, Rebecca Davitch gives a one-hundredth birthday party for Poppy, her uncle by marriage and her fellow lodger at the Open Arms – a man who had been invited into the Davitch home years ago when he was on the verge of "turn[ing] into a telephone drunk. (Calling up at all hours: 'Can I honestly be expected to go on without my Joycie?')" after his wife has died (*BWWWG* 24). Poppy has also survived the suicide of his twin brother many decades ago, a man who "wasn't a naturally happy person. Some people, they just have a harder time being happy," Poppy concludes (*BWWWG* 251). While Poppy still mourns his deceased wife, and has celebrated each successive birthday for his twin as well as himself, he nonetheless continues to relish every minute of his life and this special occasion (one everyone knows he won't even be able to remember later).

Poppy regales the assembled guests with an account of every pleasure he has experienced on his special day:

> "Well. This has been just what I dreamed of, I tell you. From the
> very start of the day, it's been perfect. Sunshine on my bedspread

when I opened my eyes; radiators coming on all dusty-smelling and cozy. Waffles for breakfast, that puffy kind that are light inside but crispy outside, and one-hundred-percent maple syrup heated first in the microwave and then poured over in a pool and left a moment to soak, so the waffles swell and turn spongy and every crumb of them is sopping with that toasty, nutty flavor." (*BWWWG* 269)

He commemorates, too, the "soft, rich lather" of his "morning shave"; the "*slip slip slip* – a peaceful sound*" of his solitaire cards; the "peanut-butter-jelly sandwich on whole wheat" he had eaten for lunch, "done exactly right: the grape jelly smeared so thick that it had started soaking through," as well as the "body-shape of warmth" of his sheets as he takes his afternoon nap (*BWWWG* 270-272). Listening to Poppy's lengthy report of his day, Rebecca finds "it was sort of like a report on what it was like to be alive . . . . Let's say you had to report back to heaven at the end of your time on earth, tell them what your personal allotment of experience had been: wouldn't it sound like Poppy's speech? . . . Why, her own report might take even longer" (*BWWWG* 273).

Being able to take pleasure in life's small moments, in its little comforts as well as its larger joys, can simply be a gift. However, it can also be learned. Rebecca knows that "she had had to labor at [her own joyousness]. She had struggled to acquire it" (*BWWWG* 247). It still remains an on-going challenge for her to turn pain and hurt into happiness for herself and others, even on the day of Poppy's one-hundredth birthday celebration (as Poppy, too, must ignore his arthritic pain and his memory problems to appreciate the many joys of life still remaining him). However, Rebecca has learned that the kind of person she has really always wanted to be, and the kind of person she will continue to strive to be (even without Joe Davitch at her side), is someone who savors life in spite of its bitterness. In Tyler's realistic fiction, happiness and heroism can still be found, but they exist in unassuming men and women who work to meet everyday challenges with grace and good cheer. Tyler redefines courage and happiness in her novels, encouraging readers to "lean into" (*SM* 213) the reality of their lives where true heroic tests and adventures abound.

Notes

43.   Pearl Tull also suggests the perversity of life's drama, agreeing with Mary Tell that "dying, you don't get to see how it all turns out. Questions you have asked will go unanswered forever" (*DHR* 30).

44.   Robert Croft argues that time is "circular and reflexive" in Tyler's novels and that this concept of time affects the structure of her works, so that "characters often find themselves back where they started" (*Companion* 11). While I agree that time sometimes appears circular to Tyler's characters, it actually is shown to be moving them forward and, as I will argue in Chapter Six, even characters who wind up back where they started usually undergo substantial change by the end of a work. Their lives at each novel's conclusion, therefore, are not merely repetitions of what has gone before, as Croft argues.

45.   Rebecca Davitch is also not prepared to find that Will Allenby has aged at least as much as she has since their freshman year in college together: "His fingers were as knuckly and wiry as ever, but there was a difference in the texture of his skin, a kind of graininess that she saw in his face, too, now that she was close enough – a sandy look to his cheeks, a trio of fine lines straining across his forehead. His lips, which had once been very full and sculptured, were thinner and more sharply defined. He was wearing . . . elderly clothes, sagging off his bony frame in a slack and elderly way." Will is also surprised by the change in Rebecca: "What happened to your long golden braid?", he asks (*BWWWG* 129).

46.   In *Back When We Were Grownups*, Rebecca Davitch remembers, too, when she "had been struck by fear as physical as a kick in the stomach" after her stepdaughter's appendix had burst: "Patch was the first stepdaughter Rebecca had loved – or the first she'd become aware of loving. . . . In some ways, she had never recovered" (273). Similarly, Charlotte Emory in *Earthly Possessions* is reluctant to accept the abandoned baby (Jiggs) Saul brings home, not because she cannot love him but because she knows she can: "But then his mother will come back. . . . We could lose him at any moment," she protests, to which Saul replies, "We could lose anybody at any moment. We could lose [our daughter] Selinda" (138).

47.   Nor can Elizabeth Abbott be fooled about old age after she has started taking care of Mr. Cunningham: "She had often wished, when things went wrong, that she were old and wise and settled, preferably in some nice nursing home. Well, not any longer"; now she sees what can happen as a person ages, how old Mr. Cunningham

"viewed his body as an acquaintance who had gone over to the enemy. Why had she supposed that people's interiors aged with the rest of them?" (*CW* 182).

48.   In *Breathing Lessons*, Ira Moran's father complains that his deceased wife Rona "died before she went through all this. . . . Wrinkles and gnarls and creaking joints and heartburn – she missed out on it. . . . It's like she didn't live a real life. . . . I mean all of life, the whole messy kit and caboodle that comes at the end," and he seems to feel "peevish" that she "had got away with something" (278). Aging is part of the full course of "real life" – and, Tyler suggests, a stage Rona might have been glad to experience, despite its difficulties, had she been given a choice in the matter.

49.   Caleb Peck differs from his brother Daniel in his acceptance of nursing homes and aging (as in so much else). Although Caleb feels angry when they take his harmonica away from him at the Evergreen Nursing Home, "as time went by he made a few acquaintances, discovered a dogwood tree in the concrete yard, and began to enjoy the steady rhythm of bed, meals, social hour, nap. He had always liked to think that he could get along anywhere." As Daniel's search for Caleb continues, and as he watches his granddaughter Justine take each setback with patience and good cheer, for once in his life Daniel "beg[ins] to relax. He began to enjoy the search itself. . . . he learned to concentrate solely on the act of traveling" (*SFC* 277; 158).

50.   Although characters often look back wistfully at their younger days, when they are given opportunities to see themselves as they were, "they yearn, significantly, to 'fast-forward' the film" (*BL* 89), as Alice Hall Petry says of those watching a movie of Serena and Max Gill's wedding at Max's funeral (*Understanding* 249). The same thing is true in *Back When We Were Grownups* when Poppy explains that his wife Joycie really was much more attractive than she appears on Hakim's videotape, telling guests to "take his word for it: this was not really the way things had been"(265).

51.   Mary J. Elkins believes that "[Pearl] understands what Ezra does not, that life is a reverberating moment and not a plot unfolding and leading to a happy or unhappy ending" (133). However, it would seem that life both has continuous moments to be experienced, as well as a plot with a final resolution (just not one, as Pearl Tull comes to understand, that individuals themselves can fully comprehend – "dying, you don't get to see how it all turns out" (*DHR* 30)). Readers, however, and those who outlive the dying person (Pearl's children, grandchildren, and estranged husband) can see how the story turns out – the full pattern of Pearl's (or any individual's) life.

Chapter Six
Countering the Status Quo

In all of her novels, Anne Tyler's characters tend to lead slipping-down lives. They grow older; undergo social and economic decline; experience family break-ups, deaths, and conflicts; as well as fail in their dreams of romance and heroic adventure (not to mention fail to live up to their illusions of an ideal past which diminishes the present moment) – only to awake and discover themselves in the everyday, real world once more. Yet the most successful of them discover that that is exactly where they want to be.

While they may often have felt powerless to change their fates or find fulfillment, many of them discover that considerable control of their lives has been in their own hands all along. Tyler's protagonists find that they always have had the opportunity to change their perspectives – on the past, the present, and the future, as Madame Olita explains to Justine Peck (*SFC* 129). Perhaps even more important, they also have always had, and will continue to have, the power of choice over their own lives – to change their families, their friends, their towns, their jobs, their goals, or to maintain those they have and start to hold them dear. While each choice exacts its own price, Tyler's strongest characters find that enduring loss and pain them-selves, as well as having to hurt others in the process, may not only be necessary but also worthwhile in order to experience their own personal growth and the greater social well-being which results from healthy individual development. As Macon Leary tells his wife Sarah, people can always "choose what to lose" (as he does when he leaves her behind to live with Muriel Pritchett) but, at the same time, thereby gain a rich sense of fulfillment in life and improved interpersonal relationships, as Macon finally does (*AT* 310). (Separation and divorce can even lead to a renewal of love and appreciation through a sense of loss, as Tyler shows in *Ladder of Years* and *The Amateur Marriage*.)

If contemporary American culture tends to inculcate passivity into its work-force and citizens, its spectators and consumers, Anne Tyler seeks to counteract society's numbing effects by returning her protagonists (and her readers) to a sense of their own inner resourcefulness, personal resiliency, individual self-worth, and ability to shape their own lives in ways that are more meaningful, productive, and harmonious (whether socially condoned or not). Her protagonists, from Evie Decker to Delia Grinstead to Morgan Gower to Barnaby Gaitlin, learn that they can be active players in their own lives – discovering their individual power of choice and their ability to exert their own personal values. They find that they may do so, as well, in opposition to their materialistic culture which defines success almost entirely in economic terms while restricting them to a narrow definition of family, as well as to outworn traditions and impossibly romantic dreams, through its advertisements, television dramas, political campaigns, and Hollywood films.

If Tyler's characters do not have the power to change their society, at least they find that they can still act within American culture in ways that will allow them to form meaningful personal relationships and perform fulfilling work to affirm their sense of self and ensure their helpfulness to others. Through constant assessment and re-assessment of their own feelings and lives, they are able, over time, to determine a course of action that is right for them. Tyler's characters, from Rebecca Davitch and Mary Tell to Ian Bedloe and Morgan Gower, find themselves in the process of constantly evaluating and re-evaluating their lives, asking themselves these essential questions:

(1)   Is the work I do useful?
(2)   Am I valued by the people around me?
(3)   Do I feel I am becoming the kind of person I want to be?
(4)   Am I living the kind of life I want to live?

For Anne Tyler's characters, answers to these questions are essential for determining the right future course for their lives – and their answers must be correct ones not according to some ideological or cultural standard but according to their own individual needs and values.[52]

Most important, Tyler never presents these internal self-examinations as narcissistic self-indulgence, but quite the opposite. As Lee Siegel has said (in responding to the works and ideas of another author from the Western tradition, Dante Alighieri, evaluating Dante's importance for readers living in the contemporary world):

> But our self-investigations are not the problem – they are essential. What we need is an improvement in the art of making them. Indeed, ceaseless self-examination offers our brightest cultural prospect. It's the only way to cut our own path through the prevailing image of a collective "self," composed of vanity and trivial appetites, projected onto us by a commercial society. If we master the art of making them, our good self-examinations will help fend off the bad narcissisms. (80)

This, too, is the message of Anne Tyler's works: that we need constant, responsible self-appraisal that will lead to individual growth, self-knowledge and self-assertion – that the collective American identity which seems to have worked so long for business and industry, for production and sales, most often demeans individual enterprise and robs people of a sense of their own self-worth.

When Anne Tyler affirms Ian Bedloe's choice of carpentry over college (and a subsequent professional career) as fulfilling, creative, healing work, or Justine and Duncan Peck's choices to be carnival workers as a fortune-teller and fix-it man, respectively, or Barnaby Gaitlin's work as a Rent-a-Back employee, defining all of these kinds of employment as worthwhile endeavors, she reveals the essential link between character formation, and reformation, and proper work that is good for the soul (however denigrated it may be by society). In doing so, she redefines tasks labeled as low-level and non-essential in contemporary society as ones that are individually and communally significant. Tyler's characters discover that they can do many things that are useful, both practically and psychologically, for themselves and for others, regardless of the cultural "value" assigned to these tasks. What is important is how the work makes them feel about themselves and those around them. If they feel they are performing necessary work that is valued by those they serve, then what they do is worthwhile both for themselves and for society. When they lose interest in their jobs, as do Duncan Peck and Morgan Gower, or feel their work is no longer seen as valuable by others, in the manner of Delia Grinstead, or even feel their work has become harmful to those they seek to help (in the case of Elizabeth Abbott), then it is time for a change.

So, too, if they cannot feel good about themselves, feel affirmed by the people around them, or feel proud of the lives they are living, again it is time, once more, for Tyler's characters to take steps to initiate change – as do (among others) Macon Leary, Rebecca Davitch, Michael Anton, Delia Grinstead, Morgan Gower, Maggie Moran, Mary Tell, Ben Joe Hawkes, and Joan Pike. Sometimes Tyler's characters decide to alter their lives by choosing a different partner – or no partner at all; sometimes they choose a different lifestyle; at other times, they re-learn the value of those around them and the meaningfulness of the tasks they perform each day, choosing to remain just where they are. Whether they ultimately create new lives for themselves, or stay in their old ones, they have acquired vital, liberating knowledge of the power they possess to change their own circumstances, both for now and in the future.

When Tyler's protagonists find pleasure in what they do and who they are, rediscovering the richness of their lives in the manner of Rebecca Davitch, Charlotte Emory, Morgan Gower, and Barnaby Gaitlin, they can experience an inner joy and spiritual renewal rarely found in the midst of the enervating effects of contemporary society. Once more, as Lee Siegel says, such an enhanced sense of self, while healthy for both the individual and for society as a whole, is seldom defined as wholesome by society's system of consumer capitalism:

> A business culture produces a condition of permanently stimulated appetite, in which any issue touching the consuming self holds the most interest and the highest value. So people – many people – turn inward to find that part of themselves that is connected to a larger life, that exists beyond their self-interest and their banal desires. And what happens then? The captains of the culture deplore all the vigilant self-absorption and defensive self-scrutiny as narcissistic. (80)

Ironically, it is only by pursuing tasks of critical self-examination and working to achieve a meaningful existence that individuals can develop a sense of the "larger life" of spiritual connectedness that takes them beyond the confines of the self.

From an enhanced sense of the potential of one's inner being comes an enhanced sense of the meaning and value of life itself, as Anne Tyler repeatedly makes clear to her readers. For example, when Charles Leary tells his brother Macon, "You're not yourself these days and this Muriel person's a symptom. Everybody says so," Macon can reply with confidence, "I'm more myself than I've been my whole life long" (*AT* 249). At the same time that Macon finds himself experiencing an expanded view of self, giving him "a sudden view of his life as rich and full and astonishing" (*AT* 285), he finds all of life, the world itself, a place of "adventure" suddenly filled with mystery, surprise, and beauty (*AT* 351). Similarly, Michael Anton comes to feel "alive and energized," as though "his life was just beginning," when he falls in love with Anna Stuart, awed that he is even "capable of such feelings" in *The Amateur Marriage* (216). Such a sense of self and life cannot be purchased at the mall, acquired by having a prestigious job, or experienced in the process of making a substantial profit. In Tyler's novels, there is no substitute for the hard work of personal development, for it seems the only avenue her characters find leading them towards a sense of enhanced self-esteem and life appreciation.

Materialism can never offer the internal richness of being Tyler's characters find growing within themselves, then progressing into their work and their relationships with others as they creatively meet life's challenges. As Margaret Morganroth Gullette explains, "nothing more exhilarating could happen to a person, personally, than to come into a better relationship to the self, build the idea of progress into one's life, and implicitly accept aging (even via suffering) as an advance" (*Safe* 167). Tyler's characters find that slipping-down materially, socially, and physically provides them with the opportunities they need for self-reflection, personal challenge, individual development, and spiritual growth – "growth in a sense of expanded usefulness, [in a sense of] spiritual redemption" (Gullette, *Declining* 88). Their lives improve as they grow older, become less respectable, less comfortable, or less wealthy, because their appreciation of self and the world has become enlarged.

It is not impossible after all, Tyler's characters find, to experience adventure and romance or achieve heroic stature in their own lives. In fact, contemporary life, Tyler suggests, offers them as many opportunities as the seemingly more glorious, legendary past for modern day travelers to become "celestial navigators" in their own lives. Tyler leads her characters – and her readers – into a sense of the adventure and possibility to be found in the familiar, everyday world around them.

In her novels, Tyler suggests several ground rules her self-examining characters learn to follow in regaining a sense of life as a meaningful quest and an heroic adventure. As Tyler's characters ask themselves who they want to be and what they want to do with their lives, they find that they must also be careful to:

(1) become active rather than passive players in their own lives;
(2) respond to internal motivators rather than external ones;
(3) disregard cultural and ideological (including religious) formulas for correct living;
(4) try not to hurt others *more than is necessary* in order to do what is required to fulfill their own needs and goals; and
(5) reach out to form meaningful connections with others (through their work, their marriages, and their extended families).

By following the above criteria, while continuing to undergo constant self-assessment and re-assessment, Tyler's characters find adventure in ordinary life – in deciding what kind of person to become, the people with whom they wish to share their lives, where to live, and what jobs to do, in their quests for a sense of meaning and wholeness in their lives. As Margaret Morganroth Gullette says, "the plot of a particular novel might move the evolving and sometimes consciously questing protagonist from randomness to meaningfulness, or from conflict to resolution, from pain to serenity, from stasis to activity, and from defeat to fulfillment, from drive to freedom, from loss to recovery" (*Safe* xiv-xv). In every novel, however, Tyler's protagonists are shown to have become *different* by the end of the work – in their outlooks, at least, if not in the actual circumstances of their lives. As Justine Peck tells her daughter Meg, "Imagine you were handed a stack of instructions. Things that you should undertake. Blind errands, peculiar invitations . . . things you're supposed to go through, and come out different on the other side" (*SFC* 229). Tyler hands her characters their sets of "instructions," "blind errands," and "peculiar invitations" in each of her novels, challenging them to grow and change through sometimes painful, frequently confusing, yet often joyful experiences.

Three of Tyler's works (from separate decades of her career) offer varied examples of characters taking three quite different journeys toward greater personal and social well-being. In *A Slipping-Down Life*, published in 1970, the teenaged Evie Decker fears becoming a spinster left to live life alone in her father's house, ending her life as an elderly woman who has missed out on all of the excitement and fulfillment life can offer. To propel her life forward, Evie takes drastic action, carving Drumstrings Casey's last name into her forehead in order to gain the attention of a musician she barely knows. In doing so, she encounters immense social disapproval. Her school teacher father is humiliated and bewildered by her sudden foolishness and notoriety (no doubt contributing to his fatal heart attack several months later); the doctor who attends to her wounds tells Evie sagely, "you'd be better off in the Peace Corps" (*SDL* 39); her friend Violet points out that Drum "is kind of trashy" with his "greasy hair" and "those tight pants. Walking that slinky way he has" (*SDL* 16-17); the Decker's maid Clotelia disgustedly asks, "*Oh*, Evie .... What call you got to act so ignorant?" (*SDL* 66); while, at school (according to Violet) Evie's peers have become both dumbfounded and intrigued, at once: "Like when the cheerleader had to get married. . . . Like when someone has crossed over where the rest of them haven't been. Getting pregnant, or dying, or that boy in the band who shot himself. Remember that? You think, 'Why, I saw him in the hallway, often. And sat behind him in algebra. But I never *knew*, and now he has gone and done it.' That's what they sound like [when they talk about you]" (*SDL* 60-61). Evie's action has been so outrageous that it must be placed in a special category of outlandish adolescent behavior.

Evie also has made herself into a social outcast denounced in the community by the newly arrived revivalist Brother Hope at the Pulqua Tabernacle of God. From his pulpit, Brother Hope refers to Evie as someone who "slashed her forehead with the name of a rock-and-roll singer" and thereby "ruined her life for nothing" (*SDL*

180). Seemingly, Evie has risked her reputation and her future, creating a scandal in Pulqua through her extreme response to Drumstrings Casey when, ironically, as the novel's first line admits, "Evie Decker was not [even] musical" (*SDL* 3).

Clearly, Evie's action is not that of a dedicated rock fan or a star-crazed teenager (for she is barely familiar with Drum's music), but the calculated risk of someone who hopes to change radically the dynamics of her life. Despite the negative reactions of others, Evie admits, "I believe this might be the best thing I've ever done. . . . Something out of character. Definite. Not covered by insurance. I'm just sure it will all work out well. . . . if I had started acting like this a long time ago, my whole *life* might've been different" (*SDL* 40). The thrust of the novel's plot proves that Evie is right. As a consequence of her bizarre action, all of the resulting publicity, and her continuing efforts to engage Drum's interest, Drumstrings Casey asks her to marry him. That he is lazy, selfish, unfaithful, and only mildly talented proves irrelevant, for it is clear that the resourceful Evie will never allow herself to become dependent on Drum – he is merely a means to the end she wishes for herself.

First, Evie Decker takes a job at the local library to help support herself and her husband; then becomes pregnant; and, finally, after her father's death, moves back into her father's house, leaving Drumstrings Casey in order to begin a new life on her own. The proactive Evie stands in direct contrast to the passive Drum who merely sits and waits, asking, "Evie . . . where has my luck gone? When am I going to rise above all this? Am I going to grow old just *waiting*?" (*SDL* 188). When Evie tells him, "You've got to pull yourself together, Drum. I keep meaning to tell you this: I'm expecting a baby. It's coming in six months or so," then offers him the opportunity to "start a new life. Give some shape to things" by moving in with her at her father's, Drum says he can't do it (*SDL* 209-11). Unlike Evie, Drum prefers to wait and hope for his life to change.

Prepared by all she has already done in recent months to move her life forward, Evie self-confidently tells Drum at the end of the novel:

> "All right. I'll go there alone."
> "You mean leave me?"
> "If I have to."
> "You don't have to," said Drum. "Evie, I don't know why you are talking this way. Is it Fay-Jean? Fay-*Jean* don't mean nothing, I swear it. Oh, how am I going to convince you?"
> "Fay-Jean. Don't make me laugh," said Evie. "All I'm asking is for you to pick yourself up and move to a decent house with me. If you don't do it, then it's *you* leaving *me*. I did give you the choice."
> "That's no choice," Drum said. "Evie, I would do almost anything for you but not this. Not get organized and follow after you this way. . . . Can't you just stay and wait till my luck is changed?" .
> . . .
> "I have the baby now," she said.
> "I don't see how that changes anything."
> "No, I know you don't. That's why I'm leaving." (*SDL* 210-11)

As Evie walks out, Drum asks, "How will you support that baby, all alone?", to which Evie replies, "I'll get along" (*SDL* 212). The reader knows that Drumstrings Casey is right when he replies, "Yes, well. . . . *That's* for sure" (*SDL* 212).

Throughout the course of the novel, Evie Decker has proved that she is capable of taking positive action on behalf of both herself and her child-to-be. She has shown that she is willing to find work she enjoys and put her skills and intelligence to good use for her own and the baby's future; further, it is clear that she is strong enough to risk parental, spousal, and social disapproval to achieve the kind of life she feels is right for them both. In the course of her personal journey, Evie earns the reader's respect for earlier actions that may have proved simply selfish and immature. She moves far beyond Drumstrings Casey in terms of her energy, her maturity, and her decisiveness, finding a way to support herself and working actively to shape an adult future that she can look forward to. Whatever life has in store for Evie Decker, she has shown herself equal to accepting its difficulties.

However, in *The Accidental Tourist*, published in 1985, the protagonist is someone who has found himself inadequate to the challenges of life. While formerly his existence has seemed merely lackluster, now, in his early forties, it has become overwhelmingly painful. Macon Leary feels lost in mid-life: his son Ethan has been ruthlessly killed in a fast-food restaurant; his wife Sarah has left him because he cannot help her feel "there's any point to life. . . . You're not a comfort, Macon" (*AT* 5); he writes travel books for a living yet hates to travel; and, looking back over his past, "he reflected that he had not taken steps very often in his life, come to think of it. Really never. His marriage, his two jobs, his time with Muriel, his return to Sarah – all seemed to have simply befallen him. He couldn't think of a single major act he had managed of his own accord" (*AT* 351). Macon asks himself, "Was it too late now to begin? Was there any way he could learn to do things differently?" (*AT* 351). In the course of the action of *The Accidental Tourist*, Macon Leary finds that the answer to these questions is, yes, he can make a new beginning and bring change into his life.

Having tested out several life alternatives throughout the action of the novel – returning to his childhood home to live with his adult siblings; living a new kind of existence on Singleton Street with Muriel Pritchett and her son Alexander; then going back to live with Sarah after she has come back home to live – Macon finally makes his decision. He tells Sarah, "I just decided [to be with Muriel permanently], Sarah. I thought about it most of last night. It wasn't easy. It's not the easy way out, believe me" (*AT* 352). While Macon knows his decision is one that will hurt Sarah after twenty-one years of marriage, and that he and Sarah are much more alike in their social, educational, and economic backgrounds than he and Muriel Pritchett could ever be, he also knows that he has made an essential choice that is the right one for him. He feels comfortable that Muriel will not prove to be the "inappropriate" and "grotesque" partner Sarah warns him she will seem whenever she appears in public at Macon's side (*AT* 352). Instead, Macon knows that he needs Muriel, a person who has never known failure (*AT* 115), "a fighter" who has confronted each difficulty in her problem-filled life with ingenuity and courage (*AT* 279), a woman who has taught him how to cope with challenges and even relish them. In Muriel's company, Macon can feel "a kind of inner rush, a racing forward" that enables him to anticipate the future and feel "the real adventure" of his life for the first time (*AT* 354).

No longer is Macon the person Sarah has criticized for being cautious and closed off: "The trouble with you is . . . you think people should stay in their own sealed packages. You don't believe in opening up. You don't believe in trading back and forth" (*AT* 321). Instead, with Muriel, Macon feels "the surprise of her, and also the surprise of himself when he was with her. In the foreign country that was Singleton Street he was an entirely different person. This person had never been suspected of narrowness, never been accused of chilliness, in fact, was mocked for his soft heart. And was anything but orderly" (*AT* 212). In his forties, Macon "slips-down" into a new, more disorganized, and less respectable life – one that will enable him to become a different person in the future, someone who enjoys traveling, someone who has become more interesting, flexible, open, and fulfilled than he ever was before.

Delia Grinstead in *Ladder of Years* (1995) is another of Tyler's mid-life protagonists who has passively fallen into her life. She feels she has never acted on her own behalf and gained a sense of achievement through her own efforts. Instead, she has relied first on her father, then on her husband Sam – waiting for Sam to ask her to marry him, give her three children, as well as provide for the family's future through his medical practice. Delia has become so passive in her life that, even as she runs away from her family, she looks at a farmhouse along the road, imagining a different life for herself inside, then thinks, "first she'd have to marry a farmer, though. You always had to begin by finding some man to set things in motion, it seemed" (*LY* 82).

Yet Delia is, at that very moment, proving that women can set their own lives into motion if they choose to do so. She has left Sam and the children behind at the beach (since she no longer feels needed or valued by them) to come to a small town to establish a new life of her own. Delia then uses the office skills she has developed in helping out with Sam's medical practice, becoming a secretary for a local law firm, living in a nearby boarding house, and developing new friends of her own. Still, Delia finds herself waiting for Sam "to come fetch her" (*LY* 126) since she regards her husband as an "unassailably self-possessed man who [once] had all but arrived on a white horse to save her from eternal daughterhood" (*LY* 212), a man so competent, so skilled (even with his newly diagnosed heart condition of angina), that he is capable of doing everything on his own, in fact even better, without her. Delia believes that neither Sam nor their virtually grown children will have missed her much at all, despite the fact that she has been away from their home in Baltimore for almost a year.

And yet, when Delia returns as an almost-overlooked guest (or so she feels) for her daughter Susie's wedding, she finds that her children have all feuded with Sam and moved out – that their household has not continued to run at all successfully without her during the past year. Delia realizes, as well, that it is not just she herself who has felt overwhelmed, inadequate, unappreciated, and lost in mid-life – but so has her husband Sam, as well. As Sam confides in her, "you get to believing you did it *all* wrong. Your whole damn life" (*LY* 307). It would seem that Delia has been very much needed – is needed right now – and yet she has felt so belittled (most significantly by herself rather than by the husband or children she blames) that she could not appreciate her own worth. When Sam makes it clear he desires her to return, asking, "was there anything that would, you know. Would persuade you to come back," Delia replies, "Oh, Sam. All you had to do was ask" (*LY* 324).

Although Delia has "ended up back where she'd started, home with Sam for good" (*LY* 326), this is one of those times when, as her friend Nat Moffat has said, "you get to what you thought was the end and you find it's a whole new beginning" (*LY* 219). Delia and her family now know that she is capable of shaping a life for herself, making new friends, taking action, even hurting others, if necessary, to act on her own behalf – not to mention risk being socially ostracized in the process. When Delia returns, she does so not out of habit, a sense of futility or fear, but because it is her choice. While her children may be "leaving. . . . going [on] without her," and she may still find it difficult "to say goodbye" to them (*LY* 326), Delia now looks forward to her future. She can feel eager to begin a new life with Sam as a confident woman who knows she is capable of surviving on her own, a woman worthy of being valued by those around her.

Because of her experiences of the past year, Delia can also feel more helpful to her three young adult children when they seek her advice. When her daughter Susie desires to call off her wedding at the last moment (the guests have already begun to arrive for the ceremony), Delia is able to assure her that that is the right thing to do. If Susie is unsure that her future husband is the kind of person with whom she should share her life, Delia knows that Susie should honor those feelings. Delia has learned the importance of making correct choices to enhance, not diminish, the self, whatever social embarrassment or inconvenience those decisions might cause. Through her own recent experience and personal growth, Delia can assure Susie that feelings of doubt must be resolved before moving on and getting involved in a lifelong relationship. Delia has found that a truly happy marriage requires more than just mutual love and respect between partners; it also requires individuals who have acquired enough self-esteem to feel worthy and capable of contributing to their future together. Now, at last, Delia has that kind of marriage – one she believes her daughter deserves, as well.

None of these three Tyler plots offers a socially acceptable morality play following American society's dictates for community respectability and ultimate happiness. Evie Decker in *A Slipping-Down Life* does everything "wrong," yet she turns out to be "right." She mutilates her face, marries a wastrel, gets pregnant while still a teenager, causes her father pain (contributing to his final coronary), then leaves Drumstrings Casey to begin life on her own as a single mother (a plot few parents would wish their adolescent children to imitate). On the other hand, Macon Leary of *The Accidental Tourist* and Delia Grinstead of *Ladder of Years* achieve adulthood feeling they have wasted the better part of their lives and become totally inadequate in middle age to meet life's challenges. As a result, they desert their spouses for good (in the case of Macon) or temporarily (as Delia does for a year) to go off to live "slipping-down lives" in circumstances much diminished from their former stations in life, yet ones in which they feel able once more to grow and develop. Delia has become so inured to social disapproval that she can even counsel her daughter to call off her wedding just minutes before its commencement. However, just as shocking to readers who reject traditional values and adhere to feminist ideology, Delia Grinstead finally decides to return to live with her husband once more. Not one of these protagonists follows a socially approved game plan for achieving a better life – nor a politically correct course of action, either – yet each one finds personal happiness.

Society benefits also, Tyler suggests, from characters' renewed sense of self-worth and revitalized pleasure in using their unique, individual talents and skills within the public sphere.[53] Evie Decker will not remain isolated in her father's house, as she has feared, but will have her baby to care for and find work to support them both within the community. Evie's ability to do this successfully has already been suggested by her agility as a newlywed in combining the domestic tasks of being a wife with enjoyable work at the local library – and finishing high school at the same time, as well. Macon Leary will now write travel books in which he will be able, for a change, to encourage his readers to enjoy going to foreign locations, feel a sense of adventure, even desire to take occasional risks, as he has begun to do himself. And Delia Grinstead will know that she is an asset to Sam's medical practice (as well as to his life). She is someone who can continue to help out in the office, as she has done for years, but now she can do so with a renewed sense of her ability to establish good relationships with patients (perhaps help Sam attract and keep new ones), having proven herself efficient, resourceful, and pleasing to others in Bay Borough. Because these characters have come to feel good about themselves, Evie, Macon, and Delia can look forward to improved relationships with those around them in the future (true of so many other of Tyler's characters at the conclusions of her novels).

In fact, Anne Tyler's gentle, comic world is one that encompasses remarkable strength. Her characters develop such force of character (although it may take many years for some of them to do so) that they find themselves able to leave those they love best (as does Mary Tell and, perhaps, he comes to feel, Michael Anton) for the sake of their own self-esteem. They are able to turn their backs on family positions, social respectability, and economic security (as do Barnaby Gaitlin or Justine, Duncan, and Caleb Peck) to follow the course of action they deem best for their own lives. And they become tough enough to hurt parents who have made sacrifices on their behalf (as do Evie Decker, Justine Peck, Lindy Anton, James Green, or Cody, Jenny, and Ezra Tull) in order to forge separate, satisfying identities for themselves.[54] While they never harm others gratuitously, and are capable of rebuilding relationships with those from whom they have long been estranged (as it is intimated that both James Green and Cody Tull may be ready to do with their fathers at the end of *The Tin Can Tree* and *Dinner at the Homesick Restaurant*, respectively, and as Caleb Peck does for a short time in his visit with Justine and Duncan Peck), Tyler's characters come to understand that positive relationships are impossible when their inner selves remain stunted and dissatisfied.

Far from offering her readers a "static, politically conservative line on life, a nostalgic vision of an America of private houses and lawns" in which "the solution . . . [lies] in endurance" (Gilbert 139; 144), Anne Tyler's novels advocate an alternative value system whereby characters learn to take back control of their lives. Because they find that remaining loyal to nuclear families, attaining respectable positions, or following society's conventions may, in fact, limit their potential, they seek other ways to affirm themselves and achieve success in life. While it is still true, as Lewis Mumford once said in *Technics and Civilization* in 1934, that "our machine-dominated society is oriented solely to 'things,' and its members have every kind of possession except self-possession" (400), exactly the opposite holds true for Tyler's characters. What they learn to hold most dear is their own self-knowledge and self worth – the "self-possession" those who look outside themselves for solutions in society rarely find.

If, as Lewis Mumford also warned decades ago, American culture continues apace to "put business before every other manifestation of life, [so that] our mechanical and financial leaders have neglected the chief business of life: namely, growth, reproduction, development, expression" (400), Tyler's protagonists, once more, ultimately escape such misdirection and neglect. They take back control of their own lives to experience the personal "growth, reproduction, development, expression" which Mumford finds central to human progress and civilization (400). They work hard to develop enriched selves, find more satisfying work, establish more fulfilling relationships with others, and achieve a fuller experience of their own and others' humanity. They take on the care and nurturance of children (many not their own), such as Simon Pike, Alexander Pritchett, Lucy Dean Bedloe's three orphans, Slevin St. Ambrose and his assorted siblings, Pagan Anton, or the three motherless Davitch girls. As they seek out trailers, shacks, and apartments in which to live, repair their crumbling brownstones, or embrace jobs as nursing home attendants, traveling puppeteers, manual laborers, or carnival mechanics, Tyler's characters survive and thrive.

Tyler's characters come to appreciate fully that:

> our success in life will not be judged by the size of the rubbish heaps we have produced: it will be judged by the immaterial and non-consumable goods we have learned to enjoy. . . . Distinction and individuality will reside in the personality, where it belongs, not in the size of the house we live in, in the expense of our trappings, or in the amount of labor we can arbitrarily command. (Mumford 399)

Tyler's characters grow spiritually, delighting in the richness of their lives, all the while appearing merely to have "slipped-down" in the material world of contemporary American society.

What middle-class readers seek in Tyler's fiction would not seem to be reassurance for continuing to lead conventional, suburban lives (for such reassurance is seldom to be found in her novels) but, rather, a vision of themselves as capable of coping with slippage, ready to take risks, and prepared to undergo significant changes – if non-consumer ones their culture discourages. As John Updike has said of *The Accidental Tourist*, Tyler offers readers her "primal faith in natural resilience and the forces of renewal" available not only to the characters of her comic works but to all of us as human beings in the everyday world we inhabit ("Leaving" 130). Tyler's healing novels seek to restore personal power to individuals whereby they can revitalize their lives in fulfilling ways, even if they are not ones their society promotes, condones, or even seems to understand.

In a letter she once wrote to her fellow writer Anthony Trollope (upon reading his latest work *Rachel Ray*), Victorian author George Eliot called his novels "pleasant public gardens, where people go for amusement, and whether they think of it or not, get health, as well" (qtd. in Hall 255). So it seems, too, with Anne Tyler's works, into which today's readers can enter and find their vitality, initiative, and hope restored. Further, we might also agree with Eliot when she added, "such things are rather a result of what an author is than of what he [sic] intends" (qtd. in Hall 255). Tyler's novels, indeed, prove to be healthy public places wherein readers can laugh, imbibe fresh air, and feel revitalized once more. In the presence of this wise and compassionate author, her sturdy and striving characters, they can feel reinvigorated. Tyler's tales direct contemporary readers, through the structure of their plots, towards a sense of their own capabilities: the achievement, well-being and pleasure they can come to know in their own lives. The "slipping-down" world of Tyler's novels offers its audience a means to spiritual renewal for the individual soul as well as for a culture needing the enrichment of a more vigorous, capable, active, and self-possessed citizenry. For those willing to turn their backs on a pre-packaged, ready for purchase (yet unsatisfying, even insulting), contemporary version of the American dream, Anne Tyler offers examples of spiritual effort, choice, power, and fulfillment by which to recreate lives into ones that are worth living and worth sharing.

Notes

52.   Tyler offers no "traditionally, generally-accepted rules" for her protagonists to follow, as Barbara Harrell Carson explains of Macon Leary and Charlotte Emory: "Each arrives at a sense of moral responsibility far more complex than that associated with the notion that endurance, self-sacrifice and adherence to commitments are, of themselves, heroic. Charlotte learns to see her relation-tangled home as a place to build rather than give up, a self. Macon reaches his decision to leave Sarah, whom he loves (in a way) . . . . because of the growth Macon experiences" (32). In *Searching for Caleb*, Justine Peck (who is far more conventional than her husband Duncan) tells him that she agrees with him in not believing in self-sacrifice

(288) – and Tyler does not advocate self-sacrifice as good for character development in her other novels, either.

53.   As Margaret Morganroth Gullette argues, in support of Tyler's basic themes, "if many of us could do this [come into a better relationship with the self], the results for society – for relationships with others, projects in the social world – would also probably be quite positive" (*Safe*, 167).

54.   Even the tender, stay-at-home Ezra Tull hurts his mother by insisting on becoming a restaurant owner rather than an educator, as Pearl Tull has wished, and entering into a business partnership with Mrs. Scarlatti (thereby creating possible scandal about their relationship to each other, according to Ezra's displeased mother) in *Dinner at the Homesick Restaurant*.

Bibliography

Primary Sources

Chopin, Kate. *The Awakening and Other Stories*. Ed. Judith Baxter. New York: Cambridge University Press, 1996.

DeLillo, Don. *Mao II*. New York: Penguin, 1992.

Moore, Marianne. "Poetry." *The Norton Anthology of Literature By Women: The Tradition in English*. Ed. Sandra M Gilbert and Susan Gubar. New York and London: W. W. Norton and Co., 1985: 1492-93.

O'Connor, Flannery. *Mystery and Manners*. Selected and edited by Sally and Robert Fitzgerald. 1957. New York: Farrar, Straus, and Giroux, 1997.

Phillips, Jayne Anne. *Interview. Listen to Their Voices: Twenty Interviews With Women Who Write*. Ed. Mickey Pearlman. New York and London: W.W. Norton and Co., 1993: 152-62.

Tyler, Anne. *The Accidental Tourist*. New York: Alfred A. Knopf, 1985.

_____. *The Amateur Marriage*. New York: Alfred A. Knopf, 2004.

_____. *Back When We Were Grownups*. New York: Alfred A. Knopf, 2001.

_____. *Breathing Lessons*. New York: Alfred A. Knopf, 1988.

_____. *Celestial Navigation*. New York: Alfred A. Knopf, 1974.

_____. *The Clock Winder*. New York: Alfred A. Knopf, 1972.

_____. *Dinner at the Homesick Restaurant*. 1982. New York: Alfred A. Knopf, 1989.

_____. *Earthly Possessions*. New York: Alfred A. Knopf, 1977.

_____. *If Morning Ever Comes*. 1964. New York: Alfred A. Knopf, 1972.

_____. *Ladder of Years*. New York: Alfred A. Knopf, 1995.

_____. *Morgan's Passing*. New York: Alfred A. Knopf, 1980.

_____. *A Patchwork Planet*. New York: Alfred A. Knopf, 1998.

_____. *Saint Maybe*. New York: Alfred A. Knopf, 1991.

_____. *Searching for Caleb*. New York: Alfred A. Knopf, 1975.

_____. *A Slipping-Down Life*. New York: Alfred A. Knopf, 1970.

_____. "Still Just Writing." *The Writer On Her Work: Contemporary Women Writers Reflect On Their Art and Situation*. Ed. Janet Sternburg. New York: Norton, 1980: 3-16.

_____. *The Tin Can Tree*. New York: Alfred A. Knopf, 1965.

Secondary Sources

Bail, Paul. *Anne Tyler: A Critical Companion*. Westport, CT and London: Greenwood Press, 1998.

Bennett, Barbara A. "Attempting to Connect: Verbal Humor in the Novels of Anne Tyler." *South Atlantic Review* 60.1 (January 1995): 57-76.

Betts, Doris. "Tyler's Marriage of Opposites." *The Fiction of Anne Tyler*. Ed. C. Ralph Stephens. Jackson: University Press of Mississippi, 1990: 1-15.

Brooks, Mary Ellen. "Anne Tyler." *Dictionary of Literary Biography: American Novelists Since World War II, Second Series*. Ed. James E. Kibler Jr. Detroit: Gale Research, 1980, vol. 6: 336-45.

Carson, Barbara Harrell. "Complicate, Complicate: Anne Tyler's Moral Imperative." *Southern Quarterly* 31.1 (Fall 1992): 24-35.

Comstock, Cathy. *Disruption and Delight in the Nineteenth-Century Novel*. Ann Arbor: UMI Research Press, 1988.

Cook, Bruce. "New Faces in Faulkner Country." *Saturday Review* 4 September 1976: 39-41. [Reprinted in *Critical Essays on Anne Tyler*. Ed. Alice Hall Petry. New York: G. K. Hall, 1992: 157-59.]

Croft, Robert W. *Anne Tyler: A Bio-Bibliography*. Westport, CT and London: Greenwood Press, 1995.

_____. *An Anne Tyler Companion*. Westport, CT and London: Greenwood Press, 1998.

Culler, Jonathan. *Structuralist Poetics: Structuralism, Linguistics and the Study of Literature*. 1975. Ithaca, New York: Cornell University Press, 1976.

DeMott, Benjamin. "Funny, Wise and True (review of *Dinner at the Homesick Restaurant*)." *New York Times Book Review*, 14 March 1982, 1, 14. [Reprinted in *Critical Essays on Anne Tyler*. Ed. Alice Hall Petry. New York: G. K. Hall, 1992: 111-14.]

Elkins, Mary J. "*Dinner at the Homesick Restaurant*: Anne Tyler and the Faulkner Connection." *The Fiction of Anne Tyler*. Ed. C. Ralph Stephens. Jackson: University Press of Mississippi, 1990: 119-36.

Evans, Elizabeth. "'Mere Reviews': Anne Tyler as Book Reviewer." *Critical Essays of Anne Tyler*. Ed. Alice Hall Petry. New York: G. K. Hall, 1992: 233-43.

Evans, M. Stanton. "Toward a New Intellectual History." *Freedom and Virtue: The Conservative/Libertarian Debate*. Ed. George W. Carey. Lanham: University Press of America, Inc, 1984.

Farrell, Grace. "Killing Off the Mother: Failed Matricide in *Celestial Navigation*." *Critical Essays on Anne Tyler*. Ed. Alice Hall Petry. New York: G. K. Hall, 1992: 221-33.

Finnegan, William. *Cold New World: Growing Up in a Harder Country*. New York: Random House, 1998.

Fowler, Roger. "Polyphony and Problematic in *Hard Times*." *The Changing World of Charles Dickens*. Ed. Robert Giddings. London: Barnes & Noble, 1983: 91-108.

Franzen, Jonathan. "Perchance to Dream: In the Age of Images, A Reason to Write Novels." *Harper's Magazine*, April 1996: 35-54.

Fredman, Alice Green. *Anthony Trollope*. New York: Columbia University Press, 1971.

Gerstenberger, Donna. "Everybody Speaks." *Anne Tyler As Novelist*. Ed. Dale Salwak. Iowa City: University of Iowa Press, 1994: 138-47.

Gibson, Mary Ellis. "Family as Fate: The Novels of Anne Tyler." *Southern Literary Journal* 16 (Fall 1983): 47-58. [Reprinted in *Critical Essays on Anne Tyler*. Ed. Alice Hall Petry. New York: G. K. Hall, 1992: 165-75.]

Gilbert, Susan. "Private Lives and Public Issues: Anne Tyler's Prize-Winning Novels." *The Fiction of Anne Tyler*. Ed. C. Ralph Stephens. Jackson: University Press of Mississippi, 1990: 136-47.

Giles, Jeff. "Errors and 'Corrections.'" *Newsweek* 5 November 2001: 68-69.

Gilmour, Robin. *The Novel in the Victorian Age: A Modern Introduction*. London and Baltimore: Edward Arnold, 1986.

Godwin, Gail. "Review of *Celestial Navigation*." *New York Times Book Review* 28 April 1974: 34-35. [Reprinted in *Critical Essays on Anne Tyler*. Ed. Alice Hall Petry. New York: G. K. Hall, 1992: 71-73.]

Greene, Gayle. *Changing the Story: Feminist Fiction and the Tradition*. Bloomington, Indiana: Indiana University Press, 1991.

Gullette, Margaret Morganroth. *Declining to Decline: Cultural Combat and the Politics of the Midlife*. Charlottesville and London: University Press of Virginia, 1997.

_____. *Safe at Last in the Middle Years: The Invention of the Midlife Progress Novel: Saul Bellow, Margaret Drabble, Anne Tyler, and John Updike*. Berkeley, Los Angeles, London: University of California Press, 1988.

Hall, N. John. *Trollope: A Biography*. Oxford and New York: Oxford University Press, 1993.

Hayward, Jennifer. *Consuming Pleasures: Active Audiences and Serial Fictions From Dickens to Soap Operas*. Lexington: University Press of Kentucky, 1997.

Hoagland, Edward. "About Maggie, Who Tried Too Hard [review of *Breathing Lessons*]." *New York Times Book Review* 11 September 1988: 1, 43-44. [Reprinted in *Critical Essays on Anne Tyler*. Ed. Alice Hall Petry. New York: G. K. Hall,1992: 140-45.]

Hughes, Linda K. and Michael Lund. *The Victorian Serial*. London: University Press of Virginia, 1991.

"Jane Austen: 1795-1817." *The Norton Anthology of Literature by Women: The Tradition in English*. Ed. Sandra M. Gilbert and Susan Gubar. New York and London: W. W. Norton and Co., 1985: 206-09.

Jones, Anne G. "Home at Last, and Homesick Again: The Ten Novels of Anne Tyler." *The Hollins Critic*, 23.2 (April 1986): 1-13.

Kilgore, Michael. "Saint Anne: Blessedly Prolific Tyler Pulls Off Yet Another Miracle [review of *Saint Maybe*]." *The Tampa Tribune-Times* 1 September 1991: Sunday Book Section.

Klinghoffer, David. "Ordinary People [review of *Breathing Lessons*]." *National Review* 30 December 1988: 48-49. [Reprinted in *Critical Essays on Anne Tyler*. Ed. Alice Hall Petry. New York: G. K. Hall, 1992: 137-40.]

Lamb, Wendy. "An Interview with Anne Tyler." *Iowa Journal of Literary Studies* 3 (1981): 59-64 [Reprinted in *Critical Essays on Anne Tyler*. Ed. Alice Hall Petry. New York: G. K. Hall, 1992: 53-61.]

Lueloff, Jorie. "Author Explains Why Women Dominate in South." (Baton Rouge) *Morning Advocate* 8 February 1965, sec. A, 11. [Reprinted in *Critical Essays on Anne Tyler*. Ed. Alice Hall Petry. New York: G. K. Hall, 1992: 21-24.]

Mantel, Hilary. "Escape Artists (review of Alison Lurie's *The Last Resort*, Ann Beattie's *Park City: New and Selected Stories*, and Anne Tyler's *A Patchwork Planet*)." *The New York Review of Books*, 5 November 1998: 23-26.

Marovitz, Sanford E. "Anne Tyler's Emersonian Balance." *Critical Essays of Anne Tyler*. Ed. Alice Hall Petry. New York: G. K. Hall, 1992: 207-21.

Mathewson, Joseph. "Taking the Anne Tyler Tour (review of *The Accidental Tourist*)." *Horizon*, September 1985: 14. [Reprinted in *Critical Essays on Anne Tyler*. Ed. Alice Hall Petry. New York: G. K. Hall, 1992: 123-26.]

McCullough, David Willis. "Anne Tyler's *Saint Maybe* (review)." *BOMC News*, September 1991: 10-11.

McPhillips, Robert. "The Baltimore Chop (review of *Breathing Lessons*)." *The Nation*, 7 November 1988: 464-66. [Reprinted in *Critical Essays on Anne Tyler*. Ed. Alice Hall Petry. New York: G. K. Hall, 1992: 150-57.]

Michaels, Marguerite. "Anne Tyler, Writer 8:05 to 3:30." *New York Times Book Review*, 8 May 1977: 13, 42-43. [Reprinted in *Critical Essays on Anne Tyler*. Ed. Alice Hall Petry. New York: G. K. Hall, 1992: 40-45.]

Miller, D. A. "The Novel as Usual: "Trollope's *Barchester Towers*." *Sex, Politics, and Science in the Nineteenth-Century Novel*. Ed. Ruth Bernard Yeazell. Baltimore and London: The Johns Hopkins University Press, 1986: 1-39.

Mumford, Lewis. *Technics and Civilization*. 1934. New York and Burlingame: Harcourt, Brace and World, Inc., 1963.

Papadimas, Julie Persing. "America Tyler Style: Surrogate Families and Transiency." *Journal of American Culture*, 15.3 (Fall 1992): 45-51.

Petry, Alice Hall. "Bright Books of Life: The Black Norm in Anne Tyler's Novels." *Southern Quarterly* 31.1 (Fall 1992): 7-14.

_____, ed. *Critical Essays on Anne Tyler*. New York: G. K. Hall, 1992.

_____. *Understanding Anne Tyler*. Columbia, South Carolina: University of South Carolina Press, 1990.

Pool, Daniel. *Dickens' Fur Coat and Charlotte's Unanswered Letters: The Rows and Romances of England's Great Victorian Novelists*. New York: Harper Collins, 1997.

Ridley, Clifford. "Anne Tyler: A Sense of Reticence Balanced by 'Oh, Well, Why Not?" *National Observer*, 22 July 1972, 23. [Reprinted in *Critical Essays on Anne Tyler*. Ed. Alice Hall Petry. New York: G. K. Hall, 1992: 24-28.]

Robertson, Mary F. "Anne Tyler: Medusa Points and Contact Points." *Contemporary American Women Writers: Narrative Strategies*. Ed. Catherine Rainwater and William J. Scheick. Lexington: University Press of Kentucky, 1985: 119-42. [Reprinted in *Critical Essays on Anne Tyler*. Ed. Alice Hall Petry. New York: G. K. Hall, 1992: 184-207.]

Salwak, Dale, ed. *Anne Tyler as Novelist*. Iowa City: University of Iowa Press, 1994.

Shafer, Aileen Chris. "Beauty and the Transformed Beast: Fairy Tales and Myths in *Morgan's Passing*." *Anne Tyler as Novelist*. Ed. Dale Salwak. Iowa City: University of Iowa Press, 1994: 125-38.

Shelton, Frank W. "Anne Tyler's Houses." *The Fiction of Anne Tyler*. Ed. C. Ralph Stephens. Jackson: University Press of Mississippi, 1990: 40-47.

_____. "The Necessary Balance: Distance and Sympathy in the Novels of Anne Tyler." *Southern Review* 20 (Autumn 1984): 851-60. [Reprinted in Critical Essays on *Anne Tyler*. Ed. Alice Hall Petry. New York: G. K. Hall, 1992: 175-84.]

Siegel, Lee. "Out of the Dark Wood: Dante and the Subversive Ego (review of *Dante* by R. W. B. Lewis (Viking 2001) and *Inferno: A New Verse Translation*, by Michael Palna (W. W. Norton 2002)." *Harper's Magazine*, May 2002: 79-84.

Skilton, David. "The Trollope Reader." *The Nineteenth-Century British Novel*. Ed. Jeremy Hawthorn. London: Edward Arnold, Publishing, 1986: 143-56.

Stegner, Wallace. "The Meddler's Progress (review of *Breathing Lessons*)." *Washington Post Book World*, 4 September 1988, 1, 6. [Reprinted in *Critical Essays on Anne Tyler*. Ed. Alice Hall Petry. New York: G. K. Hall, 1992: 148-50.]

Stephens, C. Ralph. *The Fiction of Anne Tyler*. Jackson and London: University Press Mississippi. 1990.

Sullivan, Walter. From "The Insane and the Indifferent Walker Percy and Others." *Sewanee Review* 86 (Winter 1978): 155-57. [Reprinted in *Critical Essays on Anne Tyler*. Ed. Alice Hall Petry. New York: G. K. Hall, 1992: 92-94.]

Templin, Charlotte. "Tyler's Literary Reputation." *Anne Tyler As Novelist*. Ed. Dale Salwak. Iowa City: University of Iowa Press, 1994: 175-97.

Towers, Robert. "From Roughing It (Review of *Breathing Lessons*)." *The New York York Review of Books*, 10 November 1988: 40-41. [Reprinted in *Critical Essays on Anne Tyler*. Ed. Alice Hall Petry. New York: G. K. Hall, 1992: 145-48.]

_____. "Review of *Morgan's Passing*." *New Republic*, 22 March 1980: 28, 30-31. [Reprinted in *Critical Essays on Anne Tyler*. Ed. Alice Hall Petry. New York: G. K. Hall, 1992: 103-07.]

Town, Caren J. "Rewriting the Family During *Dinner at the Homesick Restaurant*." *Southern Quarterly* 31.1 (Fall 1992): 14-24.

Updike, John. "Family Ways (review of *Searching for Caleb*)." *Hugging the Shore: Essays and Criticism* by John Updike. New York: Knopf, 1983: 273-78. [Reprinted in *Critical Essays on Anne Tyler*. Ed. Alice Hall Petry. New York: G. K. Hall, 1992: 75-80.]

_____. From 'On Such a Beautiful Green Little Planet'(review of *Dinner at the Homesick Restaurant*)." *Hugging the Shore: Essays and Criticism* by John Updike. New York: Knopf, 1983: 292-99. [Reprinted in *Critical Essays on Anne Tyler*. Ed. Alice Hall Petry. New York: G. K. Hall, 1992: 107-11.]

_____. "Leaving Home (review of *The Accidental Tourist*)." *The New Yorker*, 28 October 1985, 106-08, 110-12. [Reprinted in *Critical Essays on Anne Tyler*. Ed Alice Hall Petry. New York: G. K. Hall, 1992: 126-32.]

_____. "Loosened Roots (review of *Earthly Possessions*)." *Hugging the Shore: Essays and Criticism* by John Updike. New York: Knopf, 1983: 278-83. [Reprinted in *Critical Essays on Anne Tyler*. Ed. Alice Hall Petry. New York: G. K. Hall, 1992: 88-92.]

Voelker, Joseph C. *Art and the Accidental in Anne Tyler*. Columbia and London: University of Missouri Press, 1989.

Weisbrot, Mark. "Globalism for Dummies (from "Globalism on the Ropes," published on TomPaine.com in March 2000)." *Harper's Magazine*, May 2000: 15-19.

Wills, Garry. *Confessions of a Conservative*. Garden City: Doubleday, 1979.

_____. *Reagan's America: Innocents at Home*. Garden City: Doubleday, 1987.

Index